OXFORD HISTORICAL SERIES

Editors

N. GIBBS R. W. SOUTHERN J. S. WATSON
R. B. WERNHAM

SECOND SERIES

NOTE

This series comprises carefully selected studies which have been submitted, or are based upon theses submitted, for higher degrees in this University. The works listed below are those still in print

THE NORMAN MONASTERIES AND THEIR ENGLISH POSSESSIONS

BY

DONALD MATTHEW

OXFORD UNIVERSITY PRESS
1962

Oxford University Press, Amen House, London E.C.4

GLASGOW NEW YORK TORONTO MELBOURNE WELLINGTON
BOMBAY CALCUTTA MADRAS KARACHI LAHORE DACCA
CAPE TOWN SALISBURY NAIROBI IBADAN ACCRA
KUALA LUMPUR HONG KONG

PRINTED IN GREAT BRITAIN
AT THE UNIVERSITY PRESS, OXFORD
BY VIVIAN RIDLER
PRINTER TO THE UNIVERSITY

PREFACE

IN the course of preparing this study I have come to
live, like the Norman monks here described, on both
sides of the Channel. For want of baronial patrons and
monastic vows I have trusted to the tolerance of academic
life and the generosity of the Centre National de la Recherche
Scientifique, Merton College, Oxford, the Bryce Research
Fund of the University of Oxford, the University of
Liverpool, and Mr. G. H. S. Mills.

For more than a century English historians have been
drawn into Normandy by the fascination their Norman
ancestors have for them, and even the battle-scarred Normandy I first saw in 1955 gave me an inkling of the exaltation
they felt. In these pages I have tried to show the irrelevance
of the Channel as a barrier in the Middle Ages and the
intimate relations between England and France, in the hope
that in the future there may be less talk of the ties that bind
these countries together and more practical experience of
living in both countries. The monks of this book were at
home on both sides of the water and their example is not
without interest at the present time. I have not simply made
another wreath for the Anglo-Norman cenotaph.

For stirring in me a desire to understand the differences
that divide at a deeper level than reason I owe most to my
experiences at the universities of Oxford and Caen. Mr.
Southern suggested the original theme which I have twisted
out of recognition; in spite of this he has continued to help
me, encourage me, and inspire me, even when I have been
most unfaithful to his ideals, and it is he who has throughout
insisted on arrangement, presentation, and simplicity. He
has never sent me away on the grounds that he was too busy
and my regret is that I cannot more obviously show how I
have profited by his generosity and wisdom.

The friends I have made through my universities have
given me the grace to emerge from research more sensitive
to the living and more tolerant of the imponderable than
historical work usually allows for. I thank them for their

friendship and their efforts to keep me alive to normal human interests. I am particularly grateful to those who have helped me to enter intimately into French life.

Finally I wish to record the help I have received first, from all those librarians and archivists whose collections I have been able to use, especially Mlle M. J. Le Cacheux, Mlle J. Dupic, M. F. Blanchet, M. Michel Lepesant, M. André Leroi, Mr. Noel Blakiston, Mr. Godfrey Davis, and Mr. P. L. Hull, and second, from the following scholars, Professor C. N. L. Brooke, Miss F. E. Harmer, Mrs. Wood, Dr. J. Mason, Dr. E. B. Fryde, Mr. Cyril Hart, and Mr. Norman Blake.

D. M.

CONTENTS

LIST OF ABBREVIATIONS

Abbr. Rot. Orig.	Abbreviatio Rotulorum Originalium.
B.E.C.	*Bibliothèque de l'école des chartes.*
B.M.	British Museum, London.
B.N.	Bibliothèque Nationale, Paris.
B.S.A.N.	*Bulletin de la Société des Antiquaires de Normandie.*
Calvados	Archives du Calvados, Caen.
C.Ch.R.	*Calendar of Charter Rolls.*
C. Chan. Warr.	*Calendar of Chancery Warrants.*
C.Cl.R.	*Calendar of Close Rolls.*
C.D.	J. Kemble, *Codex Diplomaticus.*
C.D.F.	J. H. Round, *Calendar of Documents preserved in France.*
C.F.R.	*Calendar of Fine Rolls.*
C.P.R.	*Calendar of Patent Rolls.*
C.Pap.L.	*Calendar of Papal Letters.*
C.C.R.R.	*Calendar of Curia Regis Rolls.*
Davis	H. W. C. Davis, *Regesta Anglo-Normannorum Regum 1066–1100.*
D.B.	Domesday Book.
Delisle–Berger	L. V. Delisle and E. Berger, *Recueil des actes d'Henri II.*
Eure	Archives de l'Eure, Evreux.
E.H.R.	*English Historical Review.*
Exon. D.B.	*Domesday Book,* vol. iii of Record Commission edition.
E.Y.C.	*Early Yorkshire Charters,* ed. W. Farrer and C. T. Clay.
F.A.	T. Madox, *Formulare Anglicanum.*
G.C.	*Gallia Christiana.*
H.M.C.	Historical Manuscripts Commission.
Holtzmann	W. Holtzmann, *Papsturkunden in England.*
Johnson	C. Johnson and H. Cronne, *Regesta Anglo-Normannorum Regum 1100–35.*
L.R.S.	Lincoln Record Society.
Manche	Archives de la Manche, formerly at Saint-Lô.
M.A.	*Monasticon Anglicanum* (original edition, unless otherwise stated).
M.S.A.N.	Mémoires de la Société des Antiquaires de Normandie.
New	C. W. New, *A History of Alien Priories.*
N.L.	Newington Longueville Charters.

O.H.S.	Oxford Historical Society.
Oliver	G. Oliver, *Monasticon Exoniensis.*
Orne	Archives le l'Orne, Alençon.
O.V.	Ordericus Vitalis, *Historia Ecclesiastica.*
P.L.	J. P. Migne, *Patrologia Latina.*
P.Q.W.	*Quo Warranto, Placita.*
P.R.(S.)	Pipe Roll (Society).
P.R.O.	Public Record Office.
Rigaud	O. Rigaud, *Journal des Visites.*
Rot. Claus. Litt.	*Rotuli Litterarum Clausarum.*
Rot. Parlt.	*Rotuli Parlamentorum.*
R.S.	Rolls Series.
Rymer	T. Rymer, *Foedera.*
Seine-Maritime	Archives de la Seine-Maritime, Rouen.
S.A.C.	*Sussex Archaeological Collections.*
S.H.F.	Société d'Histoire de France.
S.H.N.	Société de l'Histoire de Normandie.
T.R.H.S.	*Transactions of the Royal Historical Society.*
V.C.H.	*Victoria County History.*

INTRODUCTION

ENGLAND AND NORMANDY
THE SOURCES OF THEIR HISTORY

THE principal sources of the history of alien priories are the charters preserved in England and Normandy. The earliest reference to them, about 1200, shows that the character of the records then available was similar to the character of those still surviving. Rainaldus, abbot of Saint-Wandrille, sent to the chapter of the cathedral of Salisbury the proof of his title to two churches in the diocese that he was giving to the canons: a charter of William the Conqueror, a letter from Bishop Roger to the archdeacons of Dorset and Wiltshire, a charter of Bishop Jocelyn, and papal bulls of Innocent II and Eugenius III.[1] It is possible that records of more ephemeral interest were not kept at all in the twelfth century; if they were, the abbot did not think they would interest the new owners. At a later date owners preserved memoranda about estate management, legal agreements, receipts of money, and letters from Normandy to England and from England to Normandy. No medieval history of alien priories was contemplated and learned monks of the seventeenth century usually knew little of the English chapter of their monastery's history. The documents are rare and have not come down to us complete, but those that do survive are probably a fair sample of the records ever committed to writing.

Judging from references to the dangers of sending original documents to England for lawsuits,[2] the proofs of title

---

[1] *Sarum Charters*, pp. 229–33.

[2] In 1316 Louis X of France, at the request of the monks of Montebourg, confirmed their charter of Henry I of England: 'ut litteras ipsas quas in diversis locis pro eorum conservandis iuribus tam citra quam ultra mare frequenter habent necessario deportare, periculose tamen propter viarum discrimina . . .': B.M. Add. MS. 15605, f. 13. Likewise Robert, bishop of Salisbury 1274–84, inspected Saint-Wandrille's deeds for Ecclesfield because it was dangerous to take charters oversea: B.M. Add. MS. 27581, no. 1; see also *C.P.R. 1267–72*, p. 207, for a charter sent from Cherbourg, and lost in the civil disturbances of Henry III's reign. For the difficulties of the distance of the priories see a letter printed in Martène, *Thesaurus Anecdotarum*, iv. c. 474–6.

were normally kept in Normandy, where their preservation into modern times was assured. By contrast, most of the documents in England were concerned mainly with matters of local importance, retained for use in the priories. The documents acquired by Eton College[1] and King's College, Cambridge, came from the priories, for no transfer of documents from the Norman monasteries took place, as was the case when Wykeham purchased Harmondsworth[2] from the monks of Sainte-Cathérine-du-Mont, or when Chichele bought West Mersea[3] from Saint-Ouen. The Carthusians of Shene, although they could not preserve the priories' deeds after 1539, compiled a great register of those they had found, thus summarizing more than fifteen hundred documents, mostly earlier than 1400.[4] At Warminghurst, the bailiff of Fécamp kept certain records in his chests, until a burglar destroyed them in 1400.[5] Cartularies for Blyth,[6] Boxgrove,[7] Carisbrooke,[8] Eye,[9] Lancaster,[10] Modbury,[11] Newent,[12] Otterton,[13] St. Michael's Mount,[14] Stogursey,[15] Tutbury,[16] all written in England, were evidently composed for local use.

It is not the case, however, that the Norman monks

---

[1] Eton College negotiated with Grestain for some of the property it had been granted by Henry VI, but has no documents for this property. King's negotiated with the prior of Wootton Wawen, not with the monks of Castellion: see below, p. 138, n. 3.

[2] There were papers there in the thirteenth century: *C.P.R. 1272–81*, p. 236. The Harmondsworth archives at Winchester College, however, contain only three pieces earlier than 1377.

[3] See below, pp. 129–30. The cartulary of Higham Ferrers (B.M. Stowe MS. 931) contains only fifteenth-century deeds.

[4] B.M. Cotton MS. Otho B xiv: Lire's priories provided the most : Carisbrooke about 125, Wareham more than 200, Liver's Ocle nearly 400. Ware priory had more than 550; Hayling priory 250 including 'duo libri antiqui facti in prima fundacione continentes hidas et divisiones terrarum', now unfortunately lost.

[5] *C.P.R. 1399–1401*, p. 56: this collection included court-rolls.

[6] B.M. Harley MS. 3759.

[7] B.M. Cotton MS. Claudius A vi, ed. L. Fleming, published by Sussex Record Society. [8] B.M. Egerton MS. 3667.

[9] B.M. Add. MS. 8177, copy of Chelmsford MS.

[10] B.M. Harley MS. 3764: printed by Chetham Society.

[11] Eton College Modbury charter 32.

[12] B.M. Add. MSS. 15668 and 18461.

[13] Oliver, pp. 249–59: this is a calendar of the manuscript still in private ownership.

[14] Hatfield MS. 315: fourteenth century.

[15] Eton College, published by the Somerset Record Society.

[16] B.M. Add. MS. 6714: copy of the cartulary in the College of Arms.

jealously hid away their proofs of title in Normandy and left
their brethren in England to pursue local problems by themselves. The abbot and chapter attended seriously to the
responsibilities of their English possessions and for this purpose needed to be informed about the estates. To some extent the agents were expected to keep their monasteries
informed, but agents were not perfect and some check on
their statements was essential. A number of records of local
character are therefore to be found in Normandy at the
present time which, whatever their original purpose, served
the abbots as guides to local problems. Loders priory cartulary was taken to Normandy at some unknown date and left
there. A rent-roll of Ottery manor,[1] of no more interest
than many others, perhaps witnesses to a momentary zeal on
the part of the cathedral chapter of Rouen to view the
accounts. Many documents describe manorial customs and
services[2] and an abbot of Mont Saint-Michel made a
special point of asking his prior at Otterton to send him a
copy of the customs of the manor of Budleigh.[3] With such
documents at his elbow an abbot could more seriously
appreciate what his agent's difficulties could be. The monks
of Montebourg went to the lengths of copying into the great
cartulary of their mother house, the rents, services, and
customs of Loders, giving as their reason the wish that later
generations should be informed.[4] These generations to
come were Norman; the monks in England could not have
benefited from the record, unless, as is possible, they
studied the record before leaving Normandy on their
English mission.

The monasteries which have left the most valuable records

---

[1] Seine-Maritime G 4057.

[2] e.g. Eure H 711, ff. 181–202: customs of Préaux's manors c. 1231–85. The prior
of Ware compiled a roll in 1272: 'qui . . . continent omnes redditus in anglia ad
monasterium S. Ebrulfi spectantes et omnes terras in dominico et in libero tenemento
et in villenagio cum consuetudinibus libere tenentium et villanorum': Orne H 896 =
P.R.O. 31/8/140 B, i, pp. 332–51.

[3] Avranches MS. 211, f. 101ᵛ: 'copiam . . . inquisitionibus de modo teneure
hominum nostrorum de Boudelee'.

[4] B.N. MS. Lat. 10087, ff. 253–72: 1305: 'ad ambiguitatem futurorum delendam
tam pro tenentibus quam propter lapsum temporis redditus servicia et consuetudines de Lodre et de Botenhantone et omnium ibidem tenentium tam liberorum quam
villanorum cottariorum et censarum . . . ad perpetuam rei memoriam meliori modo
quoscunque in scriptis redegi, ut hii qui in posterum venient informentur'.

in France were those of the present département of the Seine-Maritime, whose archives are now in Rouen.[1] Déville made copies of most of these documents for the Record Commission, and his transcripts (P.R.O. 31/8/140 A) were the basis of the appropriate parts of Round's *Calendar of Documents preserved in France*. On account of the confusion then prevailing in the archives at Rouen, Round was not able to check most of these copies against the originals. Since his day an *Inventaire-Sommaire* of monastic documents (instead of the more detailed *Inventaire* for the secular clergy) has been prepared and published for monasteries, alphabetically as far as Saint-Ouen. Uncalendared documents have been summarily sorted into boxes, but no progress with publication of the *Inventaire-Sommaire* is being made. It will no doubt wait upon the completion of the new *Archives* building on the left bank of the Seine.

The chief importance of the collection at Rouen is its completeness. There is not one monastery of the département which has not left some documents. Even the house of the Holy Trinity, Rouen, or Sainte-Cathérine-du-Mont, which was so ruined after the wars of religion that Henri IV gave it to the Carthusians, somehow preserved an eleventh-century cartulary, uniquely early for Normandy, which was published by Déville. With few exceptions the records now available appear to be those used by the pre-revolutionary historians of Saint-Ouen,[2] Le Tréport,[3] and Jumièges.[4] The chauvinists of the revolution who demanded the destruction of all documents relating to the English occupation of France did not destroy evidence of the Norman occupation of England. If ever there were more documents about the English property than there are now, it was the wars of the fifteenth and sixteenth centuries that must be held responsible for their loss: not the revolution.

---

[1] Under a decree of 1796 monastic archives were to be deposited in the *chef-lieux* of départements. Le Cacheux described the delays in shifting the deeds of Jumièges from Yvetot, where they had been transferred in 1792, to Rouen. They did not actually arrive until 1827: *Inventaire-Sommaire*, ii, pp. i–v.

[2] F. Pommeraye, *Histoire de l'Abbaye Royale de St. Ouen*. He provides the text of one document otherwise unknown. See below, p. 130, n. 1.

[3] F. B. Coquelin, *Histoire de l'Abbaye de St. Michel du Tréport*.

[4] *L'Abbaye Royale de St. Pierre de Jumièges* (ed. J. Loth).

The canons of Rouen cathedral transferred all their English property to English purchasers in the fourteenth century, and it is probable that they parted with their title deeds at the same time. Only in the thirteenth-century cartulary in the municipal library in Rouen (Y 44) are such documents found. The archives contain a rarer kind of material, giving insight into the actual administration of the manors in the same century (G 4037-58).

The documents of Fécamp relative to England are very inconveniently scattered through a dozen different folders in the archives, although there is one labelled 'Angleterre' (7 H 57) which contains fifty or sixty pieces. Round calendared those earlier than 1204; some of the later ones give valuable and unusual information about the final stages of the aliens' history. In addition to these separate pieces there are also three cartularies. The one in the archives (7 H 9) is a late compilation which virtually ignores England; it has no index and the writing is so crabbed that it is possible that I have missed something. The other two are in the municipal library. The first (Y 51), of the thirteenth century, contains little more than what Round calendared, but the second (Y 188) is a nineteenth-century transcript of papal bulls which cast valuable light on certain aspects of the abbey's problems. The very earliest of Fécamp's deeds are still to be seen in the Musée de la Bénédictine at Fécamp itself.[1] Considering the importance of the abbey, Fécamp has been poorly served by historians, and it is disappointing to be unable to estimate the value of the English connexion to the monks from a knowledge of their Norman position. The numerous documents for the monastery quoted in the text may not be considered typical of the other houses, for Fécamp was a specially privileged beneficiary of the Anglo-Norman connexion. Their relative importance is impossible to measure, but the documents are too valuable to be set aside.

The great Merovingian houses of the département, revived by monastic initiative in the tenth century, Saint-Ouen, Saint-Wandrille, and Jumièges, were less favoured by the

---

[1] These documents were printed by C. H. Haskins in *Norman Institutions*, Appendix B, pp. 250-64.

lords of the conquest, probably because they lacked intimate contact with benefactors anxious to draw them into the affairs of their Domesday vills.[1] Saint-Ouen's archives for England consist of a late copy of their charter from the Confessor[2] and a few odd pieces (14 H 910) about their property in Essex. Jumièges, which benefited by the Conquest's occurrence just before the consecration of the new church, never enjoyed more than one English manor and a few churches. The unknown Maurist historian of the monastery had access to some documents not now available, but many papal bulls survive in the original (9 H 18) and a few charters occur in the great cartulary (9 H 4). The latest chronicler of Jumièges's English possessions found little new material, except details from public records.[3] For Saint-Wandrille there is a great seventeenth-century cartulary (16 H, vols. 39-42) from which Gaignières copied some interesting pieces.[4] The only original documents are a remarkable collection of charters mainly of the thirteenth century, which record the negotiations between a rector provided by the pope to one of Saint-Wandrille's churches and his agents.[5] The only other ducal house in this département, Montivilliers, sold its single English manor 1237-42[6] and there is no reference to the property in the six boxes of surviving deeds in the archives. The Vicomte Goscelin founded two monasteries in Rouen, about the same time as his Duke Robert founded Montivilliers. After the Conquest, La Trinité du Mont, Goscelin's monastery for men, received an income from Blyth priory when it was founded by Roger de Busli, as well as the manor of Harmondsworth

---

[1] See below, p. 31. It is also possible that the monks deliberately adopted an estates policy different from that of their Merovingian predecessors. M. Lucien Musset noticed a tendency to concentrate on Normandy. 'Les destins de la propriété monastique durant les invasions normandes (ixe–xie siècles): l'exemple de Jumièges' in *Congrès de Jumièges 1954*, i. 49–55. 'Les abbayes normandes semblent renoncer délibérément à s'enrichir hors du duché; elles obéissent évidemment à des raisons économiques et administratives et sans nul doute aussi, à des motifs de prudence politique . . . la nouvelle constitution des patrimoines monastiques exprime et renforce tout à la fois la cohésion d'un Etat qui entend se suffire à lui-même': ibid., p. 55.

[2] See Appendix I.

[3] Sir Charles Clay in *Congrès de Jumièges 1954*, i. 277–82.

[4] B.N. MS. Lat. 5425.

[5] B.N. MS. Lat. 17133, nos. 1–34, and B.N. n.a.lat. 1657, nos. 7 and 10.

[6] *C.P.R. 1232–47*, p. 333.

from the Conqueror. The charter in which this gift was recorded was copied into the cartulary,[1] and this is the only evidence in Normandy of the monastery's English interests. A few deeds relating to this manor, mainly fourteenth century, are now at Winchester College.[2] Goscelin's house for women, Saint-Amand, preserved archives recently studied by Mademoiselle Le Cacheux, archivist of the département of the Calvados;[3] four documents concern a group of tithes in Sussex, acquired at some unknown period before the mid-twelfth century.

Of the remaining houses, Boscherville (Y 52) and Foucarmont (Y 13) have left cartularies now in the Rouen municipal library and a few original documents of slight interest to England, now in the archives; Longueville Giffard's early charters as far as 1204 have been published by Le Cacheux, and Salter published those concerning lands acquired by New College, Oxford. Odd charters from Aumâle, Saint-Victor, and Valmont survive in the archives; there is a cartulary in the Rouen library for the house of lepers at Pont-Audemer (Y 200). A modern cartulary was composed and published by Laffleur de Kermaingant from the still extant charters of Le Tréport; he missed one interesting petition to the queen of England.[4]

The archives of the Eure were already classified and catalogued when Round checked Déville's transcripts. For England there is not much material; several houses have left practically no memorials of their past: Bernay,[5] Cormeilles,[6] La Croix Saint-Leofroy, Grestain,[7] Ivry, Saint-Léger de Préaux,[8] and Saint-Sauveur d'Evreux. The monks of Saint-Pierre de Préaux composed a cartulary (H 711) containing documents for English manorial history, but the cartularies of the cathedral of Evreux

1 Davis, no. 29.

2 T. F. Kirby, 'Charters of Harmondsworth, &c.'

3 M. J. Le Cacheux, Histoire de l'Abbaye de St. Amand de Rouen.

4 See below, p. 140, n. 2.

5 The cartulary of Bernay's priory of Eye hardly refers to the mother-house or to the other priories of Creeting and Everdon.

6 The cartularies of its priory of Newent are original authorities for the dates of the abbots of Cormeilles.

7 See C. Bréard, L'Abbaye de Notre-Dame de Grestain.

8 The only document I know of about this house is B.N. MS. Lat. 17133, no. 35.

(G 6, G 122) and of Saint-Taurin d'Evreux (H 793) are of
very slight importance for this subject. The principal interest
of the documents for this département is the collection for
Castellion, particularly the cartulary of its priory of Wootton
Wawen[1] (II F 148) which has only recently been given to
the archives and was quite unknown to Déville and Round.
Important too are the deeds of Lire, including an elaborate
summary of English titles, of which the originals are most
often lost, entered into the register of the monastery (H 590,
chap. 97). The Maurist historian, Le Noir, copied a cartulary for Lire which has since disappeared; although his
manuscript is now in private hands (MS. Le Noir, vol. 23,
pp. 453-96) a microfilm of it may be seen in the archives
(Eure 1 M 2/R 1). In England the cartulary of one of Lire's
priories, Carisbrooke,[2] and the summaries of charters in the
possession of the Carthusians of Shene[3] form a valuable
collection of materials for the history of this house. Bec's
rather meagre archives have been used by Porée and Mrs.
Chibnall.

Next in importance to the monasteries of the Seine-Maritime for the value of their English archives come those of the
Calvados. One of the richest collections of documents in all
Normandy is that of the Benedictine nuns of La Trinité,
Caen. There are no deeds at all in England. In Paris there
is a twelfth-century cartulary, at least half of which is devoted
to the English manors (B.N. MS. Lat. 5650), together with
transcripts made by Léchaudé d'Anisy from originals in the
archives at Caen (B.N. MS. Lat. 10077). Most of these still
survive in the original. They belong chiefly to the thirteenth
and fourteenth centuries so that Round's Calendar gives
little idea of their interest. Their survival does make it
possible to check Léchaudé's accuracy which is a matter of
more than pedantic concern, because his transcripts in the
Public Record Office (31/8/140 B, 3 vols.) are sometimes
the only surviving record of some deeds and have been used
confidently by English historians. Some of these transcripts
have been printed in the form of abstracts, with inaccurate
and misleading names; other faults of his copies are his

---

[1] There are some charters for the priory at King's College, Cambridge.
[2] B.M. Egerton MS. 3667.   [3] B.M. Cotton MS. Otho B xiv.

omissions of passages he could not understand or overlooked and doubtful ascriptions of dates.

The other Benedictine archives are less interesting. Troarn provides a file of documents about the exchange of its lands with Bruton priory (H 7780), some of which were left out of the cartulary now in Paris (B.N. MS. Lat. 10086). The deeds of Saint-Pierre-sur-Dives, missing in Round's day, have never been found and the missing cartulary of Saint-Etienne of Caen is known only by a seventeenth-century analysis published by Déville.[1] The archives of the monks of Caen are chiefly interesting for their different versions of the great charters of the Conqueror and of Henry II. Fontenay is poorly documented and the history of its priory of Brimpsfield one of the most obscure. Even in the fourteenth century royal clerks were not well informed about its Norman connexions and left a blank in the records where the name of the mother-house was required.[2] Saint-Vigor of Bayeux and Saint-Désir of Lisieux probably never possessed English lands.

Sainte-Barbe-en-Auge, originally Benedictine, became a house of Austin canons in 1128 when it received some small English manors. In the next generation the activity of its priors, often busy in England, was the subject of its chronicle, published by Sauvage. Its archives illustrate some of the aliens' difficulties in the late fourteenth century (2 D 170). The archives of its fellow Austins, Notre-Dame-du-Val and Plessis-Grimould, hardly refer to English property. The other Austin house, Saint-Jean of Falaise, later converted to the rule of Saint-Norbert, has not preserved even the name of its English land and probably lost it at an early period.[3] The well-documented house of Saint-André-en-Gouffern appears never to have enjoyed English property, but its fellow Cistercians have left brief records of their interests: Aunay, a dignified transaction disposing for good of their property (H 1251), and Barbéry, a single charter, published by Stapleton.[4]

[1] See Déville in *Revue Catholique de Normandie*, xiv–xv (1903–5).
[2] P.R.O. E/106/5/2. See *Worcester Registers: Giffard*, pp. 368–9; *v.* P.R.O. 31/8/140 B II no. 4, p. 21. [3] *C.D.F.* 609.
[4] *Rotuli Scaccarii Normanniae*, ed. T. Stapleton, vol. ii, p. ci, n. c *ex originale*, now John Rylands Library, Manchester, Beaumont charter 43.

The archives of the département of the Orne at Alençon are all catalogued and indexed. Nothing of interest survives from the Middle Ages for the cathedral of Séez; the archives of the Bellême foundations of Saint-Martin of Séez and Almenesches are rather meagre. Saint-Martin's cartulary exists in two versions, both copies, one in the archives (H 938), the other in the Alençon municipal library (MS. 190). A fourteenth-century 'original' is confined to the episcopal archives at Séez and M. Adigard de Gautrie is working on the textual variants. Saint-Martin was one of the Norman abbeys most favoured in England, so that the loss of its archives is particularly unfortunate. Of its priories Lancaster alone has left a few minor records of general interest, preserved in its cartulary, published by the Chetham Society. The seventeenth-century antiquaries transcribed no documents for Saint-Martin, so that presumably even then there were no records for the monks' properties in Sussex and Lincolnshire, where the other priories were. Almenesches was the only Norman nunnery that certainly maintained a small priory of women in England; the rare documents for this house unhappily throw no light on this peculiarity. Most of these are at Eton College, still unclassified. Lonlay, although it had two dependent priories in England, has nothing to colour the picture that emerges from the charters of Stogursey, also at Eton, which have been published for the Somerset Record Society. Saint-Evroul, however, left a bulky collection of documents as well as a three-volume cartulary, now in Paris (B.N. MS. Lat. 11055-7). Whereas the cartulary contains mainly twelfth- and early thirteenth-century charters, the archives can boast a number of manorial deeds and three distinct rent rolls (H 896-7, 932).[1] There is also an important letter about the dissolution of the priories (H 898). For the earlier period there are a notable number of decisions given by papal judges-delegate.

The complete destruction of the archives of Saint-Lô in June 1944 could have been a disaster of the first magnitude for the history of priories dependent on the monasteries of the Côtentin and the Avranchin. The mass of documents in

---

[1] Copies of two of these are in P.R.O. 31/8/140 B, i, no. 163 (10th Yr. H. IV), pp. 351-9; no. 164 (Little MS. 21 pp.), pp. 360-76.

these archives was said to be easily the richest in France. Fortunately, copies of many documents had been made. The *Inventaire-Sommaire* had been published to include documents from Montebourg; it did not get as far as describing the English folders, but these were probably substantially revealed by Guilloreau's researches: he published the text of 140 charters in a cartulary of the fourteenth century from Loders priory, which he had collated with originals in the archives. The cartulary of Montebourg itself was at Paris (B.N. MS. Lat. 10087) and so escaped destruction. It includes a fourteenth-century description of deeds relating to England. There is a less important cartulary for this house in London (B.M. Add. MS. 15605). Probably, therefore, little was lost irretrievably for this monastery.[1]

Unfortunately the same is not true of Mont Saint-Michel, formerly the best-documented house in France. The documents had been examined perfunctorily by many antiquaries fascinated by the history of this famous monastery, but the sheer volume of material had daunted all those who might have undertaken a serious investigation as well as those whose job was to classify and publish a record of the documents in their keeping. There is no worthy history of Mont Saint-Michel. The Maurists were unable to pursue their studies there, perhaps for political reasons: the monastery became a prison. Its beautiful cartulary, written in the twelfth century, still survives, because the manuscripts from the Mont were taken to Avranches when the deeds went to Saint-Lô: Avranches MS. 209. It was from the cartulary that Léchaudé copied a large number of documents now incorporated in the Paris cartulary (B.N. MS. Lat. 10072) and in the P.R.O. transcripts (31/8/140 B, vol. 2). Of the documents formerly at Saint-Lô he can have transcribed only a fraction. Whether materials for the English property were ever abundant is of course unknown.

---

[1] An Inventaire-général written in 1720 showed that there were then documents for England: 'Angleterre: une liace de titres concernant plusieurs rentes et droits dus à l'abbaye tant à Loudres qu'en plusieurs autres lieux du royaume d'Angleterre', *Inventaire-Sommaire*, H 8154, f. 47. This *liasse* was probably the one used by Guilloreau for his collation, but there is no means of knowing what else this *liasse* may have contained that was not copied into the cartulary, or whether other *liasses* did not also contain odd documents about England.

Guilloreau, who was not necessarily an exhaustive researcher, published only thirty-three charters for Otterton priory. They may have been all he could find, or they may have been simply the contents of a folder carelessly labelled 'Angleterre', as at Fécamp. There might have been documents for the Cornish priory of St. Michael's Mount, where a cartulary was composed in the fourteenth century; it is rarely of more than local interest. Even the monks themselves may have given up all hope of controlling their documents and left them in disorder. But it is a great pity that no historian from the sixteenth century down to 1944 did what has now become impossible.

For the other houses of the Manche, the failure of the *Inventaire-Sommaire* to advance beyond the letter M is more serious still. Round's Calendar ignored all deeds later than 1206. There are only transcripts. Léchaudé's in the P.R.O. are inadequate. Charles Duhérissier de Gerville was copying documents about the same time, six volumes of which form part of the 'Collection Mancel' (belonging to the municipality of Caen but at present deposited in the archives); they are described as 'Répertoire ou recueil de chartes extraites de cartulaires ou dépôts publics et particuliers du département de la Manche'. Gerville described the archives of Saint-Sauveur-le-Vicomte as the richest collection of the Manche, after Mont Saint-Michel, with 350 charters *dont cinquante anglaises mises à part*; neither he, who was not interested in the latter, nor Léchaudé, who ought to have been, copied them.[1] It is a considerable loss. Apart from Saint-Sauveur (vol. 298), other religious who received a brief notice from Gerville include the canons of Saint-Lô (vol. 296), the monks of Savigny (vols. 298, 299), the monks of Saint-Sever[2] (vol. 299), and the nuns of La Blanche Mortain (vol. 300). Of the houses which were covered by the *Inventaire-Sommaire* only Lessay amongst the Benedictines is memorable for its documents relating to the appoint-

[1] L. V. Delisle used these charters in his *Histoire du château et des sires de Saint Sauveur-le-Vicomte*. There are a few documents for Ellingham priory at Eton College.

[2] Saint-Sever is strictly speaking in the département of the Calvados, but it belongs to the Avranchin through its original founder St. Sever, bishop of Avranches, and its refounder Hugh d'Avranches, earl of Chester.

ments of priors from Lessay, long after the formal subjection of its priory of Boxgrove is generally believed to have been abolished. Boxgrove's own cartulary hardly refers at all to the Norman monastery. Cérisy, which maintained an important priory at Monks Sherborne, has no records of its own; the priory's papers, now at the Queen's College, Oxford,[1] are silent about the mother-house. Hambye, a later foundation (1139), disposed of one of its English assets, the church of Great Massingham, to the bishop of Norwich in 1232.[2] There is nothing to show how it had been governed during the monks' period of ownership. The only records of Saint-Fromond's English assets[3] come from official records on this side of the channel.

The cathedral canons of Coutances,[4] like all the other cathedral canons of Normandy, enjoyed English manors;[5] there are no details of their administration recorded in the *Liber Albus* now in Paris (a copy made in 1841) or in the archives of the see of Coutances, which somehow survived the war. The *Inventaire-Sommaire* shows that the Premonstratensian canons of Blanchelande and Lucerne enjoyed a little revenue from England. The more important possessions of the Austin canons of Cherbourg have left few records.

The final part of this work is based principally upon hitherto unused documents from the Norman archives and upon the published and unpublished official records in the P.R.O. The most important of the latter are the Alien Priory bundles (E 106).[6] These have been used by the contributors to the Victoria County Histories but no attempt seems to have been made, even by New, to examine royal policy towards the aliens in the light of these records.

Before the death of the Conqueror some forty foreign Benedictine monasteries and cathedral chapters divided very unevenly amongst themselves property worth more than

[1] *Historical MSS. Commission Reports*, iv. 451–5.

[2] Bodleian Charters: Norfolk Charter 249. Hambye received a rent from William Paynel II, 1182–4: *E.Y.C.* VI, pp. 95–96. There was also a monk of Hambye at Debden in Essex: *Taxatio*, p. 29 (n), P.R.O. E106/7/3.

[3] Saint-Fromond was a priory of Cérisy.

[4] The cathedral of Avranches also received rents at some unknown period: see Avranches MS. 206.   [5] *C.D.F.* 958, 966.

[6] Transcripts of some of these are to be found in B.M. Add. MSS. 6164–5.

£1,000 (Domesday values) and scattered through twenty-five counties of William's English conquest. With the exceptions of St. Peter's, Ghent, Saint-Rémy of Reims, and Saint-Denis, whose endowments antedated the Conquest, and of Cluny, Marmoutier, Saint-Florent-lès-Saumur, and two monasteries of Angers and two of Le Mans[1] (where the Conqueror had pretensions to government), patronized by the invaders, all the clerical landlords were Normans. This great vested interest was preserved until the fifteenth century. During the years 1086-1204 other 'French' monasteries received gifts of land in England, sometimes on a grand scale, but the Norman possessors remained the largest single group.[2]

The better-endowed monasteries outside Normandy—Tiron, Grandmont, and Fontevrault—normally established small English priories, bound to their mother-houses by religious ties modelled on Cluny or Cîteaux. These 'orders' have only one Norman parallel, Bec-Hellouin, which fostered co-operation between its four English priories, Cowick, Goldcliff, St. Neot's, and Stoke by Clare. Most of the Norman houses did not establish conventual priories but regarded their English estates as extensions of their domain on Anglo-Norman territory. Merovingian monasteries had likewise extended their domains all over Frankish Gaul. The Channel might be a geographical inconvenience; it was no frontier. The monks treated their English like their Norman estates. In this way the monks played their part in assimilating England to Normandy by 'consecrating' the work of their benefactors. If it would be anachronistic to speak of promoting a 'national' outlook in the Anglo-Norman realm, it is permissible to discover social and

---

[1] See L. Guilloreau, 'Les Possessions des Abbayes Mancelles et Angevines en Angleterre d'après le Domesday Book'.

[2] It is convenient to refer to the foundations of the eleventh century collectively as monasteries, although collegiate churches, including cathedral chapters, were also revived at the same time. In spite of the vituperation both canons and monks indulged in at one another's expense the difference between the two was not always as profound as they might have believed, although the monks had the reputation of observing the rules of behaviour more faithfully. Both actually prayed for the souls of their founders like later medieval chantry priests and the founders chose one or the other according to their personal preferences. Several monasteries were originally collegiate churches: Fécamp, Mont Saint-Michel, Saint-Sauveur-le-Vicomte, Aumâle, Boscherville.

political connexions, which the monks, as guardians of the Normans' spiritual ideals, were bound to encourage. Alien priories were an instrument and a symbol of Norman influence. Historians habitually study monastic and secular societies separately, but with alien priories it is the interdependence of both that matters.

The Norman monastic revival of the first half of the eleventh century differs markedly in character from the English revival under Edgar.[1] The English movement owed its inspiration to Dunstan and was sustained by the enthusiasm of Æthelwold and Oswald. Its dissemination may have varied with royal favour, but its impetus was independent of the king. In Normandy contemporary enthusiasm caused monks to return and revive the abandoned Merovingian monasteries: Jumièges, Saint-Wandrille, and Mont Saint-Michel. The Norman dukes tolerated, but did not at first encourage, them. It was not until Duke Richard II took an active interest in reform that the real Norman monastic revival began. He took no Norman monk to be his Dunstan but the abbot of Dijon, brought to Fécamp to reform the ducal 'eigenkloster'. William of Volpiano held numerous abbacies in France and established a spiritual reform in all his monasteries, but at Fécamp the effective head remained not the abbot but the duke, to whom the pope sent his bull of confirmation. None of its monks persuaded Norman lords to restore former monastic lands to the church; no monks were promoted to Norman bishoprics. Later, there were monastic archbishops of Rouen,[2] but they played little part in the promotion of the monastic revival. Archbishop Maurilius had a great reputation for sanctity and austerity of life and admittedly advised upon the foundation of the monastery of Le Tréport in 1059, but if it had not been for the counts of Eu there would have been no monastery at all. The episcopate was in general energetic and secular, typified by Geoffrey of Coutances; monasticism penetrated the church through the support of the devoted Norman barons.

[1] See J. Laporte, 'Les Origines du Monachisme dans la province de Rouen', especially pp. 53–58.
[2] See D. C. Douglas, 'The Norman Episcopate before the Norman Conquest'.

Each baron strove to found his own monastery to en-
shrine his family piety, and secured for this purpose the
most reputable monks available, those of the new movements. The monks themselves accepted, they did not demand, expansion. The best-known account of a monastic
foundation in Normandy is that of Saint-Evroul by Ordericus Vitalis in the *Historia Ecclesiastica*.[1] Professor Knowles
gives the monastery a pedigree derived from Jumièges,
Cluny, and the reformers of Lorraine,[2] but it leaps to the
eye that Orderic regards the monastery as an individual
house owing everything but its monks to the founders: its
lay patrons. The Norman monasteries should be seen as the
houses of their founders, not members of reforming orders.
Benedictines abhorred mutual co-operation and it had to be
imposed on them by Innocent III. Surprisingly enough,
even Bec, the Norman monastery most distinguished for its
spirituality, began as a house of retreat for a layman and his
friends, owing nothing to the already reformed monasteries.
Moreover, it was its exceptionally ascetic practices that
attracted Lanfranc who found nothing admirable in the
Cluniac-type houses, like Fécamp, and through his intellectual reputation the monastery began to receive public
attention and to influence other houses. Bec's unusual influence upon the Norman monastic movement was in no way
dependent on the founding of 'daughter-houses'; it worked
through its abbots, its school, and the elections of its monks
to abbacies. Its two daughter-houses, Saint-Etienne of Caen
and Lessay, had nothing to do with Bec in later life.[3] The
spiritual and intellectual revival affected all monasteries, but
it did not of itself inspire new foundations. They depended
upon the generosity of laymen.

Historically, the revival of Norman monasticism began
with Richard II's eviction of canons from his father's
foundation at Fécamp and the arrival of William of Volpiano from Dijon.[4] Fécamp, far from undertaking an ex-

---

[1] Ordericus Vitalis, *Historia Ecclesiastica*, iii. 2.
[2] D. Knowles, *The Monastic Order in England*, Appendix II.
[3] J. Laporte, 'Les Origines du Monachisme dans la province de Rouen', p. 59.
[4] For William's life see Glaber, *P.L.* cxlii. 698–719. The Norman monasteries he
'reformed' are not mentioned in the life at all. W. Williams, 'William of Dijon'.

tension of its activities, had to be bought out by Count Robert from its ownership of the property where he wished to set up the nunnery of Montivilliers (1030). In the same year he founded Cérisy; Countess Judith had founded Bernay in 1015. The lesser lay foundations began with Bellême's monastery at Lonlay (1026) and Vicomte Goscelin's monastery of La Trinité and nunnery of Saint-Amand, both in Rouen (1030). The movement gathered momentum after Count Robert set out for the Holy Land and the Norman lords emulated the absent ruler by 'ducal' policies in church and state. During the years of 'anarchy' before Val-lès-Dunes (1047) it was the baronial leaders who founded the principal monasteries of the duchy. Many of these founders were still living in 1066 and they naturally shared their new wealth with their own monks. The exultant Conqueror gave the monks of Jumièges[1] the island of Hayling, just across the Channel from the Seine estuary: 'suscepto enim imperio regni michi adversantes omnes evici';[2] other benefactors might have to be generous in more outlandish places.

No doubt 'religious' motives were strong in the minds of these Norman lords. They expected the prayers of their monks for their own souls, for those of their friends and of their glorious king. They were assured by the religious ideals of the time that generosity in this world would stand them in good stead in the next. It is also probable that they took pride in their monasteries in the present as expressions of their family distinction and wealth. As a duchy they rejoiced that their reputation, born of military prowess, was baptized in prayer. After the Normans had settled in England they retained their loyalty, at least for a time, to the family monastery, which explains benefactions in England which could not have been inspired by the Conquest. Boscherville, refounded as Benedictine in 1114, Sainte-Barbe-en-Auge, refounded as Austin in 1128, even the Cistercians like Aunay, received gifts because of this surviv-

---

[1] Jumièges was not a ducal foundation, but the dukes patronized the monks when they returned from exile after the establishment of the duchy.

[2] Davis, no. 21; J. Vernier, *Chartes de l'Abbaye de Jumièges 825–1204*, no. XXIX.

ing sense of traditional loyalties. Richard I, king of England, gave Bonport a manor in England after Philip Augustus's accession;[1] Beaulieu was also endowed about the same time;[2] Barbéry may have received its only English lands after 1204.[3]

[1] *M.A.* ii. 1007.
[2] *V.C.H. Kent,* ii. 239.
[3] See above, p. 9.

I

THE PRE-CONQUEST ENDOWMENT
OF FOREIGN MONASTERIES

THE first foreign religious house to receive English property was St. Peter's, Ghent, to whom Alfred's niece Aelfryth gave property at Lewisham (Kent) in 918. In return she asked for the monks' prayers for her late husband, Baldwin II, Count of Flanders, and for her sons, Arnulf and Adelulf. Some years later when King Edgar confirmed the gifts of his kinswoman in 964, he did more than honour family loyalties; Dunstan, his archbishop, asked the king to favour the monastery where he had spent his late exile and had first experienced the continental monastic reform movement. The reputation of foreign monasteries for piety, and their relations with the families of the great, were to be the principal causes for endowing French monasteries with English property.

After Edgar's death the monks of Ghent lost Lewisham, probably in the confused period of the renewed Danish invasions, for Edward, Æthelred II's son, was made to promise to restore it whenever he could, while on a visit to Ghent in 1016.[1] About the same time, according to Vincent of Beauvais in the thirteenth century,[2] Aethelred himself visited the abbey of Fécamp in Normandy, where he had an adventure; this story appears to represent a genuine tradition, for just as Edward promised to restore their manor to the monks of Ghent, so according to Canute, who can have had no reason to invent it, Aethelred promised a gift to the monks of Fécamp. In his charter granting the monks the manors of Brede and 'Rameslie' with its 'port', Canute, probably at the beginning of his reign, fulfilled what Aethelred, by his death, had been unable to accomplish.[3]

[1] *C.D.F.* 1372–4.
[2] A. Du Monstier, *Neustria Pia*, p. 213: 1013–16.
[3] C. H. Haskins, 'An Early Charter of Canute for Fécamp'. 'Rameslie' was a Domesday manor now divided between Winchelsea and Rye.

It is most likely that Queen Emma inspired her husbands:
the first to promise the gift, the second to honour it; her own
brother was devoted to Fécamp, for whose re-foundation he
was himself responsible. Emma must have transmitted this
devotion to her English relations. Fécamp was the only
Norman house to be singled out for endowment before the
Confessor's reign.

Canute's gift was confirmed by Hardacanute in a version
of his father's charter which contained an additional clause
of privilege: 'dono . . . duas partes telonei in portu qui dicitur
Wincenesel in manu Abbatis Johannis'.[1] John became abbot
only in 1028, so that if this clause is genuine Canute added
this grant in his later years. Haskins, however, thought this
clause a forgery. If it were it was most likely added before
Hardacanute's confirmation. Yet there is no greater probability that the monks forged it than that Canute added this
further concession to his original grant. Abbot John certainly visited England in the next reign, for there is an
account of his journey in 1054, which may even be contemporary. There are two versions of this episode.[2] Both
agree that the Confessor gave the abbot at his own request
the church of Eastbourne, but one of them only[3] adds that
the king gave as well *terra carrucae sufficiens* at Lamport
and in Horse Eye and at *caestram* the same, with salt-pans
and twelve houses, all of which were held for life by two
priests, Lenigar and Eggard. A clerk Roger in 1086 held in
Eastbourne, Lamport, and Horse Eye, where various secular priests had held in 1066, and these may have been the
successors of Lenigar and Eggard. No other records link
Fécamp with this locality. The most interesting feature of
the narrative is that it explains why Abbot John came to
England in the first place: 'mare disposuit transire, terrasque
suae ditionis illa in regione sitas invisere; et pro ut compe-
tebat utiliter ordinare'.

Another doubtful gift of the Confessor to Fécamp was
Steyning in West Sussex. In a writ,[4] the form of which

---

[1] Haskins, op. cit.

[2] *Neustria Pia*, p. 223, and J. Mabillon, *Annales Ordinis Sancti Benedicti . . .*,
iv. 503.

[3] *Neustria Pia*.   [4] *C.D.* 890.

Miss Harmer finds somewhat suspicious,[1] Edward says that he has given it to the monks of Fécamp to hold after the death of Bishop Ælfwine.[2] According to Domesday, Harold held Steyning *in fine regis Edwardi* and from this Round concluded that he had seized lands belonging to the monks, in order to prevent them assisting William's invasion.[3] It is rather odd that on the very eve of the conquest, William gave Fécamp seisin of the land of Steyning by token of a knife,[4] as though by this act he defied Harold and promised to restore England and Steyning to their rightful rulers. Yet this grant need not imply that the monks had enjoyed actual possession of Steyning, but only that they had claims as good as if not better than those William himself had to England. In a later, genuine, confirmation for Steyning in 1085,[5] William says bluntly that even 'if the abbey did not hold the manor in the time of King Edward yet he gives it'. Better proof that there is justifiable doubt whether the monks had enjoyed possession of Steyning could hardly be found. The same charter likewise makes it quite clear that they had held property in East Sussex; the Conqueror exchanged with Fécamp some property, held by them in Hastings before the Conquest, for the manor of Bury; should the manor prove less valuable than the rents they had lost, he would make it good. Whether these rents represent the rights at 'Caestram' referred to in the account of Abbot John's visit in 1054, as Round believed,[6] or whether they were simply part of the revenues of 'Rameslie' manor, they were evidently real assets, which had been profitable to the monks. If they did not certainly obtain possession of Steyning before the Conquest, it cannot be maintained that Harold deliberately took it from them from fear of treachery in 1066, or even that general hostility to the Normans caused him to seize lands of which they enjoyed a 'reversion'. Surely, if Harold is to be credited with such motives, it is consistent to expect that he would have also taken the manor of 'Rameslie', which was closer to the sea and possessed of a recognized port.

[1] F. E. Harmer, *Anglo-Saxon Writs*, p. 16, n. 1.
[2] Harmer, op. cit., p. 552. If he was bishop of Winchester, he died in 1047.
[3] J. H. Round, *Feudal England*, pp. 317–31, esp. 319–20, see D.B. i, f. 17b.
[4] Davis, no. 1.   [5] Davis, no. 206. *C.D.F.* 115.
[6] J. H. Round, 'Some Early Sussex Charters', *S.A.C.* xlii. 75–77.

There is no record of Harold's occupation of this manor. His seizure of Steyning should therefore be ascribed to particular motives of which we must remain unaware.

Mont Saint-Michel, which also enjoyed ducal patronage, possessed a charter purporting to be issued by Edward *dei gratia Anglorum rex* while apparently still in exile in Normandy before 1035 judging from the witnesses of Count Robert of Normandy and Archbishop Robert of Rouen and other Norman bishops.[1] Only two other instances of Edward's name in Norman documents are known. In one he uses the title king when witnessing a charter for Fécamp;[2] in the other, a charter for Saint-Wandrille, he signs simply 'Hetuuardi'.[3] Even if there is one precedent for Edward taking the title king during the life of his stepfather, it is a different matter to exercise kingly functions, or to pretend to do so. Edward does not hint that his grant depends upon his restoration: he implies actual power. 'Si quis autem his donis conatus fuerit ponere calumpniam anathema factus iram dei incurrat perpetuam. Utque nostrae donationis auctoritas verius firmiusque teneatur in posterum manu mea firmando subterscripsi quod et plures fecere testium.' It is not possible to assume from the evidence available that a grant made in exile was renewed once Edward really did become king. In such a case it would be natural to expect the names of later English witnesses to have been added to the names of Count Robert and his bishops. Edward's gifts were considerable: 'sanctum Michaelem qui est iuxta mare cum omnibus appendiciis, villis scilicet, castellis, agris, et caeteris attinentibus'. This may indeed be the Cornish St. Michael's Mount, a small island at high tide. The charter continues: 'Addidi etiam totam terram de Uennefire cum oppidis, villis, agris, pratis, terris cultis et incultis, et cum horum redditibus adiunxi quoque datis portum addere qui vocatur Ruminella cum omnibus quae ad eum pertinent, hoc est molendinis et

---

1 This was published by Dugdale *ex autographo* without the witness of Count Robert: *M.A.* i. 551. The only early text now available, in the twelfth-century cartulary of Mont Saint-Michel, adds his name, easily overlooked when it precedes its homonym, the archbishop's: Avranches MS. 210, f. 32ᵛ. It is calendared by Round: *C.D.F.* 708.

2 Haskins, *Norman Institutions*, p. 263, no. 10: 1032–4.

3 F. Lot, *Études critiques sur l'Abbaye de St. Wandrille*, p. 54, no. 13.

piscatoriis et cum omni territorio illius culto et inculto et eorum redditibus.' These grants of land including 'towns' and 'vills' are best understood as grants of recognized 'territories' like the patrimony of a saint. There is an accepted tradition of the existence of a religious community at St. Michael's Mount from the eighth century, but the only reference to the patrimony of St. Michael is made in passing by Domesday Book and there is nothing to link the patrimony with 'Uennefire'. The Exon Domesday entry runs as follows: 'Sanctus Michaelis habet i mansionem quae vocatur Treiwal de qua abstulit Comes de Moritonio i hidam quae erat in dominicatu sancti die qua rex Edwardus fuit vivus et mortuus.'[1] The Domesday entry itself makes it clear that while the manor itself was held by the priest Brismar, the hide of land rendered geld to St. Michael.[2] Truthwall is on the mainland opposite to the Mount. Canon Taylor identified Uennefire with Winnington, a Domesday hundred, where seventeen thegns held lands which were monastic or 'meneage' in the parishes of St. Keverne, St. Anthony, Manaccan, St. Martin, and Mawgan-in-Meneage. The monks certainly held lands in this region at a later date. He also identified 'Ruminella' with Ruan Minor (the 'port' being Cadgwith in that parish).[3] Gover gives an ancient form of Ruan Minor as Rumon le Meinder (c. 1250) which seems to confirm this otherwise doubtful reading.[4] Henderson[5] was inclined to doubt these, but they are the most satisfactory solution yet offered. Nevertheless it is important to notice that Domesday does not support the view that the places of Edward's charter then belonged either to St. Michael or to the monks of Mont Saint-Michel. This fact, taken together with the suspicious form of the document, makes it unlikely that the document records a genuine grant by Edward. In the late eleventh century the monks appear to have been in

---

[1] *Exon D.B.*: Record Commission, iv. 471.
[2] D.B. i, f. 120b 2. See T. Taylor, 'St. Michael's Mount and the Domesday Survey'. [3] T. Taylor, *St. Michael's Mount*, pp. 29–30.
[4] I owe this information to the invaluable help of Mr. P. L. Hull, the archivist of the county of Cornwall, who was kind enough to supply me with information on Cornish place-names, gleaned from the unpublished notes and papers of Mr. Gover and Mr. Henderson now deposited at Truro.
[5] See note above. C. Henderson, 'Ecclesiastical Antiquities of Cornwall', vol. i (written 1923–4), in manuscript.

serious trouble with the mighty Robert of Mortain[1] and it is a tempting possibility that this charter was concocted about the same time, to defend claims to lands which their canon predecessors on the Cornish Mount may even have enjoyed, but for which the monks could find no documentary proof. This would explain the violence of 'Edward's' language; the monks may also have preferred to compose a Norman charter and not to risk too much by inventing an English one. The evidence for any grant of lands in Cornwall to the Norman Mont Saint-Michel before the Conquest is unconvincing.

The gifts of the Confessor to Saint-Ouen of Rouen and the cathedral of Notre Dame, Rouen, are recorded in unimpeachable charters, both dated, with witnesses. The charter for Saint-Ouen is the earlier. The cult of this Norman saint was not introduced by the Confessor; Levison called attention to the presence of relics at Christ Church, Canterbury, from the tenth century.[2] Yet his exile no doubt increased Edward's devotion to Saint-Ouen; the gift was made not long after his accession. The charter of benefaction survives in two forms: the first is a fifteenth-century copy of the original at Rouen,[3] the second, a later version, was seen by Philip Morant in the archives of Colchester and published by him,[4] but the document he saw has since disappeared. The important differences in the versions are that Morant did not publish the witnesses which may be seen from the Rouen text to be consistent with the alleged date, 1046, and that he gave a Latin version of the boundary description, incorporating the name of someone who is believed to have been a Domesday tenant, whereas this description is given in Anglo-Saxon and without this name in the Rouen text. Domesday shows that the monks were seised of the property in the time of King Edward,[5] and unlike the monks of Fécamp, those of Saint-Ouen never strayed from the corner of Essex where the Confessor had established them; Henry I added another manor to this original endowment

[1] See below, pp. 35–37
[2] W. Levison, *England and the Continent in the Eighth Century*, pp. 211–12.
[3] Seine-Maritime 14 H 145; see Appendix I A.
[4] P. Morant, *History of Essex*, i. 426 n. F.
[5] D.B. ii (Little Domesday), f. 22.

which was adjacent to West Mersea, and Stephen gave them the hundred rights in Winstree.[1]

The cathedral's charter was given in 1061 and survives in two forms: one without witnesses.[2] In elaborate formulas Edward describes how he had governed England for eighteen years and had at last decided to grant the vill of Ottery to Notre Dame of Rouen, in order to secure her prayers. This remained the most valuable of the cathedral's manors, even after others had increased its English possessions.

Round was responsible for championing the theory that the Confessor's religious enthusiasms caused him to endow monasteries which would help to prepare England for the coming of the Norman heir, and that Fécamp's foothold in Sussex, and Bishop Osbern's holding at Bosham, were deliberately given to aid the Conquest. There is, however, no evidence to show that William was welcomed in these districts or that bishop or monks assisted in William's plans. The fact that Edward's gifts were easy of access by boat should not be given political significance. If the only non-royal gift to a foreign monastery before 1066 was Earl Leofric's grant of lands in Staffordshire to the monks of Saint-Rémy, Reims, this may mean only that the earl had no available coastal manor to give them, not that he was too patriotic to admit potential traitors near the coasts. The Confessor was in a position to think of his monks' convenience. The Lewisham estate of the Conqueror's Flemish ally had been given in 918 and was easily reached from Flanders by sea across the North Sea and up the Thames. Fécamp's Sussex interests lay equally conveniently across the Channel from Fécamp itself, but had been given by Canute, who had every reason to discourage Norman ambitions, and every desire to promote trade and contact between the two countries. Of the Confessor's own benefactions, Mont Saint-Michel's doubtful assets in the extreme south-west could have been no help in any attack on London: a manor on Southampton water would have been far more useful; Saint-Ouen's West Mersea offers no port facilities, and although accessible from Flanders by sea, could have been less help in

---

[1] Appendix I B.
[2] C.D. 810: this gives witnesses. Rouen MS. Y 44, f. 26–26ᵛ omits them.

the Conquest than the wharves in London where Rouen merchants could be found from Æthelred's reign. The fact that these properties were all on or near the coast was important to the monks who had to come from Normandy to visit them. The significance of Harold's seizure of Steyning has already been questioned. Edward's motives were simply pious, and no subtlety should be sought in his actions. He remembered the saints he had venerated in his youth, listened with rapt attention to the saintly Abbot John of Fécamp (who visited him in England) and expressed his sympathy for the reviving monastic movement in Normandy, which excited his Norman friends, by distributing a few English lands to the Norman monks, as his predecessors on the throne of England had expressed their esteem for the monasteries of the Continent.

II

THE POST-CONQUEST FOUNDATIONS

THE effect of the conquest on English ecclesiastical history is usually described solely in terms of the policies of Lanfranc and the Conqueror himself. Inevitably contemporary witnesses were impressed by the king and archbishop, but modern critics doubt whether their influence or their opinions and actions were as profound or far-reaching as is commonly supposed. Sir Frank Stenton goes so far as to suggest that the state of the parochial clergy was hardly affected by drastic changes in all matters of external activity. Unfortunately there is little evidence to draw upon for a new picture of the effects of the conquest on the parochial clergy of the eleventh century. Nevertheless a rather neglected aspect of monastic history does make it possible to lift a little the veil that shrouds all but the brightest lights of Norman religion. Monasticism was the ideal of eleventh-century piety and a proper understanding of it can do much to illuminate the whole ecclesiastical picture. Here again the foundation of Battle abbey, the introduction of the Norman abbots and knight-service into the old English monasteries, or the influence of Lanfranc's *Consuetudines* may, not unfairly, be said to exhaust the general historian's interest in the effects of the conquest on monasticism. Stenton admits that 'the characteristic benefactions of this age are gifts of land in England to monasteries in France' but dismisses them immediately: 'the future of alien priories was to be undistinguished and it is unlikely that those who brought them into being received much encouragement from Lanfranc'.[1] Those who brought them into being included the Conqueror himself.

The interest of these alien priories, and their importance in the period of the Norman kings, lies precisely in the fact that they represent another attitude to the ecclesiastical prob-

[1] Sir Frank Stenton, *Anglo-Saxon England*, pp. 665–8.

lems of the age than Lanfranc's and Anselm's.[1] The alien priories were the foundations of the Norman families who governed the country and bequeathed to succeeding centuries a tradition of seigneurial initiative in local church affairs. The great lords did not plan national policies and their only chroniclers were enthusiastic admirers or injured enemies: in both cases monks with a narrow range of sympathies. Yet these same lords shaped the lives of their dependents and wielded unrivalled power in their districts. Of their actions little has come down, save a tradition of lawlessness; of their 'motives' it is almost presumptuous to speak. Yet in the documents of benefaction to their monks, it is possible to read an ecclesiastical 'policy' quite unlike Lanfranc's.

It is not true to say, as Stenton does,[2] that the lords of the conquest were too poor to found large monasteries in England. They had been founding them in Normandy for the thirty years before 1066 with resources inferior to their Domesday holdings. The reason why they preferred to give lands to their own Norman houses, rather than to found new monasteries in England, was because they continued to regard Normandy as their own land. They therefore expressed their piety through gifts to the monasteries which enshrined their family's devotion in Normandy. Not until the families began to identify themselves with their new homes in England did they foster English monasteries. This process of losing touch with Normandy is hardly noticeable before the death of Henry I.

Most writers on alien priories assume that these gifts of land were intended to become the basis of convents of monks, and have therefore to deplore that they did not develop in this way, or that if they did, they remained very small, as though monasteries ought to use their resources only to found new cells. Some Norman monasteries did found English priories which were able to show in the fifteenth century that their conventual life was independent and that all the monks were Englishmen. There were few of

---

[1] Anselm himself as abbot of Bec had to visit his monastery's English possessions: Eadmer, *Vita Anselmi*, i. 29–31: see also chap. 28.

[2] Stenton, op. cit., p. 665.

these houses. Most of the 'priories' had only French monks. Some were priories with three or four Norman monks who came and went at their abbot's pleasure; some were bailiwicks with monks sent to manage the property as bailiffs, sometimes with, but often apparently without, a 'fellow' to hold them to their monastic profession. In these cases the bailiff had usually to be frequently on the move, visiting manors in different parts of the country. Even the regular priories had their endowments in several counties, which meant that administration could be burdensome; only the smallest priories enjoyed a compact group of estates.

Nearly thirty Norman monasteries eventually received gifts of manors or estates in addition to churches and tithes, and so became landlords in England. About twenty-five monasteries received only spiritual revenues, with no land except a small piece of glebe land that might be attached to their churches. These spiritual revenues were generally less valuable than the possession of lands, and only the smaller Norman monasteries received them. What is surprising is that those monasteries which were best endowed with temporalities, and therefore in the most favourable situation for founding daughter priories, had they wished, did not use their wealth for this purpose. The monasteries with spiritual revenues were the principal founders of priories. This raises the question whether the lords of the conquest did, in fact, give manors for the purpose of having priories founded from the revenues, or whether they had some other motive.

Unfortunately very few charters issued by the Normans themselves have survived. Most of their gifts are known only from royal confirmations in which the benefactors appear to ask only in general terms for the monks' prayers for themselves, their families and friends, and lords.[1] Many original gifts were still made without written evidence at this time, so that it is impossible to recover the actual words used by these men and therefore to assert what their intentions were. The

---

[1] Services of prayer could be performed in the Norman house itself. For example, the young King Henry (III) was buried at Rouen, but his mass priests were supported by English revenues: *C.D.F.* 30–31, 46–50. William Paynton of Hayles gave English property to Saint-Evroul to support 'uno monacho ad cotidie celebrandum in eodem monasterio perpetuo pro anima eius et heredum suorum': B.M. Cotton MS. Otho B xiv, f. 119.

Normans were, however, men of action, not words; had they wanted to see daughter priories of their monasteries spring up in England, can we doubt that they would indeed have come into being? There is nothing to show that such priories were ever desired. The property was given to show favour to the Norman monks and obtain their prayers.

In a few special circumstances the gifts are easily explained. The Conqueror paid his debt to St. Valéry, the Picard saint, for the favourable breeze that blew him to England before Hastings, with the manor of Tackley in Essex.[1] To the monks of Jumièges who celebrated the consecration of their new church in 1067, the Conqueror was pleased to give the island of Hayling.[2] But the abbot of La Trinité, Rouen, had no particular claim upon the Conqueror's generosity[3] when he came to England with two monks in 1069; the king was in the giving mood and playfully pretended to stab the abbot's hand with a knife as he handed over the manor of Harmondsworth in Middlesex.[4] The other great monasteries of Normandy had similar proofs of their duke's continued affection; he did not seek special occasions to justify, nor specific services in return for, his gifts.

He particularly favoured his own foundations at Caen. The monks had Domesday manors in Dorset, Devon, Essex, and Norfolk worth £80 odd, apart from churches.[5] The nuns of La Trinité received no separate churches, but their manors were probably worth as much as £100 in 1086;[6] Minchinhampton and Pinbury in Gloucestershire, Tarrant Launston in Dorset, and Felsted in Essex had all been given to them at the time of William's 'Quisquis' charter of

---

[1] *Chartes des Abbés de St. Valéry*, p. 33. Appendice XIII from a fourteenth-century roll at New College, Oxford, Tackley 269: 'dux Normannie et rex Anglie Willelmus ac etiam Gwydo de Reymecurt baro suus dederunt . . . elemosinam suam . . . ex voto et promissione debita in transfretatione facta conqueste anglicane'.

[2] Davis, no. 21.

[3] Unless his service to William Fitz Osbern in Normandy earned him the king's thanks: Davis, no. 24.   [4] Davis, no. 29.

[5] D.B. i, ff. 78b, 104; ii, ff. 22, 221b. The monks received three isolated churches but retained only one. Only the tithe of Bures, not the church, was confirmed to them 1174–82: C.D.F. 459. Corsham church was given to Marmoutier: Johnson no. 593. Creech was retained: Davis, no. 397; C.D.F. 453.

[6] D.B. i, ff. 79, 104, 166b; ii, f. 21b.

1082;[1] other Domesday manors were subsequently lost or exchanged for others by the Conqueror's sons.[2]

Naturally, by comparison, other ducal monasteries benefited less, but neither revived Merovingian houses, like Saint-Wandrille, Jumièges, and Mont Saint-Michel, nor foundations of previous dukes, like Fécamp, Bernay, and Montivilliers, were ignored. Saint-Wandrille received two small manors from the king, but was richer in churches by 1086;[3] Jumièges obtained disputed possession of Hayling island and two separate churches;[4] Mont Saint-Michel acquired four small manors in Devon and a few churches;[5] Saint-Ouen and the cathedral of Rouen were confirmed in possession of the lands given them by the Confessor, and both had to await Henry I's generosity before extending their holdings in England;[6] Fécamp received or recovered the endowments it claimed by gifts of the last English kings;[7] Bernay and Montivilliers received small tokens of the Conqueror's continued esteem.[8] With few exceptions the generous king expressed his piety by giving manors to his monasteries and he showed his favour to the foundations of his barons in the same manner. Saint-Evroul was given

---

[1] Davis, no. 149.

[2] Johnson, nos. 1692, 1928. See Davis, no. 183. William II gave them Horstead (Norfolk) in exchange for two Domesday manors, 'Tembreham' and 'Becdona': these two may be Umberlei, D.B. i, f. 104, 2, and Great Barrow, D.B. ii, f. 21b. Henry I added the princely gift of Tilshead (Wiltshire), worth £100 in 1086.

[3] The manor of Dullingham (Cambridgeshire) worth £12 (D.B. i, f. 193) was still held in 1304, when it was farmed for no service. C.Cl.R. 1302–7, p. 132; the manor of 'Dunsford' in Wandsworth (Surrey) worth 20s. (D.B. i, f. 34b) was somehow acquired by Merton priory before 1180. B.M. Add. Ch. 8071, B. For the six churches, four given by the Conqueror, see Davis, no. 110; M.A. ii. 974–5; F. Lot, op. cit., p. 129. Three more churches were acquired before 1139.

[4] See below, p. 34–35. The churches were Winterbourne Stoke and Chewton (D.B. i, ff. 65, 87).

[5] Otterton worth £18, Dotton, 40s., Yarcombe, 60s. (D.B. i, f. 104, 2), and 'Fierseham', 30s. (D.B. i, f. 107). The monks retained three churches in the southwest near their estates: Martock, St. Clement, and St. Hilary, Moresk, and two other distant churches: Wath in the diocese of Durham (C.D.F. 736, 751) and Great Wilbraham in the diocese of Ely (Valuation of Norwich, p. 214). No less than six churches were disposed of by the monks: two were exchanged for land in Devon with Henry I who gave the churches to Reading abbey (Johnson, no. 1418); three were given to Selborne priory in 1232 and one other to the bishop of Exeter in 1206: see below, p. 102, n. 9.

[6] Johnson, nos. 1010, 1289.   [7] See above, pp. 20–21.

[8] Creeting (Suffolk, D.B. ii, f. 389); Waddon (Dorset, D.B. i, f. 79).

the manor of Rowell;[1] Troarn, Horsley,[2] both in Gloucester-shire; Saint-Pierre-sur-Dives, Pusey in Berkshire;[3] Préaux, five hides at Aston Tirrold in Berkshire, exchanged for a Norman property and five hides at Watlington in Oxford-shire;[4] Grestain, the foundation of his stepfather's family, several small pieces of land.[5]

The great lords imitated the king. In Domesday Grestain holds lands of the count of Mortain; Almenesches, Saint-Martin of Séez and Troarn of Roger de Montgomery; Castellion, of Ralph de Toesny, Le Tréport, of the count of Eu; Saint-Victor-en-Caux, of Ralph de Mortemer. The manor held in chief by the monks of Cormeilles in 1086[6] had probably been held of Earl Roger, who gave it to them for the repose of his father, William Fitz Osbern. Préaux, which found benefactors in several families, held all its lands from its founder's family, the Beaumonts. Saint-Evroul en-joyed the patronage of several different families from the pays d'Ouche, and was exceptional in holding lands not only from the king and its founder Hugh de Grendmesnil, and the latter's nephew Robert de Rhuddlan, but also from other great tenants in chief: Ralph de Todeni, Roger de Mont-gomery, and Hugh d'Avranches.

These gifts of land were not always large. The monks were already rivals for available favours and the Norman lords cannot really have expected that the English endowments of their monasteries would increase in subsequent generations to the point when a flourishing English monastery could develop. The rarity of early charters usually makes it im-possible to show how a monastery extended its holdings, but in a few cases, which may be taken as typical, such a course can be detected. The first specific mention of many of Saint-

---

[1] Davis, no. 40.
[2] C.D.F. 464. This manor may have previously been the property of the patron's family: the Conqueror gave it for the repose of the soul of Countess Mabel.
[3] D.B. i, f. 59b.
[4] D.B. i, ff. 60b, 157. Although the Conqueror describes the Berkshire estate as being five hides (Davis, no. 130) in 1086, the monks held only two hides of their lord, the count of Mortain, to whom their Norman estate had been given.
[5] D.B. i, ff. 43b, 222b.
[6] D.B. i, ff. 20b, 68b, 92b, 146b, 193; D.B. ii, f. 291b; D.B. i, f. 24b; D.B. i, ff. 23, 24.2, 25, 25b; D.B. i, f. 25b; D.B. i, f. 183; D.B. i, f. 18; D.B. i, f. 46b; D.B. i f. 166.

Evroul's possessions occurs in twelfth-century charters of the Beaumont family. It is improbable that the Beaumonts preferred to favour Saint-Evroul rather than their own foundations at Préaux in Normandy or Leicester in England,[1] and since the possessions can in almost every case be found in vills belonging to the monastery's patron, Hugh de Grendmesnil in 1086, it is much more likely that the monks' interests there were in fact given to them by Hugh or his son. Interesting confirmation of this theory comes from a dispute between the monks and the earl of Leicester himself about the church of Widford. It is not clear what the monks' rights were, but the church had been given to Bermondsey priory in exchange for the church of Enderby in Leicestershire by Ivo de Grendmesnil, Hugh's son, presumably after Hugh's death in 1098 and certainly before 1102 when Ivo mortgaged his estates to the count of Meulan. This exchange was ratified in 1118 by the count's son, first earl of Leicester,[2] Saint-Evroul's claims therefore went back to the eleventh century, probably to a grant from Hugh. Similarly Grestain's property can be traced to manors of the count of Mortain in 1086. Count William certainly added to his father's gifts, probably, though not necessarily, after Robert's death; anyway he must have done so before his forfeiture early in Henry I's reign.[3] The case of Lire and Cormeilles is even more interesting: William Fitz Osbern their founder,[4] was killed in 1071, and his son lost his lands by rebellion in 1075. Property which the monks were to hold for centuries must have been acquired within a decade of the conquest. In both cases the monks possessed little land and their churches and tithes are often not mentioned before Henry II's confirmation charters. Lire appears to have been the first to enjoy Fitz Osbern's patronage, receiving six churches, nearly three hides of land, and all his tithes (in

---

[1] The Beaumont confirmations probably arose out of the marriage of Robert II to Petronilla, the Grendmesnil heiress, who was the first of her house in the twelfth century to be influential enough to defend Saint-Evroul's interests.

[2] *C.D.F.* 644 (Orne H 937) 1164-7 or 1174-9, *M.A.* i. 640; *M.A.* v (1825), 88, *sub anno* 1118.

[3] The date of Count William's forfeiture was 1106.

[4] According to the *Nova Chronica Normannica* (ed. P. A. Chéruel, *sub anno* 1042) Cormeilles was the senior house, but its history is very shadowy beside Lire's, founded 1046, which received its charter in 1051 (Eure H 438; Martène, iii. 1432).

1086 these were the king's) in the Isle of Wight. In the Marches, where he received from the Conqueror his last important commission, the hitherto neglected monks of Cormeilles were given possessions in sixteen of his manors, while Lire received possessions in only six manors. Yet when Henry II confirmed the possessions of the monks of Cormeilles in 1172 they retained interests in only eight of the sixteen vills of 1086, and judging from Lire's late-twelfth-century rental it was Lire which had replaced Cormeilles in six of these eight.[1] These two sister foundations can have borne no deep love to one another, in spite of the identical circumstances which deprived them of their influential patrons so early. Fitz Osbern was replaced in the Marches by William de Briouze and he brought with him the monks of Saint-Florent-lès-Saumur whom he had already introduced into Sussex. The first surviving record of dispute between the monks of Lire and Saumur belongs to the mid-twelfth century,[2] but their rival spheres of interest probably began to intersect in the Conqueror's own lifetime.

This evidence shows two things. First, the pattern of settlement and endowment of alien monks was marked out before about 1100; second, monks from different houses were already competing for what favours the Conqueror's barons would bestow. This may be illustrated by examples of difficulties experienced by three of the most powerful Norman monasteries.

Jumièges' contest with the monks of Winchester cathedral for the possession of Hayling island lasted nearly a hundred years. The Confessor's unloved consort, Edith, had given the cathedral the island of Hayling, but the monks were seised of only half of it before 1066, because the tenant of the other half enjoyed a life-holding. The Conqueror gave

[1] Lire received no manor from Fitz Osbern, but all its churches were in vills belonging to him while he lived. Roger de Laci gave Duntesbourne worth 20s. (D.B. i, f. 166) and Hugh Asinus gave Liver's Ocle in 1100 (C.D.F. 402): these two had been tenants of Fitz Osbern. Earl Roger gave Cormeilles the manor of Newent because his father was buried there (D.B. i, f. 166): it was worth £5. Cormeilles' churches were also situated on Fitz Osbern's lands. Henry II's charter for Cormeilles is printed in Delisle–Berger, i, no. 319, pp. 466–8. Lire's rental: B.N. MS. Lat. 4221. Lire's charters: M.A. ii, 986–7 and Delisle–Berger, i, no. 65.

[2] M.A. ii, 987: 1164–6. Roger, bishop of Worcester, was consecrated 1164. William, abbot of Lire, died 1166.

the island to Jumièges shortly after the conquest[1] and issue was joined between the English and the Norman monks before Domesday.[2] William II favoured Winchester;[3] Henry I, Jumièges.[4] Henry of Blois took advantage of his brother's reign to take back Edith's gift 'et reduisit les moines qui desservoient le prieuré à une telle indigence que deux d'entre eux furent contraints de repasser la mer et de rentrer dans leur premier monastère'.[5] Innocent II requested the bishop to reconsider the plight of the Norman monks, and he relented in January 1139.[6] After Archbishop Theobald's return from Rome he found that although the bishop had received a hundred marks for his concession he still troubled the monks in their quiet enjoyment of their half.[7] In 1147 Eugenius III confirmed them in possession of the greater part of the island and all its tithe,[8] and the last that is heard of the dispute is Alexander III's reference to the rights of the monks of Winchester to the tithe of vegetables and oats there.[9]

Another beneficiary of the conquest immediately threatened in possession of its new estates was Mont Saint-Michel. The evidence for this case is meagre, but a comparison of a charter of Robert, count of Mortain, with the bare records of Domesday is revealing. The earliest history of St. Michael's Mount is involved in it. According to Domesday, St. Michael held two hides in Truthwall one of which had been taken from the saint by Robert.[10] It was therefore presumably after 1086 but before his death in 1091 that Robert restored the hide by giving up the manors of Truthwall and Ludgvan. It was a small estate worth between £3 and £5 in 1086, but this was a valuable property to the saint,

[1] Davis, no. 21: 1067.   [2] D.B. i, f. 43b.

[3] Davis, no. 483a: 1096–1100.   [4] Johnson, no. 638: 1101–3.

[5] *Histoire de Jumièges*, ii. 250–1. There are now no medieval authorities for this statement.

[6] *C.D.F.* 157; *Chartes de Jumièges* (Rouen, 1916), no. LXIII, pp. 162–3. Henry is not styled legate and the charter must be earlier than March 1139 because a witness to it, Jocelin, archdeacon of Winchester, became bishop of Salisbury before Henry lost his legatine authority. Since Theobald the archbishop left England at the end of January 1139 the charter belongs to that month, after his consecration on the 8th.

[7] *C.D.F.* 158.

[8] *C.D.F.* 159: Seine-Maritime 9 H 18: seventeenth-century copy of *vidimus* of 1531.   [9] *M.A.* ii. 977–8.

[10] See above, p. 23.

whose recorded holdings in 1086 were worth only twenty
shillings. To this gift Robert added both fairs of the Mount.[1]
Unfortunately this simple story is complicated by the mere
existence of another charter of the count's, whether genuine
or not.

This charter exists in different forms. The earliest text
now available is the copy in the twelfth-century cartulary of
Mont Saint-Michel.[2] There was an 'original' used by Dugdale[3] which Round may have seen although he does not com-
ment on its form.[4] This charter is not dated, but is witnessed
by William Fitz Osbern who was killed in 1071 and by the
Conqueror's youngest son Henry *adhuc puero*. In the charter Robert appears as one of the monks' leading benefactors.
He claims to have held the banner of St. Michael *in bello*,
as if he were specially bound to the saint. His title *ego
Rotbertus Dei gratia Moritonii comes* is very unusual. What he
gives, the monks certainly possessed then or later: 'montem
Sancti Michaelis in Cornubia cum dimidia terrae hida ita
solutum . . . ut ego tenebam ab omnibus consuetudinibus
querelis et placitis' and '*mercatum die quintae feriae*'. The
second part of the charter begins 'monachorum suffragiis
michi a Deo ex propria conjuge mea filio concesso auxi
donum . . . in manaeth tres acras terrae Traaraboth, videlicet
Lismanaeth, Trequaners, Carmelel . . .'. All these places can
be identified with lands later held by the monks,[5] but the
additional clause of privileges 'ut de nulla re regiae justitiae
monachi respondebunt nisi de solo homicidio' is probably not
genuine.[6] It is possible that Robert had been benevolent in

[1] *C.D.F.* 716.   [2] Avranches MS. 210, f. 33.
[3] *M.A.* i. 551. There is a fourteenth-century copy in Hatfield MS. 315.
[4] *C.D.F.* 715.
[5] Mr. P. L. Hull has kindly supplied me with the following identifications: they
are all in the meneage – or more anciently Manahec, the monk's land. Trevelaboth
= Traboe, in St. Keverne; Lismanoch = Lesneage in St. Keverne; Trequavers =
Tregevas in St. Martin-in-Meneage; Carmailoc = Carvallack in St. Keverne. The
manor of Traboe included lands in several districts: Lesneage, Polkerth, Tregeage,
Vean and Veor, Anhay, Mallacorne, Tregidden, Polpidnick, Polherro, Mill Mehal,
Trelamining, all in St. Keverne. Tregevas in St. Martin-in-Meneage, Tretharrup,
Tregeddras, Carvallack, Bounval, Gear Veor, Vean and Velnowth, Tucoys in
Constantine. See Hatfield MS. 315.
[6] See *P.Q.W.*, p. 109: the prior of the Mount then claimed only an assize of bread
and ale and three fairs a year in Marazion. There is no record of any other privileges
ever claimed by the monks.

1066–70, but later proved hostile, but it seems more likely that the charter does not represent a genuine grant made by Robert during his lifetime. According to Round, Robert held no important Cornish estates until after 1075, when Count Brien of Brittany, who had led the Breton contingent at Hastings,[1] lost his lands there by rebellion. It is far more probable that Brien would have given lands of the priory already existing at the Mount to Mont Saint-Michel, than that Robert, the patron of Grestain, should have done so.[2] After 1075 the monks might have hesitated to claim lands given them by a rebellious lord, particularly if they had no documentary proof of their claims. The fabrication of a charter attributed to Robert would, however, have been made only after his death, and probably after the death of Henry I, who might have remembered that he had witnessed no such document, even as a lad. The attempt to justify the grant by Robert's relation to the saint at Hastings looks very suspicious.

This suspicion is confirmed by the context of the charter in all but one of its versions.[3] Leofric, bishop of Exeter, confirmed it at Pevensey in 1085, by command of Pope Gregory and the king and queen. Only one copy of the document, a late version at Hatfield, gives the more acceptable date 1070. Even this date, although compatible with the apparent date of Robert's charter, is not without faults. Leofric died in 1071 so that if he could not have been urged by the queen, who died in 1083, to confirm a charter in 1085, no more could he have been prompted in 1070 to do so by Gregory, who succeeded Alexander II only in 1073.[4] The importance of this reference to Pope Gregory in 1070 may be seen from the reference by the fifteenth-century traveller, William of Worcester, to a document supposed to stem from this pope in the same impossible year. This pseudo-grant was compiled with a view to the pilgrim traffic

[1] But G. H. White, 'The Battle of Hastings and the Death of Harold' (*Complete Peerage*, xii, part 1, Appendix L), does not include Count Brien in his list of those present at Hastings.

[2] *Complete Peerage*, iii. 427; x. 782; *Genealogist*, N.S. xvii, 1–2.

[3] Hatfield MS. 315, f. 1. This is the exception: it gives Robert's charter without Leofric's confirmation: a version evidently prepared for submission to those who would have objected to the bishop's part: Ibid., *passim*.

[4] Leofric may have overlapped for a while at Crediton with Gregory VI March–December 1046, but Gregory VII is obviously intended here.

of the priory[1] and was presumably assigned such a date on the strength of the document of Leofric. The reference to Gregory and the assumption of privileges give the two documents something in common and both documents as they stand are palpable forgeries. Leofric's clauses granting episcopal exemption for the priory were not confirmed by bishops who regularly visited it in the fourteenth century. The clauses must have been written into the charter in connexion with this grant.

Fécamp's claims to Steyning have already been described.[2] The effectiveness of the Conqueror's support of claims to the vill derived from a dubious grant of the Confessor was balanced by the presence of William de Briouze, in the neighbouring castle of Bramber. Like other Normans from the Maine border he looked to the saints of the Loire valley when it came to patronizing monks, and it was to Saint-Florent lès Saumur that he gave his priory of Briouze, in the diocese of Séez. On his way to the Maine campaign of 1073 he added to his gifts from his new lands in England: the church of St. Nicholas in Bramber castle, six hides of land and the church of Beeding with domain-tithes from twenty of his manors: 'excepta decima illa quam Sancte Trinitatis monachi habebant . . . Dedit adhuc ejusdem ecclesiae canonicis placita hominum de christianitate et ex teloneo de Staningis et castello hoc decimam et ex suis piscationibus et venationibus decimam et eorum porcos impinguare cum suis dominicis et ejus lucos ad eorum focum et aedificationes faciendas sumere.'[3] Strictly, Fécamp's rights in Steyning were not infringed by this grant, but when monks from these two powerful monasteries settled so close together, there was bound to be dispute after dispute, and these continued on and off even in the thirteenth century.

The Conqueror himself judged one of these in an all-day sitting. Saint-Florent was not mentioned by name, but the church of Beeding, belonging to the Angevin monks, was accused of defrauding the monks of Fécamp of their rights of burial dues at St. Cuthman's. The king ordered the bodies

---

[1] See p. 70, n. A.   [2] See above, pp. 20–22.
[3] P. Marchegay, B.E.C. xl, 165–6, no. 3; Davis, no. 71; C.D.F. 1130; from quasi-original in Archives de la Maine-et-Loire and Livre Blanc, f. 116.

to be dug up and reburied lawfully at Steyning, and Herbert the dean to restore the money he had received for burials, wakes, and tolling the bells. Briouze had injured the monks' interests by enclosing a warren and a park on their land, by making a road and by diverting water to his castle, and these the Conqueror ordered him to destroy. The wood of 'Hawode', where perhaps the warren had been made, was to be divided down the middle with a hedge, so that the monks' and Briouze's respective portions should be clearly distinguished; Briouze had to give up the tolls he had collected from the abbey's men at his bridge, because they had never paid them in King Edward's time. In future he was to be allowed only half the weekly toll, and ships ascending the river to St. Cuthman's port should pay only two pence, unless they called at William's market as well, when presumably they paid more. The monks recovered their marsh, saltpits, and eighteen gardens.[1]

A few years later Rufus heard a similar suit at Foucarmont. The monks of Saint-Florent and Philip de Briouze this time took the initiative and claimed the 'parish' belonging to St. Cuthman in Bramber castle, Beeding and Bridlington in Bramber. Robert, count of Meulan, reminded the court of the Conqueror's judgement, the monks were ordered to restore what they had already received as tithes, burial dues and offerings, and the king instructed his justiciars in England to enforce his decision.[2] Probably the real principals, the abbot of Fécamp, William de Ros, and the abbot of Saint-Florent, William de Dol, settled their differences at this point.[3] The monk, Hugh of Steyning, represented Fécamp. Their arguments 'de discordia et calumpnia sepulturarum atque decimarum quae sunt in castellaria' were settled by Saint-Florent's renunciation of the church of St. Nicholas 'de castello Brembra et sepulturam atque offerentias ejusdem ecclesie de Staningis et de Belingstona decimam

---

[1] Davis, nos. 220 and XXXII. Beeding must have been a new 'parish' carved out of Steyning's jurisdiction as an Old Minster.

[2] Davis, nos. 423–4 and LXXIV: 1094–9; Johnson: errata p. 406. He repeated this order in 1099 less than five years later, perhaps as little as five months later, to Ranulf bishop of Durham: Davis, no. 416.

[3] The abbot of Fécamp did not die until 1108, but the settlement was probably earlier than that with Philip de Braoze.

in garbis et caseis et lana et agnis et porcellis et vitulis et lino et canabo'. In return Fécamp quitclaimed 'omnes calumnias que fuerunt in ecclesia Sancti Petri de Beddingis et in hyda terre que ad ipsam ecclesiam iacet et insuper concessit ei de Portes Ladda et de Sutwic et de Beddingis decimam sicut eam habebat'.[1]

Philip was himself reconciled to Fécamp in January 1103, before the king and queen at Salisbury. Philip admitted that he had ignored the decision given against his father, and did fealty to the abbot as a sign of submission and as his tenant for eighteen 'burgages' (presumably the gardens) in Steyning: 'in feodo suscipit et pro his homo abbatis devenit eique ac ecclesie fiscannensi fidelitatem fecit'. Ships were to pass freely up and down the river as in King Edward's day: 'quod si ad vadum qui dictus est pons mitti tardaverit erunt naves euntes et redeuntes quiete per eam consuetudinem ad castellum Philippi qua forent ad portum S. Cuthmanni'. The parish of St. Cuthman was divided into Philip's castle and Beeding, of which Fécamp was to have all dues as 'antequam Northmanni accepissent angliam'. The abbot's monk (notice the singular!) and his men, de mensa, were allowed to take hares in the abbot's and in Briouze's warrens, but other men of his vill caught hunting in the Briouze warrens would be judged and their fines given to Fécamp. When the abbot came in provincia, he and his whole familia might hunt there. In this manner the worst dispute with Saumur was concluded,[2] although minor frictions have left a few records behind them.[3] It was presumably as a result of their effective defence of Steyning church that the monks of Fécamp were able to cover it with

---

[1] I. Marchegay, B.E.C. xl, no. 4, pp. 166-7.

[2] So far as is known, the final clause was not implemented after Philip's exile in 1110: 'Sciendum vero quod illa omnia que de dominio fiscannensis ecclesie Philipus ab abbate propter pacem et concordiam in feodo suscepit fiscannensis S. Trinitatis ecclesie relinquit si sine legitimo herede mortuus fuerit aut si terram suam forisfecerit vel in alienam abierit': Johnson, no. 626. Philip's son William wrote to Archbishop Theobald, legate, and Bishop Hilary of Chichester 1149–61 recognizing Fécamp's liberties and confirming the earlier settlement, but reserving the rents of their stalls in his markets; this was confirmed by Henry II between March 1163, when Foliot was consecrated as bishop of London, and February 1164, when Philip, bishop of Bayeux, died: P.R.O. Cartae Antiquae C 52/18, nos. 5 and 6.

[3] Sele Cartulary, passim.

the papal privilege of exemption. The churches of the monastery enjoying this privilege were named by Paschal II in his bull of 1102: Steyning was not amongst them. It appears in Calixtus II's bull of 1119 which is otherwise identical to Paschal's. This papal exemption later gave the monks the victory in their bitter dispute with the archbishop of Canterbury, John Pecham, over the archbishop's powers of visitation. It was the only Norman monastery to defy normal episcopal visitations and the privilege covered only this church.[1]

These three cases help to illustrate the problems of Norman monks in holding on to the post-conquest benefactions, not a hundred or three hundred years later, but within a generation of the Conquest itself. Moreover these particular monasteries were the richest and most powerful of Normandy, with the most considerable property in England. The barons of the period can hardly have been encouraged by these examples to believe that smaller monasteries without their patrons' determined support might in the course of time acquire property which would eventually be enough to support a small, but regular, convent of monks. Presumably the barons gave their favourite Norman monks immediately after the Conquest itself property enough to establish the kind of religious life the barons wished to see grow in England. If several monasteries unexpectedly lost the influence of their patrons through rebellion and forfeiture it was not by any means true of them all. The Beaumonts flourished, but Préaux's English endowment hardly grew after 1100;[2] similarly the Montgomeries had planned

---

[1] J. F. Lemarignier, *Étude sur les privilèges d'exemption et de juridiction ecclésiastique des abbayes normandes*, p. 205 and n. 96. Rouen MS. Y 188, f. 78, gives the text of Calixtus's bull. The exemption was extended to the chapels of the church by Celestine III in 1192: ibid., f. 105v. The printed materials for the history of Fécamp's defence of the privilege can be found in *Chichester Cartulary*, no. 273, p. 72; Peckham, *Epistolae*, ii. 604–6, 609, 620, iii. 808, 821, 882–5; *C.Pap.L.* i. 471–2; *Martin IV Register*, nos. 447–8, p. 184; *Nicholas IV Register*, no. 199, p. 355; *S.A.C.* v. 22; *C.Chanc.Warr.* i. 12. Steyning church was collegiate and there were perhaps four prebends there: *C.Pap.L.* i. 387–8. Alexander IV called it a parish church and it was appropriated by the monks: *C.Pap.L.* i. 261; *C.P.R. 1258–66*, p. 28; ibid. *1266–72*, pp. 209, 388. See also the abbot's letter to Edward I, P.R.O. Ancient Correspondence, 47/111.

[2] Préaux received the vill of Warmington from the earl of Warwick, Henry Beaumont, as late as about 1123: *C.D.F.* 335: one hide and one virgate; Delisle–

their Norman monastery's cells in England in their earliest days of conquest.

What then were the monks intended to do with their property? This puzzling question was asked by the king in the fourteenth century, and he tried to prove that the manors had been given to found priories. The prior of Hayling defied the king's order to receive a corrodian in 1341 and was upheld in the courts because the king could not prove that the Conqueror had founded Hayling *per nomen prioratus*.[1] At Horsley Edward III instigated an inquiry into the terms of the foundation. A local inquest found that a prior, a monk, and a chaplain should keep continuous residence, that honest hospitality should be held and divine service celebrated there for the king's soul.[2] These conditions are no different from those expected of the monks of Saint-Leofroy for their only manor of Esher in Surrey, where two priests, not necessarily monks it would appear, said masses for the king's soul,[3] and which is nowhere referred to as a priory. The two monks at Horsley were a canonical minimum; the chaplain would later have undertaken the parochial duties, for which the monks had been responsible.[4] Again, in 1332, Edward III wanted to make sure by what services the monks of Mont Saint-Michel held the manors of Otterton and Budleigh. After investigation in the Book of Fees, Domesday Book, and, presumably, other sources, the king wrote to the escheator of Devonshire and declared himself satisfied that King John had founded the priory at Otterton, for the souls of his ancestors, with an endowment worth £100 to sustain *cantariam et elemosinam* with four monks *ad celebrandum divina* and for a weekly distribution of sixteen shillingsworth of bread.[5] There is no other record

Berger, ii, no. DCLXXV, p. 293: 'villa salvis berewicis quae perpendebat illi manerio'.   [1] *Year Book of the reign of King Edward III*: *15*, pp. 302–6.

[2] *Bruton Cartulary*, no. 389.

[3] D.B. i, f. 34. The manor was bought by Peter des Roches, bishop of Winchester, and given to Netley abbey: *C.Ch.R. 1226–57*, p. 251; *V.C.H. Surrey*, iii. 448. In addition the monks of La Croix Saint-Leoffroi had a rent of 100s. from Dorset: *P.L.* ccxiv. 645; P. L. Lebeurier, *Notice sur l'abbaye de la Croix Saint Leufroy*; Pièces Justificatives no. x, pp. 56–58.   [4] See below, p. 59.

[5] B.N. MS. Lat. 10072, no. 177, pp. 219–24: July 1332. It was enrolled on 1 August 1332: *M.A.* i. 569–70; *C.Cl.R. 1330–33*, p. 480. In 1374 the abbot spoke of the property as follows: 'que custodiam . . . omnium fructuum bonorum redditum

of John's interest in the priory: the manors had been given by William I and Henry I. If John did found the priory by insisting on these specific obligations, it rather suggests that for nearly a century the monks had used their manors for some other purpose. This is all that the fourteenth century could discover about these foundations.

The monks received English property to swell their endowments: they had therefore to consider how to 'realize' the value. In order to retain their ownership and to secure the profits of the manors, it was necessary to do more than collect the revenues like absentee landlords; the monasteries had to maintain monks in England who could keep an eye on the property and visit the different manors. Monks who came as landlords did not have to establish priories. They came to reap the benefits for their monasteries and cathedral chapters in Normandy,[1] just as Oxford and Cambridge colleges with distant estates did not intend a decentralization of the universities when they accepted endowments outside their cities. English manors were valuable extensions of the monastic domain and were intended to be profitable. The monastic profession of the agents obliged them to observe their rule even while on administrative duties and the monks' benefactors insisted on the performance of the work of prayer which was their spiritual protection in the conquered lands. The monks and the saints acquired a valuable stake in the new order.

A few monasteries did establish cells of monks with something like a regular monastic life. What is remarkable is that the wealthiest houses which could most easily have afforded to set up independent communities, if these had been thought desirable or necessary, are precisely the houses which did not use their more than adequate endowments for this purpose. Another fact which is more difficult

et obventionum ad prioratum de Octritonya spectantium . . . membrum ipsius monasterii ac eidem subiectum commiserat et que omnes fructus predicti ad mensam communem abbatis et conventus monasterii predicti et a fundacione ipsius prioratus pertinebant'. Coll. Mancel MS. 299, no. 22: 19 February 1374.

[1] Rouen cathedral had received lands before the conquest; the canons of Bayeux, Coutances, and Lisieux benefited from the conquest itself: those of Evreux were given Bramford, and those of Séez £10 at Bampton, by Henry I: Johnson, nos. 1673, 1830, 1711.

to interpret, if it be significant at all, is that it is not so much the least well-endowed monasteries as those which received more churches than landed estates which fostered dependent cells in England. The histories of these cells show that it was not the Norman monks themselves who fostered the foundations, but English patrons, with tenuous connexions in Normandy, who tended the nursling priories and insisted, for obscure reasons of their own, that the monks pay pensions to Normandy and receive recruits from there. Perhaps it was only a sentiment of loyalty to the 'Old Country' which kept this tradition alive, even long after political ties had severed England from the mainland.

1. Conventual priories

The definition of 'conventual' priories has given rise to a great deal of discussion. In the fourteenth century royal officials were interested in the question, and conventual priories were exempted from the acts of suppression passed in the fifteenth century.[1] The only Norman priories that escaped suppression under this clause were Boxgrove, Eye, and Stoke by Clare which had acquired status as 'denizens' before 1399, and Tutbury, Blyth, Folkestone, St. Neot's, Chepstow, and Pembroke after that time. Pembroke survived as a mere cell to St. Albans[2] and Chepstow by mere chance, as Miss Graham has shown.[3] Stoke by Clare all but suffered dissolution in 1378 when seven of its monks were expelled from England[4] and only recovered itself by finding a thousand marks to buy letters of 'naturalization' in 1395.[5] St. Neot's, also a cell of Bec, had more substantial local support, for it had been an Anglo-Saxon foundation and its patron a saint of wide fame.[6] Folkestone, formerly an Anglo-Saxon nunnery, may have benefited likewise. The nineteenth-century editors of the *Monasticon Anglicanum* quote no authority for the statement that the monks elected their

---

[1] See below, p. 110 et ff.

[2] D. Knowles and R. N. Hadcock, *Medieval Religious Houses*, p. 73; *V.C.H. Hertfordshire*, iv. 403.

[3] R. Graham, 'Four Alien Priories of Monmouthshire'.

[4] See Appendix III.   [5] See below, p. 111.

[6] *V.C.H. Huntingdonshire*, i. 385–8; M. Chibnall, *The English Lands of the Abbey of Bec*, p. 128.

own prior;[1] as late as 1371 the prior was sufficiently intimate with Lonlay, the mother-house, to act as the monastery's proctor general in England,[2] and the priory was so weak in Richard II's last decade that it was farmed by the abbey of Westminster.[3] Its survival into the fifteenth century is something of a surprise: perhaps the status of its prior saved it. From the other houses—Boxgrove, Blyth, Eye, and Tutbury—something more may be learned. A regular conventual life appears to have been led in these priories from the time of foundation; the founders in each case were not closely connected with the 'parent' monastery in Normandy. Being less interested in the Norman monks' own welfare, they regarded them rather as suitable for helping to found priories in England, because of the reputation for piety of the monasteries in the particular corner of Normandy they had come from. They were new men made rich by the Conquest itself, not like the great lords, powerful as Normans. It is true that Robert de Haia, who gave Boxgrove church to the monks of Lessay in 1105,[4] was a member of the monastery's founders' family, but the priory of Boxgrove, though it began with this gift,[5] owed its phenomenal expansion to the family of his daughter's husband, the St. Johns. The husband, Roger, and his sons, William and Robert, had so increased the endowment by 1187 that provision had been made for sixteen monks.[6] The mother-house preserved its hold by strict control over the appointment of priors which lasted till the end of the fourteenth century, but the Normans retained no other valuable privileges. Abbot Thomas succeeded in depriving even the patron of his rights; he demanded further that all new monks should be professed at Lessay. If business brought them to England, the abbot or his monks might stay for as long as a month in the priory. In spite of Lessay's controlling powers, the irremovability of the prior was the foundation of the priory's independence, and within a few years the bishop of

---

[1] *M.A.* iv (1820), p. 320. [2] *Stogursey Charters,* no. 70.
[3] *C.F.R. 1383–96,* f. 294; *C.P.R. 1389–91,* p. 230; ibid. *1391–6,* p. 213.
[4] *C.D.F.* 921.
[5] The *Historia Fundationis,* a fourteenth-century summary, says that three monks came over at the time. B.M. Cotton MS. Claudius A vi, f. 1; *V.C.H. Sussex,* ii, 59; *M.A.* i. 594. [6] *M.A.* i. 594–5.

Chichester noted that the monks at Boxgrove had not all made their profession to the abbot.[1]

Lessay had few other churches to visit in England,[2] so that the Normans rarely came over to interfere in the priory of Boxgrove. In 1338 the prior tried to secure the exemption of his priory from royal seizure because his monks were Englishmen and not Normans, and he had more difficulty in explaining away his own provision by the papacy[3] than his legal dependance on Lessay.[4] Boxgrove never appears after this date on the lists of alien priories, but Lessay certainly did not lose its right to appoint priors. So far from it being true, as the prior of 1338 asserted, that the monks of Boxgrove elected their own prior, three monks from the priory had been summoned to Lessay in 1321[5] and made to swear that they would never again oppose elections of priors. The death of the prior Richard du Bonhomme on 7 January 1363 was reported at Lessay on 26 February, and a new prior was elected there on 7 March. Ten days later the abbot wrote to the bishop, informing him of the election, and the latter admitted Robert du Tot, a monk of Lessay, as prior on 31 May.[6] This appointment from Lessay may have been possible because of the peace between England and France; similarly Prior Jean de la Londe, who died about 1396, had been prior of Port Bail, a Norman priory, before being sent to England, and his successor William Briens was elected at Lessay in 1397.[7]

Bernay's part in the foundation of Eye priory is extremely obscure. Although the priory was founded in the Conqueror's lifetime there are no records earlier than the beginning of the twelfth century,[8] and Bernay is not men-

---

[1] C.D.F. 930: 1204–7.

[2] It possessed a few churches in Lincolnshire, but lost them, possibly to another de Haia foundation, Barlings priory: M.A. ii. 643–4.

[3] Prior Lawrence left England in 1316 and was still away in 1319, if not in 1320. If he died near Avignon, this would have given the papacy legal reason to provide a new prior: C.P.R. 1313–17, p. 439; ibid. 1317–21, pp. 310, 438.

[4] C.Cl.R. 1337–39, p. 662; M.A. i. 596; C.P.R. 1338–40, p. 325; P.R.O. S.C. 8. 160/7959. The prior did not pay the alien's tenth in 1345; see below, p. 96, n. 5.

[5] Manche H 4686: from the Inventaire-Sommaire.

[6] Ibid. H 4687–90, 4693.

[7] Ibid. H 4691–2, 4694–6.

[8] Johnson, no. 780; M.A. i. 356; V.C.H. Suffolk, ii. 72.

tioned in connexion with it until Henry II confirmed to the abbey not only the manor of Creeting but also 'prioratum de Eye cum omnibus pertinentiis suis'.[1] There are no archives of Bernay: royal documents reveal that priors were later appointed at Bernay, so that the abbey's rights were probably similar to those of Lessay over Boxgrove. The priory's own cartulary makes no mention whatsoever of Bernay, and popes regularly addressed their letters direct to the priors.[2] All this suggests that although Bernay's authority was undisputed, its practical influence was slight. The priory owed its survival to the size of its convent and its vigorous efforts to recover prosperity after the expulsion of some of its monks, those from Bernay, in 1378.[3]

Tutbury was founded directly by Henry de Ferrers, possibly in 1089.[4] The first, ambiguous, appearance of the 'mother-house', Saint-Pierre-sur-Dives, was about 1145 when Abbot Haimo wrote to his beloved brethren at Tutbury about the rebuilding of the monastery;[5] the second was in the 1160's when Abbot Richard was the first (as Prior Fulk, the second) of those who witnessed a charter of William, Earl Ferrers.[6] As in the case of Eye, the papacy wrote directly to the priors.[7] Even Saint-Pierre's rights to appoint priors had to be shared with the patrons. Although it appears that the abbot appointed a prior outright in 1263,[8] a document first produced in the fourteenth century claimed that the earl had the choice of one of three monks presented to him by the abbot under an agreement concluded by Earl William, which must therefore have been earlier than 1254.[9] In 1337 Henry, earl of Lancaster, who had become the patron, brought an undignified episode to the courts. The abbot had obliged the earl by nominating the earl's own clerk as prior; the sub-prior protested against the appointment

---

[1] Delisle–Berger, i, no. XCV: 1156–9.
[2] B.M. Add. MS. 8177: *passim.*
[3] Appendix III; see below, p. 110.
[4] *M.A.* i. 354: 'Anno milleno domini quater atque viceno Tuttsburiesque novo domus est fundata patrono.'
[5] L. V. Delisle, 'Lettre de l'Abbé Haimon'.
[6] J. P. Yeatman, *Feudal History of the County of Derby*, i, pt. 2, p. 289, from a charter at Hardwicke Hall: *H.M.C.* iii. 45.
[7] B.M. Add. MS. 6714, f. 1.   [8] *C.Cl.R. 1261–64*, p. 283.
[9] *M.A.* iii (1820), pp. 395–6. The last Earl William died in 1254.

of this unsuitable person and procured his resignation but the earl's rights were undoubted and the sub-prior lost his case.[1] The abbot had little say in the running of the priory and on this occasion weakly submitted to the patron's whims. Tutbury was the priory of the earls of Derby, not of the abbots of Saint-Pierre.[2]

The foundation of the priory of Blyth is more closely associated with its 'mother'-house than these two other examples. Before 1102 Roger de Busli gave to La Trinité, Rouen, the church and all the vill of St. Mary of Blyth: 'hec omnia supradicte Blida ecclesie ad edificationem loci et victum et vestitum monachorum ibidem deo eiusque genitrici secundum voluntatem abbatis servientium concedo in perpetuum'. In return the monks of Rouen received forty shillings of English money every year.[3] The priory was big enough to secure some independence, but the abbot sent monks and appointed priors to the house and the archbishops recognized the abbot's responsibility for discipline.[4] Here no powerful layman came between the priory and the monastery. Its size, not its independence, secured it exemption from confiscation.

If these were the only priories to survive the dissolution they were not the only 'conventual' ones. The prior of Modbury successfully showed as late as 1438 that he was no 'dative' prior but had security of tenure; nevertheless his priory was dissolved after his death. Throughout its history the priory's patrons played an important part in its life. Ralph and Rainald de Valletorta made the original

---

[1] *Year Book of the reign of Edward III: 11-12*, ed. A. J. Horwood, p. 21. The monks of Tutbury petitioned Edward I or Edward II to appoint a commission of *oyer et terminer* to settle their disagreements with the earl of Lancaster, but details of the case are wanting: it may have been connected with the patron's rights: *Rot. Parlt.* i. 477a = P.R.O. S.C. 8. 10/488. Two monks came to England in 1336, perhaps in connexion with this: *C.Cl.R. 1333–7*, p. 692.

[2] But Robert de Ferrars destroyed Tutbury priory for no obvious reason in 1260: *Annales Monastici*, i. 49.

[3] Johnson, no. 598; *Nova Chronica Normannica* (ed. Chéruel), p. 8: 1090. B.M. Harley MS. 3759, f. 106.

[4] A bull of Lucius II may have been designed to protect the abbot's rights: *V.C.H. Nottinghamshire*, ii. 84. The abbot ratified even a small agreement between the priory and the monks of Garendon (Leics.): *C.Ch.R. 1327–41*, p. 479. There were as many as twelve monks with the prior at the end of the thirteenth century: P.R.O. Ancient Petitions, S.C.8. 314/22.

gifts at the beginning of the twelfth century, but it is un-known why the Valletorta brothers chose Saint-Pierre-sur-Dives as the mother-house. Abbot Haimo (1140–8) obliged by sending a prior about the same time as the monks of Modbury claimed the tithes of Baldewyn de Londebroc *parochianus ecclesie de Motberie*, so that a small priory was certainly in existence by the middle of the century.[1] Al-though the abbot never grovelled as he did before the patrons of Tutbury it is probable that the humbler status of Modbury's patrons, rather than any difference in the re-lationship of the Norman monastery to the priory, was responsible for this.

There were other priories with a small, regular, 'conven-tual' character. Monks Sherborne had slender connexions with the mother-house, Cérisy: a relationship established by the founder, Henry de Port, for no better reason, as Round showed, than that his family came from that part of the Bessin where Cérisy was situated.[2] At Stogursey a priory came into being within twenty years of the original gift of the church: 'deo et sancte Marie de Lonl'(ay) et monachis deo et sancto Andree apud Stokes servientibus.' The founder, William de Falaise, evidently wanted the monks to serve in his chapel privately, for he added to the endowment with church, land, tithes, pasture, and wood from the Quantocks 'capellacionem nostre domus quantum in villa fuerimus'. Patrons played an active part in the priory's affairs but did not save it from dissolution in the fifteenth century.[3] At Wootton Wawen the monks of Castellion may have had a freer hand, but as late as the 1430's the prior resisted attempts to suppress the abbot's authority with the powerful help of the priory's patron, the earl of Stafford.[4] Unfortunately too little is known of the

[1] See p. 71, n. B.

[2] H. E. Salter, *Oxford Charters*, Sherborne, no. 1: 'donavi . . . deo et sancto Vigori Cerasii tali consideratione quod abbas conventum monachorum apud pre-fatam sireburnam poneret qui deo ordinate deservirent. Porro etiam suffragente deo me ipsum donavi ad obitum meum ibidem ad sepeliendum'. *c.* 1120–30. J. H. Round, 'The Family of St. John and of Port'.

[3] *Stogursey Charters*, no. 1: 1100–7; ibid. 51, no. 9: 1120; ibid., nos. 9, 12; *Bath and Wells Registers: Drokensford* (Somerset Record Society), i. 287, 261; *C.P.R. 1330–2*, pp. 288, 352; *C.F.R. 1337–47*, pp. 278, 292.

[4] See below, pp. 138–39.

priory's history to assess the continuous importance of the Stafford family.

For other priories no documents give the same glimpse of relationships between the mother-house and the patron, but it is tempting to suppose a connexion between those houses which did certainly contain more than two monks and the presence of a great layman who took an interest in the priory as a religious house. Lancaster priory contained at least four monks in 1378. Roger of Poitou invited to the north the monks of Séez, whom his family had patronized since his father's marriage to Mabel of Bellême, and gave them the church at Lancaster in 1094. About the same time he referred to the 'prayers and benefits of the monastery' there; the meanings of 'church' and 'monastery' were not clearly distinguished at that time and as late as 1282 the ambiguity survived because monks were still performing parochial functions in this priory church: Roger's original gift of the *church* was sufficient to found a 'priory'.[1] Carisbrooke priory had as many as six monks in 1260 and may have received patronage from the lords of Carisbrooke castle from the time of Fitz Osbern's mandate in the island.[2] St. Michael's Mount was endowed for thirteen monks in 1135, but by the fourteenth century numbers can rarely have risen above four or five monks. Judging from the charters of the priory, the earls of Cornwall retained an interest in the priory.[3] Arundel priory must have been intimately bound up with the earls of Arundel from its beginnings to its final conversion into a chantry.[4] Pembroke, another Montgomery dependency of Saint-Martin of Séez, was founded by Arnulf de Montgomery 'at Pembroke, a castle of his' which, whether it was in, or only beside, the

---

[1] See Appendix IIIa. *C.D.F.* 664–5; *Lancaster Cartulary*, pp. 139–40: 1282.

[2] *V.C.H. Hampshire*, ii. 230. Isabella de Fortibus, lady of Carisbrooke, had rights as patron in the priory, which she surrendered in the thirteenth century. M. Michel Lepesant has recently published most of a damaged library list from Carisbrooke priory which proves that there were religious works in the priory and that one of the priors had himself made a digest of certain biblical commentaries: *Annales de Normandie*.

[3] *C.D.F.* 729. In 1324 there was a prior, three monks, one perpetual clerk, and one man sent by the king—a corrodian: P.R.O. E/106/6/11, 2 November. For the charters see *M.A.* vi (1820), 988.

[4] See below, pp. 115–16.

castle was easily dominated and befriended by the lords of the castle.[1]

Elsewhere patronage by certain families must be presumed: the Stutevilles in Stratfield Saye,[2] the Beaumonts in Wareham,[3] the Quincys in Ware,[4] the Mortemers in Clatford,[5] the Lovels in Minster Lovell,[6] the earls of Lincoln in Haugham.[7] A good illustration of the difference between these priories, which were often founded as such by the specific wish of the original benefactor, and the estates, which were never called priories, is to be seen in the distinction between Coggs priory, although it never had a flourishing conventual life, and Fécamp's estates, known as the bailiwick of Warminghurst.[8] In the twelfth century the monks' agent is often styled prior of Coggs, but by the thirteenth century the bailiwick is sharply distinguished from the priory and the prior cuts a miserable figure beside the bailiff.[9]

ii. *Other priories*

Some Norman houses supported priories with a definite conventual character, but the majority had only estates run by single monks as bailiffs with or without the companion

---

[1] *C.D.F.* 666, 670; *M.A.* iv (1820), p. 320.

[2] Eton College, Stratfield Saye Charters, *passim*. The religious character of the priory was emphasized by the reception of relics from Normandy: ibid., no. 24.

[3] Jocelin bishop of Salisbury's charter suggests that Robert, earl of Leicester, replaced secular canons by monks during his episcopate: B.M. Cotton MS. Otho B xiv, ff. 32ᵛ, 35; E. Levien, 'Wareham and its Religious Houses'.

[4] *V.C.H. Hertfordshire*, iv. 455: the countess of Winchester built a hall in the priory for her retinue.

[5] Eton College charters: Clatford and Hullavington, *passim*.

[6] See below, p. 58; *C.C.R.R.* iv. 260, 305.

[7] *Lincoln Registers: Gravesend*, p. 71; *Sutton*, i. 131.

[8] The Manasses Arsic who renewed his charter for Coggs priory in 1103 had acquired his lands only about ten years before, as a result of the forfeiture of Odo of Bayeux: *C.D.F.* 120; a slightly different version of these texts is given by *M.A.* i. 573–4 from P.R.O. C 52/18, no. 9. *V.C.H. Oxfordshire*, 379, ii. 161–2. It was said of a Manasses that 'tota suspirat intentio ut ad eum revertatur tota sui predecessoris hereditas': 'Epistolae Fiscannenses', *Revue Mabillon*, xi (1953), 29–31. Contrary to the opinion of the editor, this is probably the Manasses who farmed Oxfordshire in the early years of Henry II: *P.R. 7 Henry II*, p. 25; *P.R. 12 Henry II*, p. 118. The writer of the letter suggested that the abbot take up the matter with his cousin, Henry II, who brought pressure to bear on his farmer to leave the monks in peace, as a charter of Manasses makes only too clear: *M.A.* i. 573 from P.R.O. C 52/18, no. 8. [9] See below, pp. 94–95.

they were canonically required to keep. There are lone monks recorded in Domesday[1] and judging from the large number of single monks who applied for permission to leave the country in 1378[2] the majority of monasteries maintained agencies in England staffed with one monk. In the thirteenth century Archbishop Rigaud of Rouen tried to put an end to abuses of this kind, when he heard that monks from Aumâle, Boscherville, Noion, Sainte-Cathérine of Rouen, and Valmont were alone in England, but one of these monks, Eustace of Aumâle, was hardened enough to send back to Normandy the fellow monk who had been sent out to keep him company on the archbishop's instructions.[3] Edward II interceded for another lone monk, on Saint-Pierre-sur-Dives' manor of Wolston, and obtained for him the right to hold his office for life and not at pleasure, which can hardly have been good for his discipline or the monastery's interests.[4] The agents of Saint-Martin of Séez at Atherington, of Grestain at Wilmington and of Mortain at Withyham were alone in 1326[5] and only once in his comparatively well-documented history does the bailiff of Warminghurst refer to his fellow.[6]

The monasteries with the greatest endowments in England did not establish priories on the lands given to them directly and unconditionally; but estates offices situated conveniently for the administration of the property were also called priories. The case of Lire has already been quoted.[7] There were four distant groups of estates: Carisbrooke priory, which attended to the Berkshire properties as well as those of the Isle of Wight; Wareham in Dorset; Hinckley in Leicestershire; and a group in the west country, which is occasionally called the priory of Liver's (that is Lyre's) Ocle. This last was certainly not a priory in a conventual sense:[8] Carisbrooke certainly was; the other two may have been.

---

[1] D.B. i, ff. 23b, 34; *V.C.H. Surrey*, iv. 113: this regards *per Ingulphum* as indicating the derivation of Saint-Wandrille's gifts, not the way it was held. See also above, p. 40.　　　　　　　　　　　　　[2] See p. 71, n. C.

[3] Rigaud, pp. 76, 118, 129, 191, 316, 103, 110, 608. Lone monks had been condemned at the third Lateran Council in 1179: Mansi, XXII, c. 224, canon 10.

[4] *C.Cl.R. 1313–18*, pp. 440, 468.

[5] P.R.O. C 47/18/166: 3 September 1326; see below, p. 89, n. 6.

[6] Seine-Maritime 7 H 57: in 1245.　　　　　　　　　[7] See above, pp. 33–34.

[8] *C.F.R. 1383–91*, p. 356; ibid. *1391–9*, pp. 186–7, 218.

Similarly the property of Préaux was managed from four priories. Monks' Tofts in Norfolk was founded in the church and manor at Tofts given by the count of Meulan in 1093 and possessed a church at Haddiscoe, a mile or two away.[1] Warmington, a Midland priory, was much more scattered probably because it was founded so much later, by the count of Meulan's brother, the earl of Warwick; it comprised the manor and church of Warmington, land close by in Arlescote and Shotteswell, a hide of land at Ullesthorpe, and a church at Willey, more than twenty miles away. To the south of this was another grouping of five hides of land at Watlington and churches at Aston Tirrold and Newbury.[2] The priory of Spettisbury in Dorset included revenues from tithes in Charlton Marshall and Sturminster Marshall.[3]

Even where several 'priories' may not have come into existence, the benefactors may have deliberately tried to give property which the monks could manage without too great inconvenience. I have already suggested[4] that Mont Saint-Michel disposed of churches which were not conveniently placed, when buyers presented themselves, and Saint-Evroul probably leased the remote church of West Kirby to the monks of St. Werburgh, Chester, because it was on the fringe of the monastery's relatively densely placed Midland estates.[5] Grestain acquired several small estates from the king, Count Robert and Countess Matilda of Mortain, rather widely scattered in Suffolk, Buckinghamshire, Sussex, Hampshire, and Wiltshire; from Count William of Mortain it received churches concentrated on or near Watling Street, in Hertfordshire, Buckinghamshire, and Northamptonshire, and crowded into a narrow strip of land between the East-bourne–Lewes road and the sea.[6] The less well-endowed monastery of Saint-Sever received from its refounder, Hugh of Avranches, the vill of Haugham in Lincolnshire with

---

[1] C.D.F. 326, 329; Ramackers, *Papsturkunden*, no. 192: 1179.

[2] C.D.F. 355, 334, 335.

[3] C.D.F. 325: 1087–1100. They must also have received land there because the 'manor' was restored to them in 1317, *C.Cl.R. 1313–18*, p. 495, and lands are referred to in the *Rotuli Normannorum*, p. 122, and in *Taxatio*, pp. 178, 184b. C.D.F. 111.

[4] See above, p. 31, n. 5.

[5] Orne H 901, a grant by Abbot Richard 1137–40, confirmed by Hugh, earl of Chester: 1153–81. The rent was paid at Peatling in the *domus monachorum*.

[6] *M.A.* ii. 982–3.

seven churches in the diocese of Lincoln, and four hides
of land at Henstridge, Somerset, and one church at Fife-
head Magdalen in Dorset.[1] A little later Stephen, count of
Aumâle, added to the endowment of his monastery of
Saint-Martin-d'Auchy-lès-Aumâle about twenty churches in
England: four in Suffolk, the rest in Holderness.[2] What
is interesting is the repetition of this theme: the presence
of the monks in those areas where the benefactors had important estates, especially the probable site of their *caput
baroniae*, and the gifts of churches there.

Saint-Martin of Séez found in the Montgomery-Bellême
family three important benefactors. To Roger, earl of
Shrewsbury, the monks owed their lands in Sussex: eleven
hides at Climping, two at Eastergate and the vill of Fish-
bourne with four churches there; and their property in
Cambridgeshire: churches and the priest's land at Shingay
and Arrington with the tithe of Orwell.[3] His sons, Roger
of 'Poitou' and Arnulph de Montgomery, used the monks
of Séez to establish priories in their remote outposts—at
Lancaster[4] and Pembroke[5] respectively. These foundations
were principally in churches and tithes. The origin of the
Lincolnshire priory of Winghale is more obscure. Roger of
Poitou gave churches there at the time of the foundation
of Lancaster priory,[6] but the place next occurs in a charter of
his nephew William, count of Mortain, who granted Winghale to the priory of Mortain and its mother-house, the
abbey of Marmoutier.[7] The Touraine monks must have
lost them as a result of Mortain's forfeiture: in the thirteenth
century the monks of Séez supplied priors to the church.[8]

The monks of Séez therefore established priories conveniently for the administration of these diverse lands. The
geographical limits of the priories of Arundel, Winghale,
Lancaster, and Pembroke are fairly clear; the limits of the
bailiwick of Atherington in Sussex are unknown. The bailiff

---

[1] *C.D.F.* 615: 1158. A later confirmation of Earl Hugh II gives a slightly different
list of churches, omitting the one in Dorset: Collection Mancel MS. 299, p. 1706.
[2] *M.A.* i. 587–8; ii. 999–1000; *E.Y.C.* iii, no. 1304. Longueville Giffard, also
founded later, received many churches.   [3] *C.D.F.* 656–7.
[4] *C.D.F.* 664.   [5] *C.D.F.* 666, 1098.   [6] *C.D.F.* 664.
[7] Johnson, no. 680; *C.D.F.* 1208, 1210.
[8] *Lincoln Registers: Hugh de Welles*, iii. 132–3; *Grosseteste*, p. 62; *Gravesend*, p. 71.

probably managed all the property not specifically allotted to the priories themselves. The bailiff of Atherington's function would be similar to that of his neighbour, the bailiff of Warminghurst, who administered all Fécamp's property, except what belonged to the priory of Coggs, or to that of the bailiff of Ogbourne who managed the lands belonging to the abbey, as distinct from those belonging to the priories, of Bec.[1]

At Arundel Roger de Montgomery had a castle in which Saint-Martin was already privileged by 1086.[2] A monk of Séez in 1087 acknowledged receipt of the gift of the manor of Tottington, by placing a branch of cherry, not in the local church, but in the monks' manor church of St. Mary Eastergate.[3] Was this perhaps an embryo priory church at that time? There was at Arundel in the late eleventh century a collegiate church,[4] and it is possible that the monks of Séez acquired a protective interest in it, similar to that enjoyed by the monks of Fécamp in the church of Steyning, twenty miles away.[5] This collegiate church at Arundel became the basis of St. Martin's priory in the mid-twelfth century; before that time the monks presumably managed their estates without a regular priory organization. The abbot of Séez in 1380 believed that his priory of five monks at Arundel had in fact replaced the canons in Roger de Montgomery's own lifetime,[6] and his tenants at Arundel told the king's commissioners in the same year[7] that Roger had the priory built 'in quodam loco ubi nil nisi toftum habetur', and that the five monks under their leader Gratian came from Normandy to live in the priory when it was completed in 1102.[8] Fortunately it is not necessary to decide between these equally erroneous accounts; some charters survive in the Chichester

---

[1] See M. Chibnall, *The English Lands of the Abbey of Bec,* part 1 and pp. 39–40.

[2] D.B. i, f. 23; for *castrum* see Round, *V.C.H. Sussex,* i. 385.

[3] D.B. i, f. 25b; *C.D.F.* 655.

[4] These were probably the *clerici* of St. Nicholas who held six hides in Harting in 1086: D.B., f. 23.2.

[5] See above, pp. 40–41.   [6] *C.Pap.L.* iv. 239–40.

[7] M. A. Tierney, *History and Antiquities of the Castle and Town of Arundel,* ii. 576–83, and Appendix VII: Esch. 3 Rich. II, no. 160.

[8] The activity of the monks' patron Robert de Bellême at this time drove the abbot of Séez into English exile; it was hardly a suitable time for the establishment of a priory.

cartulary to show that the monks were not established at Arundel until much later. At the end of 1149 Eugenius III authorized Bishop Hilary to install monks in St. Nicholas's church once the canons had died,[1] and the letter sent to the bishop by William, earl of Chichester, shows that the church belonged already to the monks of Séez.[2] After negotiations with the chapter of Chichester,[3] which feared the loss of its own influence over appointment of canons, the monks were allowed to occupy the church. There is nothing to suggest that they already possessed a priory in Arundel. Presumably this transfer took place shortly after 1149. At the time of Richard II's inquiry the local jury insisted that the monks were moved from their priory *ad rectoriam ecclesiae S. Nicholai Arundelliae* with the consent of Hugh, earl of Arundel, and Ralph, bishop of Chichester, in 1178, but there was no Earl Hugh or Bishop Ralph in that year. The jury of 1380 had therefore no access to documents giving an accurate account of the final departure of the canons. The foundation of Arundel priory was dependent, not on the monks' possession of estates in Sussex, but upon the condition of a collegiate church belonging to the monks of Séez. The monks had probably maintained a house for the management of their property, but Eugenius III does not refer to it as a 'priory'; Arundel priory, like so many Norman monasteries, was founded to replace an existing community of canons.

There are other examples which suggest that priories were founded in or near the founders' castles or *capita baroniae*. The connection between Fitz Osbern's movements and the endowments of his monasteries has already been pointed out: Lire's priory at Carisbrooke and Cormeilles' priory at Chepstow were both in the vicinity of his castles.[4] The reason why Nigel de Mundeville and his wife Emma called monks of Lonlay to found a priory at Folkestone,[5] or Henry de Ferrers

---

[1] Holtzmann, ii, no. 59.

[2] *Cartulary of the High Church of Chichester*, no. 298.

[3] Ibid., nos. 263, 298, 160, 64, 113, 117.

[4] J. H. Round, 'The Castles of the Conquest'. A late authority shows that a monk of Chepstow was obliged to say mass three times weekly in the castle chapel. This tradition was probably older, not an innovation: *C. Inq. post mortem*, iv. 299.

[5] *M.A.* i. 560–2. The original priory at Folkestone was moved from the site of the castle lower down towards the town in the twelfth century.

monks of Saint-Pierre-sur-Dives to Tutbury,[1] or Robert
Malet monks of Bernay to Eye,[2] appears in every case to be
that it was there that the founders had built castles. Roger de
Busli, who subjected Blyth priory to Holy Trinity, Rouen,
established it near Blyth castle at Tickhill.[3] The monks of
Saint-Evroul set up their priory, not in Leicestershire where
they and their patrons had their most extensive lands, but
at Ware, a valuable estate near London, which Hugh de
Grendmesnil had bought specially and where Round suggested that he kept residence.[4]

Even in the next century there seems to be still a connexion between castles and churches. Lire's 'Beaumont'
priories were built near the castles of Wareham[5] and Hinckley;[6] the monks of Modbury acquired the church near
Trematon castle about the same time[7] and there is a document showing that William, count of Eu, planned to introduce monks from Le Tréport into the collegiate chapel of
his castle at Hastings, as the prebends became vacant.[8]
William de Falaise established monks of Lonlay at Stogursey, where he had a residence, if not a castle.[9]

The connexion between these benefactors and the Norman monasteries is not always clear. If more was known
about lesser Norman families it might be possible to trace
their origins, as Round explained why in the similar case of
Monks Sherborne priory the Port family turned to Cérisy
to help with the foundation.[10] Whatever the relationship,
these benefactors appear to have wished to establish a community of monks around their residence. Round has pointed
out that *castellum* may mean town as well as castle at this
period,[11] so that when Henry de Ferrers speaks of Tutbury
priory *apud castellum meum* this may not be so precise as it

---

1 Ibid., p. 354.　　　　2 Ibid., p. 356.　　　　3 Ibid., pp. 553–4.

4 *V.C.H. Hertfordshire*, i. 283, and the example of William de Briouze who added
monks from Anjou to his castles at Bramber and Monmouth: P. Marchegay, 'Les
prieurés anglais de St. Florent lès Saumur', *B.E.C.* xl (1879).

5 *V.C.H. Dorset*, ii. 121.　　　　6 *V.C.H. Leicestershire*, ii. 52.

7 Eton College, Modbury Charter no. 1, *c*. 1140.

8 *V.C.H. Sussex*, ii. 113. The document, still in the archives of the Seine-Maritime
18 H 2, was transcribed by Déville, P.R.O. 31/8/40 A, p. 359.

9 Stogursey Charters no. 1: 1100–7. See above, p. 49.

10 See above, p. 49, n. 2.

11 J. H. Round, 'The Castles of the Conquest'.

looks. Nevertheless it is probable that the monks were established for the spiritual needs of the 'castle'. There is a connexion between the growth of a priory and the laity's expectation of 'parochial' service.

The gift of a church was more often the beginning of a recognizable priory than the gift of land was. As late as 1160 William de Solariis gave the monks of Saint-Sauveur-le-Vicomte the church of All Saints and the chapel of St. Mary, Ellingham, with land *ad edificandum domuum suarum*.[1] In the new priory the monks shortly after agreed that 'facient celebrare in prenominata ecclesia de Elingeham unam missam pro animabus patris matrisque mee [of Hugh de Godeshulle] omniumque fidelium defunctorum. Facient etiam ibidem recitare singulis dominicis diebus nomen meum et nomina patris et matris mee in perpetuum.'[2] At the church of Minster Mathilda Lovel made her gifts to the monks of Ivry on condition that 'semper unus vel duo monachi de supradicto cenobio ibidem Deo deservire valeant'.[3] These are late instances of the foundation of priories on the simple condition of undertaking the service of existing churches. By the mid-twelfth century this practice was thought irregular and a 'vicariate' was established in All Saints, Ellingham, about a dozen years after the monks' arrival[4] and the monks of Ivry employed a secular vicar to perform their duties at Minster within twenty years of Mathilda's benefaction,[5] but it is interesting that, in spite of this, the original benefactors founded their priories on the assumption that the monks could serve the churches.

At Modbury there was apparently only one church for the parish and the priory. The monks may have assumed parochial responsibilities at first; the first mention of a vicar shows that about 1190 he was a mere chaplain living in the priory.[6] At Chepstow the vicar also lodged in the priory.[7]

---

[1] *C.D.F.* 979: 1160; Eton College, Ellingham Charter i and x. 45: 1163.
[2] Eton College, Ellingham Charter no. 8.   [3] *C.C.R.R.* iv. 260, 305.
[4] Eton College, Ellingham Charter no. 2: 1173/4.
[5] *C.C.R.R.* iv. 260, 305.
[6] Eton College, Modbury Charters, nos. 3 and 4: 1188–90: 'ita quidem quod liceat monachis qui ibi moram fecerint capellanum suum in domo sua secum habere quem secum in victualibus exhibeant vel ei exterius certam assignent portionem cumque admoveant vel amoveant assensu episcopi vel officialis sui prout ecclesiastico honori sibi noverint melius expedire'. See above, p. 49.   [7] *C.Pap.L.* v. 253.

These facts suggest that the parish was not separate from the priory, although the monks appointed a priest, at a later stage, to assume the parochial duties as such. At an earlier period, however, it seems probable that the monks themselves assumed the parochial responsibilities. The monks of Saint-Etienne at Caen accepted the church of Bures on condition that 'they deemed the church fit for the service of God and the honourable life of monks'.[1] An early charter of a bishop of Hereford, of which the text has unfortunately disappeared, seems to imply that the monks of Lire were themselves to serve the churches of his diocese.[2] At the end of the thirteenth century the monks of Lancaster still undertook services for the parish, without recourse to a vicar.[3]

If the monks of the late eleventh century did serve parish churches we have an explanation for the considerable gifts of churches. The monks served the churches of their own manors, which were subsequently 'bailiwicks' rather than priories; they served as castle chaplains; and their priories proper began with parochial service in the parish-priory church.[4] The sources are scanty and it is dangerous to argue from silence. I do not want to suggest that monks were intended to serve in all the churches that they received, but that they were expected to serve in the principal church of the area of their endowment, where a 'priory' came into being, and it is possible that they also served in nearby churches through one of their number. The real difficulty is that too little is known about the parochial clergy in the mid-eleventh century, because records only become abundant in the late twelfth century, when attempts were being made to change the system. Probably when the Normans came to England parishes were served by ordained peasants whose rustic ministry of the sacraments had to be supplemented by visitors from Old Minsters, or simply from monasteries, who

---

[1] *C.D.F.* 1409: 1069–79; *D.B.* ii, f. 435b; *C.D.F.* 452: the church was lost by the monks who retained only the tithes.

[2] Eure H 590, chapter 97, no. 13: Bishop Robert de Béthune (1131–48) refers to a charter of Bishop Gerard (1096–1101).

[3] *Lancaster Cartulary*, pp. 139–40: 1282.

[4] For parish-priory churches see New, p. 19; *C.F.R. 1337–47*, pp. 33, 281, 282, 305, 399. For indirect evidence of the survival of this practice in 1295 see below, p. 82.

supplied the ministry of the word.[1] It is hard to believe that the conquering Normans would have been content with no more fervent spiritual counsellors than country priests. They would have naturally turned to the monks who were in the high noon of their glory and esteem in Normandy. The monastic traditions of the English church put no barriers in their way. Even at a later period monks were connected with the parochial ministry, and this practice was probably more, not less, common before the twelfth-century bishops began to introduce changes into their dioceses. Hugh de Aspeleya admitted the monks of Castellion to the service of his own chapel when he or his wife were in the county *per monachum sive capellanum eorum* and acknowledged the general rights of the monks' parish church of Wootton Wawen. Since there is no evidence that there were two churches in Wootton Wawen the priory church evidently served as the parish church at this time.[2] The monks of Stogursey took the tithes and oblations of the chapel of Aller in Sampford Brett because they undertook the duties of the chapel *in quatuor festivitatibus anni singulis annis*, and if they served the chapel they presumably served their own parish church which was the priory church.[3] The monks of Lire had some unspecified right to the chaplaincy of Wilton Castle which suggests a similar service.[4] At Carisbrooke the parish responsibilities were assumed, without reference to a parish priest, by the prior, although there is also a hint that the church was at one time served by two clerks who trespassed on the rights of the monks.[5] Evidence enough has been adduced to show that several priories were founded in

[1] e.g. Walter Daniel, *Vita Ailredi*, p. 28, for Ailred's sermons to the clergy.

[2] Eure II F 148, f. 30ᵛ: the settlement was approved by John, bishop of Worcester, probably 1151–8, because in 1178 the church of Wootton Wawen was appropriated and a vicariate established suggesting that the priory was separated from the parish: ibid., f. 23 : 3 November 1178.

[3] *Stogursey Charters*, no. 11, pp. 10–11: before 1197.

[4] Eure H 590, chapter 97, no. 72: an agreement whereby Abbot R. renounced the rights of his monastery and provided part of the chaplain's endowment; the tithe of an acre of the demesne of Wilton *cum tota vestura sine aliquo retenimento*.

[5] B. M. Egerton MS. 3667, nos. 14, 174 (ff. 70–71). Abbot Hilderus accepted a pension of 30*s.* p.a. from each of two clerks until their death or entry into religion at the request of Baldwin, earl of Exeter, whose clerks they were: ibid., f. 17, c. 1142–8. This incident may have interrupted the life of the priory during the civil wars of Stephen's reign.

parish churches, and since it is clear that no new church was built in the parish, either for the laity or the monks, it is certain that the same church was used by both. Admittedly at Modbury a parson is mentioned at the end of the twelfth century, but had there been a parson since the beginning of the priory?[1] The foundation of priories might mean the creation of new parishes around them. Local worship was therefore concentrated in the monks' church, as at Horsley, where Henry I, not the local bishop, granted the *monasterium* and parish to Troarn, absolutely free from all subjection to the church and parish of Avening.[2] In 1174 Saint-Evroul's church of Rowell was separated from the church of Hawling, but in this case, perhaps because of its late date, the clerk of Hawling enjoyed some rights in Saint-Evroul's church, and the monks were required to establish a vicariate, so that the new parish was not actually served by them.[3] Yet, where monks did have a church or chapel of their own, whether it was called a priory or not (and monks settled anywhere would tend to have a chapel in their *curia*), this centre of monastic worship, however debased, became a centre for parish worship also. There would be no point in Jocelin, bishop of Salisbury, allowing the monks of Avebury to have their own chapel in their *curia* provided that it did not prejudice the position of the parish church (which was the property of Cirencester abbey) unless such curial chapels did in fact become rivals of parish churches.[4]

To bring this long inquiry to a close perhaps two illustrations of the foundation of priories in Normandy itself may help to confirm the theory. Coquelin, the Maurist historian of Le Tréport, has a pleasant story to describe the beginnings of the monastery's priory of Sainte-Croix. Robert I, count of Eu (1036–90), accompanied the hearse of his wife Beatrice on its way to Eu for burial. At Flamangeville, where the cortège halted a while, Robert founded a priory. 'Il donna le lieu ou elle s'estoit faite à l'abbaye du Tréport y feit bastir une eglise et ordonna qu'un des religieux y demeurast; et

---

[1] See above, p. 58, n. 6. The church was to be appropriated after the parson's death and the new vicar was to live in the priory. Eton College, Modbury Charters, nos. 3 and 4: 1188–90.

[2] *C.D.F.* 475. [3] *C.D.F.* 645. Cf. ibid. 650.

[4] *V.C.H. Wiltshire*, iii. 392. Jocelin was bishop 1142–84.

pour sa subsistance et son entretien qui luy seroit envoié du
monastere donna la terre pour une charrue et une parte de sa
garenne.' By the seventeenth century there was in addition
to the prior 'un chapelain qui dessert la dite chapelle dont la
nomination et presentation du prieuré et la chapelle appartient à l'abbaye du Tréport'.[1] A later age had insisted on the
appointment of a secular priest to carry out the service which
an earlier period had wanted performed specifically by a holy
monk. The other example comes from the history of Troarn
as described by Sauvage. Examining the origins of Troarn's
priory Le Désert he refers to the dedication of the church
there in 1115. It was 'le plus éloigné des prieurés troarniens
sis dans le diocèse de Bayeux (et) fut établi par les moines
euxmêmes. . . . Sans doute il est assez difficile de démêler si
cette dédicasse se doit entendre de l'église paroissiale ou de
l'église du prieuré. Mais il nous semble qu'il faut confon-
dre toutes deux. Au Désert, comme à Tailleville, comme à
Cogny, ce furent les religieux qui à l'origine desservirent la
paroisse. Plus tard la celle, la grange d'exploitation se déve-
lopa et devint un prieuré, les moines abandonnèrent l'office
curial'.[2]

These two examples from Normandy itself do not show
foundation of the 'priories' most historians seem to expect.
The priories grow out of the monks' performance of pious
duties for the grieving Count Robert or of simple service in
the parish church. It seems to me that the best explanation
for the fact that the Norman priories in England, as distinct
from the bailiwicks, grew out of the ownership of churches
must be sought on the same lines.

First, there are the disputes about ownership of property
which show that the Normans can hardly have expected
their priories to grow in successive generations. Second,
there is the remarkable fact that the monasteries with the
best endowments were precisely the monasteries which did
not found priories. Third, there is the close association between priories and less important Norman lords who invited
monks from their own part of Normandy to settle in or near
the lords in England, probably in order to obtain the
spiritual consolation that in the eleventh century only the

[1] Coquelin, pp. 211–12.   [2] Sauvage, *Troarn*, p. 185.

monks could give. Fourth, there is the probability that priories, or at least agencies, were established in different parts of the country where the properties were grouped conveniently for administration. If the monks received a church in the district they used it for their own worship, and at first, before bishops came to insist on the institution of secular priests, rectors or vicars, the monks attended themselves to the spiritual responsibilities of the parishes. It is possible that benefactors intended to secure a monastic ministry by causing a small monastic community to be set up, like the earlier Anglo-Saxon collegiate churches or Old Minsters, which could look after the spiritual needs of a number of churches in the vicinity. It is at least notable that the real conventual priories were given, on the whole, many more churches than were the other monks. This may simply mean that the benefactors of the convents had less land to give. It could also mean that they gave churches for this further purpose, even if in later times, when conditions had changed and writing begins to record those changes, this purpose was forgotten. Even where the monks did not receive a church on their manor, they probably set up a chapel for their own worship, which would become the nucleus of the priory and which might in some circumstances lead to the creation of a new parish: this means that the monks had acquired a parochial responsibility.

This last argument is controversial and inconclusive, but before leaving the matter altogether I would like to point out that the chief argument against it is the reflection of the prejudice that monks were cloistered and did not participate in the affairs of the church in the parishes. In the Conqueror's lifetime a movement of ecclesiastical reform sought to improve the status of the priesthood which ultimately undermined a tradition of the Dark Ages, that monks were the holy men of the church. The creation of a celibate, educated priesthood helped to define the parochial structure of England which was still not clear in 1086.[1] It is not therefore possible to view the appearance of the Norman monks in the parishes at that time as an infringement of the rights of the secular clergy. The distinction which we draw

[1] W. Page, 'Some Remarks on the Churches of the Domesday Survey'.

between the secular and the regular clergy was much less sharp in the eleventh century. The tradition of both the English and the Norman church allowed the monks a distinguished part in the general life of the church, and in England bishops were often wedded to sees where the *familia* was monastic. Lanfranc did nothing to reverse this practice. His monasticism had brought him out of the cloister into William's court, even before 1066. The truth is that eleventh-century monasticism was not retiring: it set the tone of the whole church. Colleges of canons were replaced by monks in Normandy, but new orders of secular clergy adopted monastic type rules for their different way of life. The whole ideal of the church was monastic.[1] It is true that Berlière came to the conclusion that the evidence for monastic service of parish churches was so scanty that it must have been exceptional,[2] but all evidence for parochial history is scanty as early as this. What is certain is that monks like the Blessed Vitalis were the popular preachers of their day and that the new canon law had to prohibit monks from administering communion, hearing confessions, and preaching, because that was one of their common functions at the time. Reformers had new ideas, but they did not waste their fulminations on rare abuses. Whatever we may think of the rightness of the reformers, we cannot deny that there was a real religious sentiment in the defenders of an older order.

Although there were a few genuine conventual priories mothered by the Norman monasteries, the majority were priories of a different type. The monks themselves did not pretend that they were other than they were. The abbot of Cormeilles told Edward I, in spite of the existence of Chepstow and Newent 'priories', that 'il ne ad nulle fille mesun en Engleterre mes (ce) qu'il ad en Engleterre si tient il en demeigne, remuable a sa volunte'.[3] The bishop of Hereford described the 'priories' of his diocese in these terms:'Preterea sciendum est quod abbas de Lyre . . . et ejus conventus habent plures ecclesias parochiales et appropriatas . . . et unum procuratorem cum unico socio monacho qui ipsas custodit, set nullam domum nec ecclesiam conventu-

---

[1] J. C. Dickinson, *The Origins of the Austin Canons*, pp. 215, 231.
[2] U. Berlière, 'L'exercice du ministère paroissial'.   [3] *Rot. Parlt.* i. 274.

alem seu collegiatam . . . habet; . . . similiter abbas et conventus de Cormeliis . . . habent . . . unum ballivum monachum cum uno socio monacho qui prior vulgariter nuncupatur'.[1] There were other priors who could write as Saint-Fromond's prior wrote to Edward I about his 'priory-parish church' of Bonby: 'issicom il nest pas en cas des autres que unt lour celles et lour covent en Engleterre quil ne ad nul recec' en Engleterre fors une graunge ou unques meisone ne demorra quest al eglise . . . '.[2] It was these modest priories which the Normans 'founded' so numerously after the conquest.

III. *The value of the English property*

If the monks were not intended to use their English property principally for the erection of conventual priories, it was because the possessions were directly valuable to the Norman house. Rigaud's register proves that the loss of English revenues in the thirteenth century caused considerable suffering to some Norman houses. At Saint-Wandrille the payment of debts depended upon receipt of the English pension; at Aumâle the English rents at least helped to reduce the debts.[3] At Noion the number of monks in this priory of Saint-Evroul declined because the English revenues were not paid.[4] The monks of Boscherville told the archbishop that although they had four monks in England they had themselves received nothing for a long time.[5] The monks clearly wanted more than English cells; they wanted to see a surplus in Normandy.

Payments of money to Normandy are called 'apports' in English documents of the fourteenth century and were

---

[1] *Hereford Registers: Swinfield*, pp. 356–7. Newent priory had in 1327 *una curia cum aula, camera, capella, etc.* P.R.O. E 109/9/1: 30 January 1327. M. Chibnall, *The English Lands of the Abbey of Bec*, p. 136, describes the 'priories' as 'Priories only in name, existing solely to minister to the material needs of the monks of Bec'.

[2] P.R.O. E 135/22/71. The abbot of Sainte-Cathérine of Rouen describes the prior of Harmondsworth as *commonachus noster custos manerii nostri de Hermondesores.* P.R.O. Ancient Correspondence, xx. 86: 13 October 1299.

[3] Rigaud's *Register*, pp. 224, 497.

[4] Ibid., p. 499: 'solebant esse plures (monachos tres) sed redditus quod habebant in Anglia non habuerunt per annos aliquot propter guerram ideoque erant pauciores': 1264. It was the same story in 1266: p. 544. Noion expected £100 from England, p. 192: 1253.   [5] Ibid., p. 501: 1264.

definitely interrupted during the French war, and judging from Rigaud's register were subject to delays even in the thirteenth century, if they did not cease altogether. These apports varied considerably in value from house to house: those which maintained fully conventual priories in England received from them only nominal sums as a token of subjection, but those with 'bailiwicks' expected to receive all the English revenues for themselves. It was therefore the greatest Norman houses with the least important priories that gained most from these properties. Saint-Etienne of Caen had £220 from England compared to a Norman revenue of 4,000 pounds tours; La Trinité, Caen £160 and 2,500 pounds tours; Saint-Pierre-sur-Dives 30 marks or £20 and 2,000 pounds tours;[1] Saint-Victor-en-Caux £100 and 450 pounds tours;[2] a much smaller house, Almenesches, 25 marks and 750 marks.[3] These are the only comparable figures and they exhibit a range of proportions from 1 : 5 to 1 : 30. These figures are difficult to evaluate because of the variable relationship between pounds sterling and pounds tours at this time. Usually four pounds tours are calculated to one pound sterling. On this basis the abbot of Saint-Evroul who declared in the fifteenth century that confiscation meant a loss of £2,000 to his monastery every year[4] would not seem to diverge substantially from the rent rolls of his house which show an estimated revenue of about £500 sterling in 1409.[5] However, in two undated documents of the late fourteenth century the monks of Boscherville multiplied their English revenues nine times[6] and the nuns of Saint-Leger of Préaux six times[7] to find their French value.

[1] Rigaud's *Register*, pp. 77, 94.

[2] Ibid., p. 318. This entry may be calculated in pounds tours throughout.

[3] Ibid., p. 236.

[4] Martène, *Thesaurus Anecdotarum*, i, cols. 1746–8. According to Le Couteulx the monks of Jumièges enjoyed a revenue of 730 aurei from Hayling priory: *Annales Ordinis Cartusiensis*, vii. 418.

[5] Orne H 932. Receipts (debts are not mentioned) amounted to more than £550. In 1272 they amounted to about £300: Orne H 896.

[6] Rouen MS. Y 52, f. 42ᵛ: 'La declaration de ce qui appartient aux religieux de saint george de baugerville prez Rouen pour tout quilz en ont au royaume dangleterre tant du don du Conquerant que de Guillaume chambellan heredital de normandie apresent comte de Tancarville . . . Summa viijˣˣ i livres x s qui valent en tournois mil iiij liii lirres x s'.

[7] B.N. MS. Lat. 17133, no. 35: 'et vault chacun acre . . . et labourable viij d a la

The monks lost their revenues when they had become particularly valuable in France.

Clearly the monks calculated their English property's value in money terms. Rent lists for Lire's churches and tithes,[1] Saint-Martin of Séez's property in Sussex and East Anglia,[2] Newent priory,[3] as well as for Saint-Evroul,[4] provide money calculations; the manor-bailiff's account for Ottery St. Mary[5] gives a glimpse of current, although minor, expenses as well as income.

How easy did the monks find it to export their money revenues? Most sources speak only of interruptions of payments, but these, like the entry in the Sainte-Barbe chronicle that English coin of Stephen's reign was so valueless as not to be worth exporting,[6] imply that conditions were exceptional. What does become clear from a number of documents is that the monks relied on merchants for carrying their money and perhaps also for a form of banking transaction, particularly after the king began to have monks inspected at the ports in case they tried to carry coin oversea.

As early as the reign of Henry III the canon of Rouen at Kilham in Yorkshire suggested to his chapter that a merchant might collect *denarios vestros* instead of his committing them to the uncertainties of land and sea.[7] This may mean either that a merchant had forms of protection not open to monks or that a merchant would be prepared to make payments in Normandy in exchange for collecting English revenues without transferring the money itself. Italian bankers acted for the papal chaplain when Saint-Wandrille appointed Hugo Rubeus, Innocent IV's nephew, as parson of Ecclesfield,[8] and there is no reason why merchants should

monnoie du pays qui val ycy iiij tours; . . . il appartient au dit manoir xv livres de sterling, qui val en francs iiij^xx et x livres tournois; . . . et vault . . . c sous de sterling qui vault en francs xxx livres tournois et les aller querir nos hotes et tenants de stoure peraulx et quant ils sont venus eulx ont ving sols de sterling pour leurs despens qui vallent vi livres; . . . (*verso*) chacun tenant du manoir de Stourperaulx doit iij denier qui vaut xviij deniers tours'. Reference to the manor of Stower Provost, now a manor of King's College, Cambridge.

[1] B.N. MS. Lat. 4221.   [2] Orne H 938, no. 264.
[3] B.M. Add. MS. 15658.   [4] Orne H 896-7.   [5] Seine-Maritime G 4057: 1278.
[6] *Ste Barbe-en-Auge, Chronique*, p. 34.   [7] Seine-Maritime G 4049.
[8] B.N. MS. Lat. 17133. See J. Eastwood, *History of Ecclesfield*, p. 508. For a nearly contemporary grant of a benefice by Jumièges see Seine Maritime, 9 H 4, nos. 512-17, ff. 286-8.

not have acted in a similar capacity for Anglo-Norman affairs. Once the war began the monks experienced further difficulties because the English government opposed the export of specie. The abbot of Mont Saint-Michel was often in need of money[1] and pestered his English agents for it even when they could not afford to send him what he wanted.[2] One agent expresses his fears of the official attitude, and although royal records do not corroborate him in detail he probably told the truth as he believed it.[3] The date of his letter is not given, but it appears to refer to Edward II's early years during a truce in the war. After 1337, when war was continuous for twenty years, payments came to an end almost completely[4] as the monks of Grestain complained to Clement VI.[5] The treaty of Brétigny offered a respite and in this period there is direct evidence for the use of merchants as intermediaries.

In the winter 1367–8 a merchant of Lucca, Simon Bothell, received, through his English attorney, 164 marks from Philip Arnulphi, the bailiff of Warminghurst, on behalf of the abbot of Fécamp and in May 1368 he received another 170 marks.[6] In 1366 two messengers had come to collect money and one of them, Stephen de Vallecomitis, described as *armiger et nuntius abbatis*, went to England expressly to receive the year's profit of 340 marks. Stephen was said to require horses in order to visit St. Thomas's shrine at Canterbury which indicates that he did not arrive in England as was normal, through Dover, and that he may have tried to pose as a pilgrim. The abbot perhaps tried to

---

[1] P.R.O. 31/8/140 B ii, pp. 362–3, no. 171; B.N. MS. Lat. 10072, pp. 217–18, no. 174.

[2] The prior of Otterton, Richard de Albodoyto, told his abbot that the condition of the priory did not allow him to send a halfpenny to Normandy, let alone pay ten marks to the peasantry: 'immo si essetis in partibus a vobis exigerem vel prioratum vestrum penitus relinquerem': *Otterton Charter*, xxiv.

[3] See p. 71, n. D.   [4] For an exception see below, p. 96, n. 2.

[5] H. Denifle, *La Désolation des Eglises*, ii, 75, n. 1: 'cum in regno Anglie habeant unum domum . . . et census redditus et proventus ad summam 90 lib. sterl. . . . ascendentes et plurium duodecim ecclesiarum parochialium patronatus . . . nichil omnino inter Francie et Anglie reges guerris durantibus gaudere potuerunt a longo tempore': 14 July 1348.

[6] Seine-Maritime 7 H 57. Bothell is described as a merchant of R. but he was a merchant of Lucca: see A. Beardwood, *Alien Merchants*, p. 197. He was found guilty of smuggling in 1364; ibid., pp. 11, 13.

smuggle his income out of England in this guise, and when he returned the next year, Stephen brought messages both written and oral 'qui vobis dicet voluntatem nostram super missionibus et expensis et aliis nostris negotiis'. The merchant Bothell may have received the money.[1]

In spite of the clear evidence for the use of money payments, other goods found their way to Normandy. Manuscripts were written in England for Sainte-Barbe and Saint-Martin of Séez;[2] a monk of Préaux presented his monastery with a pyx when he returned from a period of duty.[3] The more frequent references to English produce are, however, to food-supplies. The Normans could not base their domestic calculations on these, but certain food supplemented local supplies. John forbade the export of corn at the beginning of the thirteenth century, which may or may not imply that export was common,[4] but there were special concessions at some times.[5] Bacon and cheese and salt were easily exported and desirable imports.[6] The monks must have sold their tithes:[7] even in the twelfth century the agent of Fécamp expected to collect a sum of money from a tithe-collector.[8] But the farm stock could be increased from the tithes and as the prior of Otterton, echoing the bishop of Exeter, told his abbot: 'de bobus et aliis estoramentis ipse dixit quod ita adherent glebe quod terra absque ipsis non potest excoli et quod est hoc thesaurus monasterii quia oportet quod prior quomodocunque contingat teneat aut dimittat in statu eque bono aut meliori'.[9] There are references to the monks' sheep:

---

[1] Seine-Maritime 7 H 43: the visit of Pierre de Salevert, 2 December 1366; ibid. 7 H 57: Stephen de Vallecomitis, April 1366.

[2] L. V. Delisle, *Histoire Littéraire de la France*, xxxi. 281; *Catalogue Général des Manuscrits des Bibliothèques Publiques de France*, Départements, ii. 470, n. 6.

[3] Eure H 711, f. 63ᵛ: 'adam secum abstulit et dedit deo et ecclesie S. Petrie de pratellis eucaristiam ubi corpus domini debet esse super altare'.

[4] *Rot. Claus. Litt.* ii. 47b.

[5] *C.P.R. 1364–67*, p. 128.

[6] *Rot. Claus Litt.* ii. 47b; *C.P.R. 1364–67*, p. 106; *C.D.F.* 661, 233. The agent of the abbess of Saint-Amand in the twelfth century sent her a small cheese from England as a gift, regretting that it was no larger. Seine-Maritime fonds Saint-Amand, Liasse Angleterre.

[7] *C.D.F.* 120, 661: what else could monks do with foals and stag-skins?

[8] 'Epistolae Fiscannenses', *Revue Mabillon*, xi (1953), 29: 'Cum aput Cantuariam ubi tota est reddituum nostrorum numerositas eosdem redditus quesiturus perrexissem'. For these tithes see C.D.F. 373.   [9] *Otterton Charter*, xxxi.

the abbess of Caen had about 800 sheep on the Wiltshire manors of Tilshead and Tarrant in 1299;[1] Boscherville had nearly as many at Avebury in the same county in 1253;[2] Saint-Ouen had four sheep walks and more than four hundred sheep in Essex in 1202.[3] Such figures are not impressive beside the size of the flocks of the English Cistercians, but the alien monks played a role consistent with their general size. England supplied them with additional resources. After the Conquest the property might serve for the monks' footwear[4] or for the *camera*.[5] Pierre Roger, abbot of Fécamp, before he became archbishop of Rouen or Clement VI, thought that his English woodlands, if cut,[6] might raise 2,000 pounds (tours?). Their English estates were indubitably valuable to the monks, and this was the justification of the endowments. The conquest of England enriched Normandy as long as the political connexion was preserved. The loss of Normandy made aliens of the exploiters, but for two hundred years longer they defied the normal consequences of the change, protected by their religious character.

NOTES

A. William of Worcester, *Itinerarium sive Liber Rerum Memorabilium*, pp. 101–2. 'Universis sanctae matris ecclesiae presentes litteras inspecturis vel audituris salutem: noverit universitas vestra quod sanctissimus dominus papa Gregorius anno ab incarnatione domini millesimo septuagesimo ad ecclesiam montis Sancti Michaelis in tumba in comitatu Cornubiae gerens eximiae devocionis affectum pie concessit ecclesiae predictae quae ministerio angelico creditur et comprobatur consecrari et sanctificari omnibus fidelibus qui illam ecclesiam cum suis beneficiis et elemosinis expecierunt seu visitaverint tertiam partem penetenciarum suarum eis condonari. Et ut inconcussum et inviolabile sic tenus permaneat; auctoritate dei patris omnipotentis et filii et spiritus sancti omnibus successoribus suis interdixit nequid contra hoc decretum usurpare presumant. Ista verba in antiquis registris de novo in hac ecclesia repertis inventa prout hic in valvis ecclesiae publice ponuntur. Et quia pluribus istud est incognitum ideo nos in Christo dei famuli et ministri hujus ecclesiae universitatem vestram qui regimen animarum possidetis ob mutue vicissitudinis obtentum requirimus et rogamus quatenus ista publicetis in ecclesiis vestris ut vestri subditi et subjecti ad majorem exortacionem devocionis attentius animentur et locum istum gloriosum perigrinando frequentent ad dona et indulgencias pre-

[1] Calvados, La Trinité, Caen, Carton 1 Angleterre: see also E. Power, *The Wool Trade*, p. 33, for numbers of sheep on the twelfth-century manors.
[2] Rouen MS. Y 52, f. 180.   [3] *C.D.F.* 104.   [4] *C.D.F.* 666.
[5] B.N. MS. Lat. 5650, f. 19^v: English manors given *ad cameram autem et ad ligna*.
[6] Seine-Maritime 7 H 43: 1326. Cf. *C.Pap.L.* ii.488: 1328.

dicta graciose consequenda'. William of Worcester visited the Mount in 1478. He does not mention the appearance of St. Michel to Aubert, bishop of Avranches, which was the Norman legend of the foundation of Mont Saint-Michel; instead he writes as though the next appearance of the saint after the famous Apulian visitation was *in tumba in Cornubia juxta mare*. He may not have known that the Tumba was in Normandy. The document he quotes gives no idea of date at all. What is clear is that Gregory must already have been associated with the priory before Leofric's confirmation was copied into the Avranches cartulary. How long it had been written at that time, *c.* 1160?, it is impossible to say.

B.   Rainald was living in 1123: Johnson, no. 1391. His son Roger (1125–62) confirmed the original grants: Eton College, Modbury Charter no. 1, *c.* 1140. The claim for tithes appears in a charter of Robert, bishop of Exeter, 1138–43: ibid., no. 32/2. Haimo sent a letter of introduction with the prior: ibid., no. 32/29: 'Pro eo donacioni vestre de qua plene confidimus presentamus dilectum fratrem nostrum H. dictum Anglicanum latorem presentium . . . ad regimen prioratus nostri et vestri Modbyr' quem ei quamdiu vixerit tradimus liberaliter admittatis et ei si placet divine pietatis intuitu consilium in negotiis impendere dignemini tantum inde interventu nostro faciatis quod liberalitatem vestram teneamur in domino commendare bene et diu valeat excellencia vestra'. In spite of the phrase used here, ibid., no. 24 shows that the prior's status was not so secure; 'si vero aliquo tempore post decessum dicti prioris vel eius amovicionem de voluntate sui abbatis'. For two letters from abbots to the patrons in the first half of the thirteenth century see ibid. 32/30 and 32/28. The endowment was sufficient for only three monks in the fourteenth century: Bishop Grandisson sent a fourth monk back to Normandy: *Exeter Registers: Grandisson*, ii, f. 104b. For the dissolution see below, pp. 136–7.

C.   A letter written by the subprior of Winchester to the abbot of Saint-Sauveur-le-Vicomte in the mid-fourteenth century shows a monk of Ellingham priory visiting Normandy to report on the prior: 'Domine reverende inquiretis diligenter causam adventus fratris Ricardi Roulond injungentes sibi in virtute obediencie quod dicat vobis veritatem privatim qualiter se habet prior suus in partibus nostris et hoc diligenter; intelligentes sane quod habetis responderel de anima illius prioris una cum vestra juxta regulam sancti Benedicti unde cum ceperint oriri vitia vel peccata radicitus amputanda sunt, ne fixis firmatisque radicibus noxios ramos mittent, et in ramis mali operis fructus ferant (?). Prior desiderat solitariam vitam habere nec vellet habere socium de habitu et secundum sanctum Benedictum multa pericula sunt solitario proxima, primum quod sibimetipsi in omnibus actibus suis placet, et nullum alium habet qui opus ejus probet'. P.R.O. 31/8/140 B III, pp. 44–45, no. 21, copied by Léchaudé d'Anisy from a document formerly in the Archives Départementales de La Manche.

D.   *Otterton Charter*, xxxi: 'et bene scio quod procurator eius habet pecuniam sed non est ausus mittere ultra mare. Et ego nolo eam recipere nec me ponere in periculo sicut omnes priores de Anglia. Quia justiciarii domini regis venerunt inquirere super illos qui miserant pecuniam ultra mare citra quatuor aureos et omnes fuerunt accusati et in prisione detenti apud Londoniam per sex septimanas et adhuc in curia remanent domini regis; et intendunt prelati et barones super hoc ordinare. Et ego solus per misas et costagia permaxima et dona facta justiciariis et inquisitionibus ad valorem xx marcarum una cum patrie familiaritate evasi cum timore et tremore quia volebant mihi imponere facta antecessoris mei et si esset presens tunc temporis non recessisset de manibus eorum cum quinquies centum marcis ut asserebant. Et heu me! quod unquam intravi Angliam quia undique mala perturbant: a monasterio quia non possum ad presens subvenire'. The prior is presumably Robert Lovel (1310–16) writing shortly after his appointment. He did visit his monastery in 1312: *Exeter Register: Stapeldon*, p. 303.

III

THE NORMAN MONKS AND THE ANGLO-FRENCH WAR

I. 1204–1294

Not until the thirteenth century was there any noticeable influence of public events on the lives of the Norman monks. The rebellions of Odo of Bayeux may have cost the canons of Bayeux their English property, for Domesday is the only record of them;[1] the Angevin conquest of Normandy in 1141 may have added to the difficulties of monks living in lawless England.[2] The turncoat William de Beauchamp took advantage of Stephen's weakness to persecute the canons of Sainte-Barbe-en-Auge,[3] and the anarchy is the best explanation for the destruction noticed on their English manors by the monks of Fécamp and Mont Saint-Michel in Henry II's early years.[4] The anarchy did not interrupt relations between England and Normandy altogether, however, for Abbot Hilderus of Lire visited the Isle of Wight in the forties, probably at the time of the consecration of Quarr abbey.[5] Not surprisingly there is no clear royal policy of hostility to the Norman enemies.

With John political considerations weighed more in his treatment of the Norman monks after 1204. Even before the fall of Rouen the king began to survey the value of the Normans' English lands,[6] and either at this time or later

---

[1] D.B. i, f. 31b.

[2] There is nothing to show what attitude Geoffrey Plantagenet adopted.

[3] *Chronique de Ste Barbe-en-Auge*, pp. 43, 64; L. Voss, *Heinrich von Blois*, Appendix IXa, p. 170.

[4] For Fécamp: A. Saltman, *Theobald Archbishop of Canterbury*, no. 109; 'Epistolae Fiscannenses', *Revue Mabillon*, xi (1953), 29–31. For Mont Saint-Michel: *C.D.F.* 734.

[5] T. Madox, *Formulare Anglicanum*, no. CCCCXCVII: 1140–7.

[6] *Rotuli Normanniae*, p. 122. 'Rotulus de valore terrarum Normannorum incepto anno regni regis Johannis sexto': i.e. June 1204. The seizure was made whilst Peter de Stokes was sheriff of Northamptonshire: he was sheriff until Easter 1204: *C.C.R.R.* vi. 85–86. The record could be a few months later than the actual seizure.

the lands were seized and the export of revenues forbidden[1] although some of them were released to the agents of the monasteries in return for a fine. The prior of Frampton offered 100 marks for the custody of the abbot of Caen's manors[2] and paid half this sum on 5 October.[3] The official entry states that he was to 'farm' the lands from the king at £80 a year six months after paying the second half of the fine, but no record of this second payment survives, unless the prior's gift of an unvalued palfrey the following year be a substitute.[4] Other monks paid regular sums to the king. These may have been the whole priory revenues or the 'apport' only. The prior of Coggs paid 100 marks for the custody and promised to answer for the revenues: 'respondebit domino regi ad summonitionem suam de exitibus illis salvo sibi et sociis suis rationabili estuverio suo';[5] the prior of Loders, after giving two palfreys for the custody, promised to account for the revenues of the abbot of Montebourg: 'pro tenendis terris quas prius tenuit de terris abbatis de Monteburgo, ita quod de tanto respondebit in camera domini regis de quanto solebat respondere abbati de Monteburgo'.[6] Similarly the king ordered the sheriff of Hampshire to release to the king's chaplain 20s. a year which the prior of Ellingham 'reddere consuevit abbatie Sancti Salvatoris de Normannia qui modo sunt in manu nostra quia illos ei dedimus'.[7] It was the money which had gone abroad that the king wanted.

The records give no general picture of John's policy towards the Norman monks, but it is probable that all suffered equally.[8] Grestain paid no fine for the custody but answered for the revenues, since the abbot and the English

---

[1] *Rot. Claus. Litt.* i. 60b, 66; *Rot. de Oblat. et Finibus*, p. 335. Roger de Eston was accused of sending money abroad: 'quod nequiter ipse portavit xx marcas de denariis suis ad inimicos domini regis ultra mare plus quam ii annis transactis' (1210), *C.C.R.R.* vi. 85–86. [2] *Rot. de Fin.*, p. 199.
[3] *Rot. Claus. Litt.* i. 10b. [4] *Rot. de Fin.*, p. 312.
[5] Ibid., pp. 319–20. The prior was Michael, the abbot's nephew. He paid 40 marks in 1206 and 60 marks in 1207: *Pipe Rolls 7 John*, p. 110; *8 John*, p. 62; *9 John*, p. 39. [6] *Rot. de Fin*, p. 313.
[7] *Rot. Claus. Litt.* i. 77: 25 January 1207.
[8] The monks of Mont Saint-Michel obtained custody of their lands after April 1205 when the prior of Otterton paid 10 marks: *Rot. de Fin.*, p. 328; the abbot of Saint-Pierre-sur-Dives recovered lands 'per finem quem fecerat cum domino rege': *C.C.R.R.* vi. 85–86.

monks had to promise to send nothing to Normandy and were allowed only their *victum*.[1] Sainte-Cathérine of Rouen recovered custody of Blyth priory on the same terms a few months later;[2] the abbot[3] and abbess[4] of Préaux and the abbot of Saint-Wandrille[5] paid fines for the custody without committing themselves to future payments; the abbot of Savigny may have avoided even that.[6] In one case the canons of Evreux paid £100 for the custody of Bramford manor and were promised payment of the arrears of the revenues by the king.[7] Not all the Normans recovered their own quickly, however, for the sheriff of Oxfordshire still held the lands of the canons of Séez in March 1205 when two of them were granted their reasonable board and *estuverium*[8] and as late as 1211 John collected 100 marks, a palfrey, and two tuns of wine from the abbot of Fécamp for the restoration of the abbot's lands and confirmation of his privileges.[9] In this case John's distrust was perhaps justified by the abbot's dominant position on the south coast.

John found other excuses, like the interdict, for a second seizure of at least the manors of the abbot of Caen, only one year after restoring them to him.[10] Other victims were the prior of Beckford and the abbots of Préaux and Saint-Wandrille.[11] John 'sold' the manor of the canons of Coutances, Winterbourne Strickland, to Robert de Berners in return for a farm of the revenues;[12] why the canons were treated in this fashion the records do not say. More intelligible was John's compensation of those who claimed to

[1] *Rot. Claus. Litt.* i. 16: 20 December 1205.

[2] Ibid., p. 66: 8 March 1206.

[3] *Rot. de Fin.*, p. 431: April–December 1208: he paid 40 marks.

[4] Ibid., p. 339: 1206; she gave a palfrey.

[5] *Rot. Claus. Litt.* i. 114b–115b: 2 May 1208; the fine was not paid and his lands were distrained for it.

[6] Ibid., p. 60b: 26–28 December 1205.

[7] *Rot. de Fin.*, pp. 435, 440: 1208.

[8] *Rot. Claus. Litt.* i. 23: 17 March 1205.

[9] Delisle, *B.E.C.* lxv (1904), 390–7; *Pipe Roll 11 John*, p. 4: the pipe rolls show that only £55 was paid: *Pipe Rolls 12 John*, p. 86; *13 John*, p. 127. The manor of Bentworth, said to be the archdeacon [*sic*] of Rouen's, was in the hands of Geoffrey de Caleto *de voluntate domini regis* in 1213: *Rot. de Oblat. et Finibus*, p. 512.

[10] *Rot. Pat. Litt.*, p. 70b: restoration April 1207; *Rot. Claus. Litt.* i. 110b taken again; *Rot. Norm.*, p. 126: restored.   [11] *Rot. Claus. Litt.* i. 113.

[12] Ibid., p. 47b: 26 August 1205. For the case of the canons of Lisieux see ibid., p. 62b: 16 January 1206.

have lost lands in Normandy with Normans' lands in England.[1]

Was John simply interested in making as much money as he could out of the monks' embarrassment or was he try-ing to frighten them into loyalty with the threat of complete confiscation? The monks were probably not regarded as potentially dangerous, although the governments of John's successors and later the Commons both pretended to be extremely fearful of monkish connivance with the enemy. In both cases the fear was probably a pretence used to cover aggressive attacks upon the monks' property. In the course of the two centuries following 1204 the privileged monks came to be thought of as no better than 'Frenchmen'.[2] John had not reached this stage. He trusted the alien prior of Stogursey to destroy the castle there[3] and the prior of Wareham enjoyed the custody of the convent of Shaftesbury during a vacancy:[4] hardly the favours enemies would receive. The only doubtful evidence of monks dealing with the French enemy comes from the early years of Henry III when the prior of Eye received from Louis of France, as late as July 1217, a quitclaim of the priory's debt to a Jew of Norwich, Isaac ben Nuru,[5] which shows that even after Lincoln the priory continued, like others in East Anglia, to support a failing cause.

Typical of the slow growth of the realization that relations between England and France must be very different after the loss of Normandy is the anomalous position enjoyed by the abbot of Fécamp in the Cinque ports until 1245. After the failure of the expedition to Poitou in 1242 Henry III accepted the loss of his French provinces as irreparable and the Normans' surviving English lands were seized in 1244.[6] This deprived Foucarmont at least of all its English pro-perty, which consisted of tithes from the estates of its

---

[1] *Rot. Claus. Litt.* i. 40b: 3 July 1205: Séez and Montivilliers.

[2] They were called *ultramarini* in John's reign; in the fourteenth century *alienigenae*.

[3] *Rot. Cart. Johannes*, p. 190, 1.

[4] *Rot. Pat. Litt.* i, part 1, p. 197.

[5] B.M. Harley MS. 312, no. 27, f. 79b: 18 July 1217: a copy made in 1636 'ex Registro Malet pervetusto MS. Prioratus de Eya'.

[6] Matthew Paris, *Chronica Majora*, iv. 288.

patrons, the counts of Eu.[1] At the same time the king forced
the abbot of Fécamp to accept the manors of Cheltenham
and Slaughter with their hundreds in Gloucestershire[2] and
the manor of Navenby in Lincolnshire and to surrender most
of his property in Rye, because in the king's view the abbot
could no longer fortify the towns of Rye and Winchelsea
as befitted their importance:[3] clearly a reference to the
abbot's foreign allegiance, not to his ecclesiastical dignity,
for the abbot had been an effective castellan under Richard
I. The king's entry into Rye had been planned twenty years
before under Hubert de Burgh. The pope wrote, probably
at the government's request, urging the abbot to surrender
the town because the king would favour the monastery if his
wish was granted, but nothing came of this move[4] and
Henry III actually confirmed the abbot's position in 1238.[5]
His change of policy towards the Norman monks in the
Cinque ports reflects the altered approach to foreign affairs
after Taillebourg.[6]

The abundance of royal records in the thirteenth century
discloses the government making petty but tiresome demands upon the foreign monks, but native houses suffered
similarly from royal demands for livings or pensions for
clerks, corrodies for retired servants, and other payments.
The Normans were not discriminated against, but they were
made to share in the burden that the increased cost of
government placed upon those susceptible to royal pressure.
Although this became most obvious when the war put the
aliens at the king's mercy, the defensive position of the
monks may be detected in their reactions to more common
demands.

---

[1] See p. 105, n. A.

[2] The abbot of Fécamp petitioned the king in 1302 because his hundred of
'Salemannesbury' lost business since Count Richard of Cornwall [sic] had bought
the manor of Netherswell and had removed his men from attendance at the abbot's
hundred: P.R.O. Ancient Petitions S.C. 8 316 E 217.

[3] C.P.R. 1232–47, p. 458; C.Cl.R. 1242–7, p. 484; C.Ch.R. II, p. 80; the monks
kept some property outside the port in Rye: C.Cl.R. 1247–51, p. 49.

[4] Rot. Claus. Litt. ii. 148: 20 February 1226; C.Pap.L. i. 111: 14 May 1226. There
is a general letter from the Abbot Richard I to Hubert de Burgh, but it is too vague
to be certain whether it refers to this episode: P.R.O. Ancient Correspondence i. 90:
1222–7.   [5] C.Cl.R. 1237–42, p. 88.

[6] See in general Sir Maurice Powicke, The Thirteenth Century, p. 104.

The bailiff of Fécamp was the only one to resist pressure;[1] Edward II coldly told the archbishop of Rouen that his right to demand a benefice for his clerks was not a matter of the archbishop's grace but the king's undoubted right.[2] Sometimes the king speaks as though his clerks deserved a reward for gratuitous services they had performed for the monks,[3] and abbots refer to corrodians as though they performed some service in the priories,[4] but this is a matter of appearances. At most these phrases prove that both sides recognized an abuse needing excuse.

More controversial were the king's claims to privileges during vacancies. Mrs. Wood has recently examined this question with regard to the thirteenth-century monks[5] so that only a few details need be added from the Norman records.

In the case of monks who held their lands in chief, the king's rights were normally clear: he enjoyed the revenues during a vacancy and new abbots paid a 'fine'. After the death of Abbot Henry of Fécamp, the king's cousin, in 1189, his English lands were accounted for at the Exchequer and the new abbot, Ralph de Argenciis, had to pay the huge fine of £2,000 (presumably calculated for both his Norman and his English lands) to Richard I *pro benevolentia Regis habenda*; it was paid in instalments over eight years.[6] There is no record of the sums demanded of thirteenth-century abbots for their English lands, but Henry III was so anxious to take advantage of vacancies that he several times anticipated an abbot's death.[7] Ironically, the one time the abbots of Saint-Ouen, Saint-Wandrille, and Jumièges pro-

---

[1] *C.Cl.R. 1307–13*, pp. 434, 436; *C.Cl.R. 1313–18*, p. 96.

[2] *C.Cl.R. 1307–13*, pp. 344, 554.

[3] *C.Cl.R. 1307–13*, p. 288. Generally the king produced no excuses: *C.Cl.R. 1237–42*, p. 132; *C.P.R. 1247–58*, p. 360; *C.Cl.R. 1259–61*, p. 262; *C.Cl.R. 1296–1302*, p. 205.

[4] Avranches MS. 211, f. 147ᵛ: Edward III's valet was to perform the same services at St. Michael's Mount as Edward II's had done: 1333. There are several examples of corrodies in the documents, e.g. B.M. Add. MS. 18461, ff. 91ᵛ, 91, 90ᵛ, 76, 76ᵛ. In official records they also occur: *C.Cl.R. 1313–18*, p. 437; *C.Cl.R. 1330–3*, p. 314: Eye; *C.Cl.R. 1313–18*, p. 596; *C.Cl.R. 1333–7*, p. 293: Hayling; *C.Cl.R. 1307–13*, p. 159; *C.Cl.R. 1313–18*, pp. 83, 221, 436; *C.Cl.R. 1318–23*, p. 706; *C.Cl.R. 1324–7*, p. 354: other priories.

[5] S. Wood, *English Monasteries and their Patrons*, chapter v.

[6] *Pipe Rolls 34 Henry II*, pp. 5–6; *1 Richard I*, p. 130; *9 Richard I*, p. 221.

[7] *C.Cl.R. 1237–42*, p. 217; *C.Cl.R. 1247–51*, p. 478.

tested to the king that Abbot William Vaspail continued in health, he was in fact on the point of dying.[1] In 1309 the monastery's bailiff was granted custody of the lands, saving 'incidents' to the king, for a period of nine months until the new abbot could come and make fine with the king; if he delayed coming after that period the bailiff was to offer the king £100 for the right to the custody for a further three months.[2] In this case the king surrendered his claim to the revenues during the vacancy. The archbishop of Rouen received from Henry III the arrears of his revenues from the time of his consecration, showing both that the king had taken charge of the estates during the vacancy and pocketed the revenues until the new archbishop had been enthroned.[3]

Other monasteries also held their lands subject to these royal demands. The abbess[4] and abbot[5] of Caen came to England at the earliest opportunity to do homage for their lands; so did the abbots of Bernay[6] and Sainte-Catherine of Rouen[7] and the abbess of Préaux.[8] Some of them had to travel long distances into England or Scotland to find the king,[9] and it is not surprising that the king was asked to allow abbots to do homage in Normandy to persons representing the king.[10] In spite of the clear obligation of the abbess of Caen to do homage, however, the king found it necessary to ask whether he was entitled to the revenues of her estates during the vacancies;[11] this was because the king's profit by the vacancy was not always the revenues, but sometimes the 'fine' or some other consideration.[12] Although the

---

[1] C.Cl.R. 1256–59, p. 885. The prior of Coggs tried to avoid the consequences of abbatial vacancies by claiming that he was a perpetual prior, in which case the lands of his cell would fall into patronal custody only during priors' vacancies.

[2] P.R.O. E 135/18/5. Abbot Thomas de S. Benedicto died 4 April 1309.

[3] Rigaud's Register, p. 36.

[4] C.P.R. 1258–66, p. 673; C.P.R. 1327–30, p. 109.

[5] C.F.R. 1272–1307, p. 291.

[6] C.P.R. 1216–25, p. 476; C.P.R. 1225–32, p. 23; C.P.R. 1232–47, p. 363.

[7] C.Cl.R. 1231–4, p. 109; C.Cl.R. 1264–8, pp. 320–1.

[8] Rot. Claus. Litt., p. 139; C.Cl.R. 1242–7, pp. 523, 540; C.Cl.R. 1330–3, p. 38.

[9] e.g. C.Cl.R. 1234–7, p. 505; C.P.R. 1301–7, pp. 219, 221–2, 246; C.P.R. 1334–8, p. 311.

[10] C.F.R. 1307–19, pp. 309, 325; C. Chanc. Warr. i. 463.

[11] C.F.R. 1272–1307, p. 273; C.Cl.R. 1264–8, pp. 327, 432. She claimed to hold by free alms: Rot. Parlt. i. 331 = P.R.O. S.C. 8 286/14257.

[12] See Wood, op. cit., pp. 86–89.

abbot of Sainte-Catherine of Rouen did homage, there was doubt about whether he paid a fine.[1] Doing homage was required of the abbot of Saint-Ouen who held by free alms and whose prior enjoyed custody during vacancies,[2] whereas the agent of Jumièges claimed that not only did the monks hold their lands by free alms, but also that the abbot was not required to do homage.[3] There was genuine confusion about the monks' form of tenure[4] and about the obligation to do homage.

The cases of the abbots of Préaux and Saint-Pierre-sur-Dives reveal the confusion which uncertain rights caused. The abbot of Préaux was asked if he held his lands by barony or not,[5] but his answer does not exist. His tenants told him that 'abbas in creatione sua veniens in Anglia solebat accedere ad dominum regem faciendum ei facetiam sed nesciunt quid nec quantum'[6] without referring to the nature of his tenure. Abbots tried to resist the king's claims. In 1267 an abbot paid £40,[7] but the new abbot of 1284 denied that the abbot's lands had formerly been taken into the king's hand and Edward I ordered an inquiry.[8] Edward II admitted in 1317 that he had no rights in vacancies[9] yet he was in possession of the lands and revenues in 1320 when the new Abbot Ralph arrived.[10] Each abbot had to defy the king afresh because the king's rights were not precisely defined: he took all he could get.

A detailed letter from the abbot of Saint-Pierre-sur-Dives to his English agent gives an interesting view of a Norman abbot trying to understand his position. In the abbot's view it was tenancy in chief even of one small manor which rendered him liable for homage and its consequences: 'et facere homagium regi et servire eidem et regine Anglie et familiis eorundem in magnis donis et pensionibus suis clericis prout omnes abbates faciunt qui debent homagium

---

[1] C.Cl.R. 1261–64, p. 159.

[2] C.Cl.R. 1247–51, p. 204; C.Cl.R. 1330–3, p. 25; C.D.F. 104.

[3] C.Cl.R. 1313–18, p. 25.

[4] The monks of Mont Saint-Michel were said to hold the manors of Otterton and Sidmouth in chief and by free alms at different times: Feudal Aids, i. 325, 365.

[5] P.R.O. 3/8/140 A, no. 215.

[6] Eure H 711, f. 200.   [7] C.P.R. 1267–72, p. 115.

[8] C.Cl.R. 1279–88, pp. 273–4, 302; the new abbot therefore refused the usual grace.

[9] C.Cl.R. 1313–18, pp. 495, 510.   [10] C.F.R. 1319–27, p. 15.

regi'. Abbot James was so determined to resist the king that
Edward I was obliged to examine the nature of the tenancy
of the manor of Penquit in Ermington. The abbot's pre-
decessor, Nicholas, was said to have done homage for it.[1]
According to the inquiry of 1304 the manor had been given
in free alms more than a hundred years before and the king
was entitled to keep the revenues during vacancies of the
priory of Modbury.[2] A more careful examination of the king's
rights eighteen months later qualified this privilege: 'nichil
tamen debet de exitibus inde medio tempore provenientibus
sibi usurpare ad opus domini regis eo quod dominus rex
tempore vacationis ejusdem Prioratus nullos exitus capiet'.[3]
Yet another inquiry made in 1318 decided that Penquit was
indeed held in chief, but that the king was not entitled to
revenues in vacancies.[4] Edward II, perhaps even more in-
sistent, was met by desperate resistance and was forced to
concessions. Monks denied that they owed homage and
refused to accept royal interference in vacancies. The abbot
of Aumâle claimed to hold in free alms, without homage,
admitting no royal rights in vacancies[5] although under
Henry III and Edward I abbots had done homage to the
king as they had done homage to their patron, the count of
Aumâle.[6] At Newent Edward II had to withdraw his claims
to rights during vacancies of the priory because abbots held
by free alms, priors were removable at will, and royal
records since Richard I's reign proved the monks' con-
tentions.[7] At Eye the prior insisted that the king was
entitled to no more than the sign of dominion enjoyed by the
escheated Malets.[8] Edward II was checked on this front, but
the beginnings of the long war with France opened up new

---

[1] Eton College, Modbury Charter, no. 314.
[2] Eton College, Modbury Charter, 32, no. 7: 1 March 1304.
[3] Ibid., no. 6: 26 September 1305.
[4] Ibid., no. 8: 1318.
[5] *C.F.R. 1319–27*, pp. 131–2; *C.Cl.R. 1318–23*, pp. 464–5; *C.Cl.R. 1327–30*, pp. 224, 571; *C.Cl.R. 1330–3*, p. 46.
[6] *C.Cl.R. 1242–47*, p. 337; *C.Cl.R. 1272–9*, p. 195; *C.F.R. 1272–1307*, p. 98. The abbot of 1285 refused to do homage: *C.Cl.R. 1279–86*, pp. 323, 374.
[7] *C.P.R. 1317–21*, pp. 524–5; B.M. Add. MS. 18461, f. 51b.
[8] *C.P.R. 1313–17*, pp. 11, 53–54; *C.Cl.R. 1313–18*, p. 9. The prior died on 17 July 1313; a new prior from Bernay received the temporalities on 10 August: a delay of only twenty-four days.

possibilities of trespassing upon the monks' property, held in free alms or not.

II. 1294–1360

Edward I's war with Philip IV begins a new period in the history of the alien monks. After 1294 hardly a decade passed without the monks feeling the heavy hand of the king on their property. The spasmodic tyranny of Henry III gave way to thorough exploitation. The Hundred Years War separated England from France and forced the monks to choose between English and French 'citizenship'; their status as churchmen could not protect them. Henry III had not hesitated to arrest the goods of all French monks *cedentibus vel decedentibus* in 1245;[1] Edward I during wartime regarded all French monks as potential enemies. As in other aspects of his policy Edward did not allow the distinction between clerk and lay to limit the competence of his authority. French monks in England had less clerical behaviour to show than many clerks; they led no regular monastic life but lived like laymen and drained English revenues away to the comfort of the king's enemies. Edward's policy was drastic enough to serve as his successors' model and was based upon the view that birth determines loyalty.

The war with Philip began when Edward was condemned as a defaulter and his duchy of Aquitaine declared confiscated, 19 May 1294. In the next few weeks retaliation at the monks' expense followed. However, as early as mid-June at least one agent, the bailiff of Warminghurst, was restored to the custody of Fécamp's lands, promising to answer for all issues except his reasonable expenses.[2] Another priory, West Mersea, was entrusted to a third person at the beginning of July, allowance being made for the prior and monks.[3] The next month Edward followed up these measures by

---

[1] *C.Cl.R. 1242–7*, p. 337: 27 August 1245: 'occasione precepti de terris abbatum priorum et aliarum personarum ecclesiasticarum de partibus transmarinis cedentium vel decedentium capiendis in manum regis'.

[2] *C.P.R. 1292–1301*, p. 74. He shared the custody with Luke de Vyenne. The abbot of Fécamp may have had to petition for this restoration of custody: P.R.O. Ancient Petition 322 E. 518.

[3] *C.F.R. 1272–1307*, p. 340: 6 July 1294.

ordering a nation-wide survey of alien property and mov-
ables, which was presumably carried out in the summer
months.[1] On 28 September most priors or bailiffs received
royal letters of protection[2] and once the inquests were made
the priors recovered the custody,[3] paying a fine for the
privilege and promising to answer for the revenues at the
exchequer. One roll for Edward's twenty-third year records
payments by all priors, county by county, of two sums: *de
subsidio regi concesso* and *de redditu transmarinis* presumably
at Hilary or Michaelmas 1295.[4] That the 'subsidy' is a fine
and not, for example, the moiety of the Holy Land tenth
offered by some priors in September 1294[5] is proved by an
entry on the papal taxation returns: 'eodem anno solverunt
certum finem ad Scaccarium pro omnibus bonis suis tam
spiritualibus quam temporalibus'.[6] The *redditus transmarinis*
is the sum sent abroad by the monks in England, not the
whole revenues of the priory: in other words, the Norman
apport.[7]

In September 1295, when Edward feared a French invasion, he was not satisfied with this financial pressure: he
appointed 'guardians' to prevent the monks speaking with,
or giving messages to, strangers, to pay the monks eighteen
pence a week for food, and to find English monks or secular
priests to perform services in conventual or parish churches
in the aliens' place.[8] A week later the king became worried
about the position enjoyed by some monks established near
the coasts and sheriffs were instructed to move them inland
in case they helped French raiders. English monks in the
communities were not to be disturbed but were to receive
the custody of the lands; if there were no English monks,

---

[1] P.R.O. E 106/2/1-6, 9: the returns were to reach the exchequer by 7 December.
[2] *C.P.R. 1292-1301*, pp. 90–97.
[3] The prior of Newent recovered the custody in October: B.M. Add. MS. 15668,
f. 32; B.M. Add. MS. 18461, f. 92ᵛ.
[4] P.R.O. E 106/3/10.
[5] *C.P.R. 1292-1301*, p. 91.   [6] *Taxatio*, p. 176.
[7] This is confirmed by a list of apports drawn up the next year, 24 Edward I:
P.R.O. E 106/3/19, m. 1. This gives identical figures with the roll of P.R.O.
E 106/3/10. Edward III also had compiled a list of 'ancient farms': P.R.O. E106/10/7.
[8] See above, p. 59. P.R.O. E 106/3/19, p. 3: 21 September 1295. The guardians
were not actually appointed until 4 November. Cf. Bartholomew Cotton, *Historia
Anglicana*, pp. 300–2, 302–4.

secular clerks would take their place.[1] This order did not affect other inhabitants of the priories, or tenants or property belonging to the monks more than thirteen miles from the coasts.[2] Where the foreign monks had other property in England not so close to the sea, they were required to move there[3] but no provision was made until November for those monks who had nowhere else to go. The prior of Birstall and the prior of Blyth, with twelve monks, were then to move up country to Saint-Wandrille's priory of Ecclesfield, near Sheffield; the prior of Newent, and seven [sic] of his fellows from the Severn valley were to go to Castellion's priory of Wootton Wawen, perhaps because these monks were neighbours in Herefordshire; the prior of Beckford and his fellow from the same region, to Winchcomb abbey; the prior of Tofts and his fellow from Norfolk to Gloucester Hall, Oxford; the prior of Wareham and three monks, and the prior of Stogursey and his monks to Clatford, the alien priory of Saint-Victor-en-Caux. These were only some of the proposed moves;[4] unfortunately the effectiveness of the order is doubtful. The various measures ordered since the invasion scare were summarized and the guardians' duties more exactly described on 16 November,[5] but two days earlier the bailiff of Warminghurst, for his abbot of Fécamp's better interest and his own comfort, proposed to buy exemption from these orders. Once granted his request he found security for the payment of £300[6] and other priors quickly followed suit. The prior of Wilmington offered £165. 10s. 10d.;[7] the prior of Otterton quaintly asked *quod possit reddere regi per annum* £80. 13s. 4d.[8] These payments all represent small but significant advances on the sums

---

[1] P.R.O. E 106/3/19, m. 2: 28 September 1295: 'religiosos alienigenas habitantes iuxta costeram maris et prope litus maris seu aquamque ducat ad mare . . . a locis in quibus sic morantur sine dilatione faciatis penitus amovere . . . quod naves et batellos universos . . . ubicunque in mari seu etiam in alia aqua eos inveniri contigerit absque mora ad terram trahi . . . .' [2] Ibid., m. 2d: 26 October 1295.

[3] *Abbr. Rot. Orig.* i. 90.2–91.1. [4] P.R.O. E 106/3/19, mm. 4, 6d–7.

[5] *C.F.R. 1272–1307*, pp. 362–6: the monks were allowed 1s. 6d. a week for food and 10s. a year for clothing and foot-wear. They were to take their own beds and books at their own expense. Inventories of their valuables were to be made.

[6] P.R.O. E 106/3/19, mm. 4, 5. His apport was £266. 13s. 4d.

[7] Ibid., m. 5: Grestain's apport was £100.

[8] Ibid., m. 5d: Mont Saint-Michel's apport was £73. 6s. 8d.

mentioned in the documents of the previous year. The king appears to have held out for a more substantial profit than before in return for relaxing the more stringent measures of control. One month later the bailiff of Warminghurst took the custody on condition that he account for all revenues at the Hilary session of the exchequer, and was given the revenues collected by the king during the period of royal custody; other priors did the same.[1] In view of this rapid change of front, it is probable that few if any monks were in fact removed from the coasts. When the king was seen to be in earnest, the monks offered to buy their exemption. The guardians must have set about their work during the month of November and their depredations no doubt helped the monks to reconsider the position. The aliens of the Isle of Wight complained that the guardians there had taken and sold their goods and left nothing out of which they could pay the fine required for taking the custody.[2] The prior of Newent, if he ever went to Wootton Wawen, had returned before the end of the year, when he offered the king £26 to recover the custody.[3]

The subsequent history of Edward I's relations with the alien monks is not so easy to write. Apparently at the beginning of 1297 the king again took the custody out of the hands of the priors and had the value of their property reassessed. The prior of Blyth petitioned in the midsummer parliament of 1302 for a redress because five and a half years before (that is early in 1297) his goods had been valued too highly by the king's officials.[4] In May 1297 the priors were restored to the custody,[5] perhaps at higher

---

[1] The priors found securities for £120 from 14 December: P.R.O. E 106/3/19, mm. 15–16. They were restored 15 December: *C.P.R. 1292–1301*, pp. 175–7.

[2] P.R.O. E 106/3/19, m. 10: the keeper of the religious houses of Hampshire, Simon Stalle, was to hold them until Easter (1296 or 1297) when the monks could pay the fine. The king's servants, who must be the guardians in this case, ejected the servants of the earl of Cornwall from Eye priory on 29 November 1295. The king's excuse, the war, was more compelling than the earl's—a vacancy in the priory: Midgeley, *Ministers' Accounts of the Earldom of Cornwall*, p. 156, n. 2.

[3] B.M. Add. MS. 18461, f. 92ᵛ.

[4] P.R.O. S.C. 8 (Ancient Petitions), 315 E 162. See also ibid. 314 E 122.

[5] *C.P.R. 1292–1301*, pp. 241, 270. The names of the priors who made fine and found security were printed by W. Prynne, *History of King John, Henry III and Edward I*, iii (London, 1670), 706–7. The original document survives in P.R.O. Chanc. Misc. 18/1/2.

rates which the new assessments had been made to justify. There are, however, no surviving records of annual payments at the exchequer, although there is evidence that 'fines' were paid in the years 1297–1301.[1] The two kings agreed to a series of truces from the end of 1297 and the suspension of the war afforded some monks a little relief. In April 1298 the abbot of Fécamp recovered his property but continued to make payments to the king until he was excused because of special services he had performed for the king: 'in nostris agendis liberalem atque gratum (esse)'.[2] Other abbots, without special reasons for indulgence, may not have benefited. Again in 1299, the bailiff of Warminghurst had to pay a fine to recover the custody of Fécamp's lands, but the reason is not given.[3] About the same time all the alien monks jointly petitioned not to be bound to continue the payment of fines to the exchequer from the time when the pope had made peace between the kings.[4] The king was reluctant to surrender any claims for revenue that he could make against the alien monks. There is only one record of a sheriff accounting for the goods of a priory, as late as 1299,[5] but there were priors who continued to pay their surplus revenues at the exchequer as late as 1303 when peace was definitely concluded. Several petitions were presented at the midsummer parliament of 1302 against the excessive sums exacted by the king.[6] The abbess of Caen obtained a special concession after the king's marriage to Margaret of France,[7] but other houses were still denied the

---

[1] P.R.O. E 106/4-5: 25–29 Edward I.

[2] *C.Cl.R. 1296–1302*, p. 240. Abbot Thomas presented a petition to the king asking to be excused payment of £451. 4s. for the one and a half years he held the custody between royal seizures. This period must be between December 1295 and May 1297: P.R.O. S.C. 8 (Ancient Petitions), 346/1366. Thomas became abbot in 1298.

[3] *C.Cl.R. 1296–1302*, p. 348: abbot Thomas may have come to do homage in 1299.

[4] The petition is undated but its position in the file indicates the year 1299: P.R.O. S.C. 8 (Ancient Petitions), 312 E 32.

[5] P.R.O. E 106/4/13: 27–28 Edward I: the goods of the priory of Ware.

[6] P.R.O. S.C. 8, 314: E 108 (Tutbury), E 110 (Wolston), E 128 (Blyth); P.R.O. S.C. 8, 315: E 162 (Blyth), E 152 (Séez), E 190 (Arundel); P.R.O. S.C. 8, 316: E 218 (Aunay). P.R.O. S.C. 8, 324: E 611: the petition of the prior of Ellingham that he and his two monks *sunt morz de meseyse* because the king demanded 20 marks a year from revenues worth 25 marks. This is earlier than the others, probably, because he asks for redress for the love of God and *pur lanime la Reyne*, i.e. of Queen Eleanor who died in 1291. The king was once more holding Fécamp's lands in September 1302: *C.P.R. 1302–7*, p. 63.　　　　[7] *C.Cl.R. 1296–1302*, p. 368.

possibility of exporting their revenue. By August 1303, however, the prior of Frampton was aware of the possibility of recovering direct administration of his property and appointed an attorney to receive it from the Chancellor 'et ad faciendum omnia alia que forma pacis inter dictos reges . . . exigit et requirit'.[1] The abbess of Préaux also was excused further payment of the farms from the time of the peace settlement, but not until the following reign[2] which suggests that the treatment of aliens was not uniform and that the king held on to their property longer than might otherwise appear. The prior of Newent was still assessed for a payment of £120 a year in 1305.[3] The fragmentary records of the latter years of Edward's reign do not reveal the whole extent of royal control and individual examples do not necessarily show the general fate of the monks.

In Edward's last parliament the statute affecting payments of apports to monasteries oversea, first discussed in 1305, was finally promulgated. The statute is formally explicit and has commonly been interpreted to mean literally what it says that 'censum aliquem sub nomine redditus tallagii aporti seu impositionis cuiuscunque vel alias nomine escambii vendicionis mutui vel alterius contractus' were no longer to be paid abroad. Mr. New pointed out, however, that the statute arose as a result of complaints against the abbots of Cluny and Cîteaux who provoked the opposition of patrons to the export of wealth because the fulfilment of religious obligations was impaired.[4] The statute itself concentrates on exceptional levies. Abbots, including Benedictines, had imposed taxes on their subject houses contrary to the laws and customs of England and parliament agreed to prohibit all 'abbates priores magistros custodes religiosarum domorum vel locorum' from exacting payments 'causa visitationis aut alio colore quesito'. The statute speaks of abbots as though they had laid new burdens upon the cells, not of traditional payments: 'ne de cetero tallagia census imposi-

---

[1] P.R.O. Ancient Correspondence, xxviii. 75.

[2] C.Cl.R. 1307-13, p. 391; C.Cl.R. 1302-7, p. 304; Rot. Parlt. i. 465.

[3] B.M. Add. MS. 18461, f. 92. He owed and paid £48. 19s. 8½d. arrears of farm in 1303: ibid., f. 92ᵛ.

[4] New, p. 61; Rot. Parlt. i. 178b; Memoranda de Parliamento (1305), petitions 126, 485-6: 26 September 1305.

tiones aporta seu alia quecunque onera aliquibus monasteriis prioratibus seu aliis domibus religiosis eis ut predicitur sic subjectis imponant vel faciant aliqualiter assidere'. Abbots were allowed to visit their dependencies but not to exact a fee for visitation: 'preter rationabiles et moderatas eorum expensas deferrant vel deferri procurent'.[1] The framers of the statute had in mind extraordinary payments by conventual priories to the mother-houses of their orders and the enforcement of the statute would have been dependent on the legal action taken by patrons who resented the taxes, so that most Norman priories should not have been affected by it. Apart from the letter of the prior of Otterton, which may belong to this period,[2] there is only one document showing that payments to Normandy were interrupted because of this statute and this also shows that the king did not intend the statute to interfere with the monks' enjoyment of their normal revenues. The prior of Beckford, the agent of the canons of Sainte-Barbe, pleaded the statute as his excuse for not paying the monks of Cormeilles the due farm for Beckford church. The abbot of Cormeilles promptly appealed to Edward I, who wrote from his deathbed requiring the prior to resume payment of the farm to the monks.[3]

Edward II's government can be detected in a number of petty exactions,[4] but it is not until the outbreak of war in the

---

[1] *Rot. Parlt.* i. 217; *Statutes of the Realm,* i. 150–2: 'per singula monasteria et domos eis subjecta in Anglia Hibernia Scotia et Wallia diversa tallagia census et impositiones graves et importabiles Domino Regi Magnatibus suis inconsultis fieri statuerunt et pro suo libito ordinarunt contra leges et consuetudines dicti regni'. An interesting story from St. Albans shows that a contemporary bishop of Lichfield and Coventry tried to obtain a pension for three lives from the monks but was opposed on the grounds that patrons objected to unaccustomed dues levied on cells: Thomas Walsingham, *Gesta Abbatum Monasterii S. Albani,* ii. 90–94, esp. 91.

[2] See above, p. 71, n. D.

[3] P.R.O. S.C. 8 (Ancient Petitions), 2/60. *Rot. Parlt.* i. 274–5: 'Et quia intentionis nostre non existit quod prefatis Abbati et Conventui de predicta firma per predictam ordinacionem seu statutum injurietur in hac parte maxime cum firmam illam non tamquam superiores vestri seu a subditis suis de vobis percipere debeant et consueverunt set potius a firmariis suis ut predictum est; vos mandamus quod si ita est tunc prefatis Abbati et conventui de Cormeliis firmam cum arreragiis ejusdem persolvatis ad terminos consuetos prout ipsam retroactis temporibus eis consuevistis et hoc nulla tenus omittatis, ne querelam inde amplius audiamus'.

[4] See above, pp. 77–81. *C.P.R. 1307–13,* p. 115; *C.P.R. 1313–17,* p. 263; *C.P.R. 1317–21,* p. 227; for the royal 'borrowing' from aliens see *C.P.R. 1313–17,* p. 281, *C.Cl.R. 1327–30,* p. 6.

summer of 1324 that the records again become continuous enough to prove that the government took more than a temporary interest in the possibility of squeezing the foreign monks. Although measures were taken against aliens in general on the outbreak of war, the king wrote and explained to the sheriffs that the monks were simply to swear oaths of fealty and give security for good behaviour and their lands were not seized at first.[1] By the end of the summer, however, the policy of Edward I had been revived and guardians of the monks and their property were appointed to keep the monks away from strangers, to move those who lived too near the coasts inland, and to manage the revenues which were to be divided evenly amongst the monks, the guardians, and the exchequer. New extents were to be made and farmers were then to be selected, leaving the monks their third of the revenues for the upkeep of the buildings.[2] These measures were the equivalent of the *dragonnade*; the monks, threatened with secular overseers, promptly offered more than their predecessors had done to Edward I for a renewal of the grants of custody to themselves. The figures are striking and suggest that the royal officials consulted the rolls of the earlier reign in order to determine the new rates. Grestain had received an estimated English revenue of £100, had paid Edward I £165. 10s. 10d. and offered Edward II £170. Fécamp received an estimated 400 marks, paid 450 in 1295 and offered 500 in December 1324. The agent of Fécamp even went further and contributed supplies for the king's journey to Gascony: 240 quarters of corn, 200 quarters of oats, and 50 quarters of beans. The following July the government received a money payment instead: 9s. for the corn, 4s. for the oats, which were paid with £112 in October

---

[1] Rymer, iv. 72: 1 July 1324: that this order did not apply to the religious was explained by the government in August: *C.Cl.R. 1323–27*, pp. 210–11.

[2] Rymer, iv. 87, 96: 28 September, 12 October. P.R.O. E 106/5/2, m. 1–1d: 8 October. Salisbury Registers: Morival, i, ff. 236, 274b: the priors of Loders and Stogursey went to the alien priory of Monks Sherborne; the monks of the diocese received 40s., not 10s., as the king required, for clothing. The bishop of Chichester sent his report on the monks of his diocese (all of whom lived too near the coast for the government's liking) in April 1325: P.R.O. C. 47/18/3. The king's order that extents be made and returned to Westminster by 6 December or the Hilary session is probably copied directly from Edward I's similar order indicating these dates as a time limit: P.R.O. E 106/5/2, mm. 3–3d, 4.

'pro bonis suis per unum tallagium de scaccario levatum'.[1] Although a general rise in prices had occurred since 1295, these sums hardly represent a new assessment to allow for inflation. The fact that the offer of these farms follows measures of increasing severity proposed by the government during the autumn months of 1324 suggests that the government was deliberately trying to frighten the monks into buying their freedom.

The list of priors who reacted to the king's pressure is long but not complete. The exceptions are not numerous and clearly special circumstances explain their absence from the lists. The property of the canons of Rouen, for example, was given in custody to Peter Galicien, admittedly one of the canons, but also the king's trusted diplomatic agent, and he enjoyed the custody, not on the canons' behalf but on his own: 'pro bono servicio et ac in recompensationem dampnorum que occasione guerre, etc., concessit ei centum libra Le extenta annuatim de dono regis'.[2] A more common reason for the non-appearance of the priors as royal custodians was the poverty of the priory which prevented the priors from accepting the king's offers. One of the priors at Upavon obtained the good offices of the earl of Winchester, Hugh Le Despenser, and recovered the custody a little later than the others.[3] Those priories which did not appear on Edward I's rolls were exempted, and Haugh and Edith Weston admitted that they were too poor to pay the dues.[4]

Within a few months, however, Edward II and Charles IV had patched up their quarrel and the aliens breathed again.[5] The renewal of the war, which was to cost Edward his throne, presumably put the monks once more in the king's hands, but only the order for removing the monks from coastal sites indicates the government's precautions.[6]

[1] P.R.O. E 106/5/2, mm. 4, 17: 10 December 1324. B.N. MS. Add. 18461, ff. 81v–84v. See Appendix II.

[2] P.R.O. E 106/5/2, m. 15d; Abbr. Rot. Orig. i. 284, c. 1; C.P.R. 1324–27, pp. 88, 171: he went to Spain on a mission in February 1325.

[3] C.P.R. 1324–27, p. 105.   [4] P.R.O. E 106/5/2, m. 25d.

[5] Ibid. m. 16d. See M. Chibnall, The English lands of the Abbey of Bec, p. 123, for Edward II's suspicions of the monks.

[6] C.Cl.R. 1323–37, p. 636: September 1326; Annales Paulini, p. 213; New, p. 63. The bishop of Chichester's report on this order is dated 3 September: P.R.O. C 47/18/6.

The guardians' appointments may have been renewed since it was one of the first acts of the new régime in 1327 to restore the custody of the monks' own priors, who were required to pay, not the farms, but the apports, as in 1294.[1] Queen Isabella was a friend to the monks, and her government indulged them. No records for the decade of peace with France have survived so that payments to the king probably ceased. Yet the monks' exploitation of their English property was not easy. If the abbess of Caen, through Isabella, was allowed to sell her goods and send the proceeds to Normandy,[2] the proctor of Saint-Pierre-sur-Dives was refused permission to take money to his monastery when he went to Normandy.[3] Other monks were allowed only named, reasonable expenses on leaving England[4] and the government did not relax its scrutiny of the monks' property.[5]

Whether or not money had been allowed out of the country 1327–37, the king forbade the export of money in January 1337 as war with Philip VI threatened to break out.[6] In the summer all alien property, religious included, was seized by the king.[7] From the first, it was the king's intention to allow the monks to farm their own lands, and for the purpose of arranging the terms the priors were summoned to Westminster for late July.[8] Most of them immediately offered a fine for permission to receive the custody, agreed to answer at the exchequer for the revenues, and to sever relations with Normandy.[9] A few extents were made,

[1] *C.Cl.R. 1327–30*, pp. 18–19, 58, 252, 284.

[2] *C.P.R. 1327–30*, p. 100. Isabella's later influence can be seen, for example, in *C.F.R. 1337–47*, p. 299. Queen Philippa also interceded: *C.P.R. 1334–38*, p. 451. The abbess of Caen came in June to do homage: *C.P.R. 1327–30*, p. 109.

[3] *C.Cl.R. 1327–30*, p. 229.

[4] *C.P.R. 1324–7*, p. 540; *C.Cl.R. 1330–3*, p. 419; *C.Cl.R. 1333–7*, pp. 106, 119, 484, 555, 657, 676.

[5] For contemporary inquiries see *Exeter Registers: Grandisson*, iii. 760; see above, p. 68.

[6] *C.Cl.R. 1333–7*, p. 643; 15 January. The order was reissued in a more stringent form: *C.Cl.R. 1337–9*, p. 414: 9 May 1338.

[7] Rymer, iv. 777: 1 July 1337. This order was, however, still not enforced in Lincolnshire, Northamptonshire, and Rutland thirty-two months later: *C.F.R. 1337–47*, p. 159.

[8] For Monday after the feast of St. Mary Magdalen, i.e. 28 July.

[9] *C.F.R. 1337–47*, pp. 28 ff. 'Protections' were issued on and after 28 July: *C.P.R. 1334–8*, pp. 483–4.

but not on the wide scale of 1294 and 1324:[1] the precedents of thirteen years before were sufficiently recent to make further investigation superfluous.

At first the king was content with farms identical to those of 1324, but he soon showed a wish to increase them. In addition he expected the monks to contribute to the clerical tenth. The prior of Hayling refused to do this, lost the custody of his monastery's property, and fled to Normandy.[2] He was not reinstated until the aliens were generally excused paying the tenth in March 1338.[3] It may be that the king's concession was wrung out of him by other priors' refusal to contribute. It was to the king's advantage to use the priors as his own servants, for exchequer administration was cumbersome and was used only as a last resort to force the monks to better terms.

Although some priories clearly could not afford to meet the king's demands,[4] it is interesting to notice that hardly a quarter of the Norman priories, and those almost invariably the smallest and weakest, ran up debts to the exchequer. If a prior unwisely claimed that his priory could not bear the increased burden, the king quickly offered the farm to his clerks: no method could more rapidly have persuaded the monks to accept the responsibility. The alien prior of Lapley (a dependency of Saint-Rémy of Reims) paid double his farm of 10 marks after 1341 in order to take the priory out of the destructive hands of royal clerks: this the king allowed for the ironical reason, 'in consideration of his poverty'.[5] The prior of Wolston, who was already in arrears on a farm of £30 by 1340, refused to pay £40 until two years of exchequer custody convinced him that his personal control would do less harm.[6] The prior of Newent endured the custody of the earl of Derby a mere four months[7] and the prior of Otterton took only one month[8] before capitulating to the king's greedy demands. The prior of Tutbury tempted the king with payments in advance, to get rid of the king's clerks.[9]

---

[1] P.R.O. Chancery Misc. Bdle, 18/1/10-17. At Hullavington the extent was made by a clerk who stayed at the priory one week. Eton College, Hullavington Charter no. 18.   [2] *Histoire de Jumièges*, ii. 81.

[3] *C.P.R. 1337-9*, p. 333.   [4] See p. 105, n. B.   [5] *C.F.R. 1337-47*, p. 212.

[6] *C.Cl.R. 1339-41*, p. 106; *C.F.R. 1337-47*, pp. 261, 361, 362.

[7] Ibid., pp. 265, 281, 299.   [8] Ibid., pp. 165, 176.   [9] Ibid., p. 175.

Presumably the clerks lined their own pockets by these commissions: the efforts of the priors to avoid them suggest that opportunities for peculation were not resisted. In one case a king's clerk, Richard of Wath, vigorously defended his right to retain the custody of Avebury priory, when the prior tried to outbid him.[1]

The priors' acceptance of these higher rates was dictated by the fear of the custody of outsiders, not by realist calculation of the resources of the priory. In spite of the prior's confidence in 1340,[2] Tutbury's farm had to be reduced from 100 marks to 60 in 1342.[3] As the forties passed into the fifties, reduced rates of farm become more common. Wolston's farm, raised to £40 in 1344, fell to £20 in 1353 and to £13. 6s. 8d. in 1357;[4] Aunay's, raised from £46 to £50 in 1342, fell to £30 in 1355, and the prior was accused of dissipating the revenues in 1358, and of owing £315 in arrears by 1360.[5] At Eye and Lancaster even the royal clerks could not keep up the inflated rates.[6] Not all debts were as considerable as those of Aunay, but Pembroke's debt of more than eight years' farm,[7] Llangenith's of nearly fifteen years,[8] and Winghale's of more than fifteen[9] were debts slowly accumulated. Modbury owed only for two and a half years in 1356,[10] Creeting for little more than one year,[11] Fécamp for six months.[12] Stogursey[13] and Haugh[14] were simply pardoned

---

[1] C.F.R. 1337–47, p. 234: 22 July 1341: Richard paid £10 more than the farm of £24 and had to find sustenance for the monks; ibid., p. 237: 8 August, after eighteen days the prior was prepared to pay another £2 to avoid occupation, and the government snapped up his offer, specifically revoking the grant to Richard. Ibid., p. 241: 23 August, Richard offered as much as the prior and secured the farm: the shamefaced entry on the rolls says that the king had overlooked Richard's grant: a bare-faced lie.

[2] Ibid., p. 175.   [3] Ibid., p. 294.

[4] Ibid., p. 362; C.F.R. 1347–56, pp. 65, 381; C.P.R. 1354–58, p. 503.

[5] C.F.R. 1337–47, pp. 35, 274; C.F.R. 1347–56, pp. 73–74, 425–6; C.F.R. 1356–69, p. 69; C.F.R. 1369–77, pp. 15, 83.

[6] C.F.R. 1337–47, p. 258; C.F.R. 1347–56, pp. 183, 446–7; C.F.R. 1356–69, pp. 12, 24.   [7] C.F.R. 1356–69, p. 115.

[8] C.F.R. 1369–77, p. 117.

[9] C.F.R. 1369–77, p. 159.

[10] C.F.R. 1356–69, p. 24.

[11] C.P.R. 1358–61, p. 356.

[12] Seine-Maritime 7 H 623: 30 November 1363: the abbey owed £271. 12s. 6d.

[13] C.F.R. 1377–83, p. 194: 1380: the debts contracted before 1360 were pardoned.

[14] C.F.R. 1356–69, pp. 91–92: 1359. The prior of Ellingham was pardoned his in the same year: C.P.R. 1358–61, p. 178.

their arrears; Hayling pleaded destruction by the sea to excuse its debts;[1] Carisbrooke demanded payment of a rent of £9. 5s. from the king's sheriff if it was to be able to meet the king's farm of £113. 6s. 8d.[2] On the whole the larger priories weathered the storm better than the smaller ones,[3] and it is remarkable that not until the fifties do general reductions in the rates of farm appear.

The king was not alone responsible for the priories' difficulties. The agent of Lire blamed royal clerks for their destructiveness in 1355,[4] but he had himself been accused of selling his monastery's goods and sending money oversea in 1339.[5] If priors did not bring down the king's wrath upon the priory by deliberate cheating, some priors were wasteful, old, incapable or ill,[6] and their weakness did their priories no good. Moreover the plague created general difficulties. In general, however, the system worked well and the exceptions confirm the general impression. A prior of Lancaster lost the custody for a time when he was accused of plotting to defraud the king of his rights of presentation to a vacant living;[7] the bailiff of Warminghurst fell into disfavour for a short time because of his suspicious behaviour;[8] the prior of St. Michael's Mount was accused, but acquitted, of having sent his brother from Mousehole harbour to Normandy with secret letters and £60 in gold and silver and of having received two of the king's enemies and supported them at Trevabon for more than two weeks.[9] Yet the king was not normally vindictive. The priors were his agents during the

---

[1] C.F.R. 1347–56, p. 446: 1355.

[2] Rot. Parlt. ii. 188: 1347 = P.R.O. S.C. 8, 206/10262.

[3] Otterton: C.F.R. 1337–47, p. 267; C.F.R. 1347–56, p. 322. Frampton: C.F.R. 1337–47, pp. 31, 272. Ware: C.F.R. 1337–47, pp. 176, 267; C.F.R. 1356–69, pp. 165, 393. The prior of Harmondsworth paid a farm of £80: C.F.R. 1337–47, p. 28. He asked for some remission because the rent exceeded the annual value; an inquiry was ordered: Winchester College, Harmondsworth 73, f. 3, 21 April 1340. The complaints are not mentioned again and the farm was still £80 in 1352: C.F.R. 1347–56, p. 325. It was reduced to 80 marks in 1369: C.F.R. 1369–77, p. 22.

[4] C.F.R. 1347–56, pp. 427–8.

[5] C.F.R. 1337–47, p. 143. Cf. p. 314. The prior of Abergavenny also took jewels to France.

[6] C.F.R. 1347–56, pp. 67, 97, 251, 352, 431; C.F.R. 1337–47, pp. 278, 280. Salisbury Registers, Wyville, ii, f. 264: the destruction caused by the wasteful prior of Wareham.   [7] C.F.R. 1337–47, p. 404.   [8] See below, p. 95.

[9] C.P.R. 1354–8, p. 460: 1 June 1355–16 October 1356.

war. When Abbot Simon of Caen died in 1341, the over-
zealous escheator of Berkshire seized the abbey lands, but
was rebuked by the king because the prior of Frampton was
already 'keeping them for the king'.[1] When the abbot of
Montebourg sent a new prior of Appuldurcombe in the
belief that the old one was dead, it was the king who prevented the entry into England of the new prior to protect
the position of the old.[2] During vacancies in the priories,
another monk was entrusted with the custody until a new
prior should be sent from Normandy: there was no attempt
to take new appointments out of the hands of the monastery.
At Tofts the prior made a fellow monk joint farmer with him
three months before his death, so that there should be no
hiatus.[3] The only sign that the government may have stimu-
lated an independent movement of Norman monks comes
from a few papal documents, designed to prevent the arbi-
trary removal of priors, presumably by Norman abbots.
This may indicate that the priors defied the abbots and tried
to cover themselves against deprivation by appealing to the
supreme ecclesiastical authority.[4] Two of the priors, Frampton and Loders, were trusted by the king to defend their
manors against possible French attacks by sea,[5] so that their
relations with the government were exceptionally good. This
episode is obscure. Before jumping to hasty conclusions it is
sensible to consider that abbots may well have encouraged
their monks in England to remain on as good terms as
possible with the king, since during war-time direct administration from Normandy was impossible. The situation was a
difficult one for the abbots, and there is nothing to show that
they provoked their priors by attempting to replace them on
grounds of disloyalty.

An example of a possible difference between a prior and
his abbot comes from the relations between Coggs priory
and Fécamp. Although the prior of Coggs in the early

---

[1] *C.Cl.R. 1341–3,* p. 306.   [2] *C.Cl.R. 1343–6,* p. 92. Cf. *C.F.R. 1337–47,* p. 124.
[3] *C.F.R. 1337–47,* pp. 87, 94–95.
[4] *C.Pap.L.* iii. 187; *C.Pap.Pet.,* p. 26: Frampton; *C.Pap.L.* iii. 116: Loders, 1344.
Oliver, op. cit., pp. 248–9: Otterton, 1358. The prior of Ellingham appealed both
to the archbishop of Canterbury and the pope in 1363 after seven years of office
for protection of his status as prior: Eton College, Ellingham Charter, no. 21.
[5] Rymer (Record Commission), ii. 2, p. 1062.

thirteenth century had acted as agent for all Fécamp's English property, by the fourteenth century there was a clear distinction between the administrations of the prior and of the bailiff of Warminghurst who acted on behalf of the abbot. The prior was responsible only for the exiguous estates of the priory.[1] For some reason the king became suspicious of the bailiff in 1340 and entrusted his administration to the prior, until an inquisition should prove the bailiff's better claim.[2] The bailiff was probably reinstated, because a year later he was arrested for sending bows and arrows to Normandy,[3] but in the meantime the prior had retired, possibly because he was accused by the abbot of having conspired with the king against the bailiff and the monastery. In his place the abbot sent a monk from Normandy, William Hamon. Within a few years this monk became the king's surgeon, was 'naturalized' although a Norman by birth, and went with Clarence to Ireland.[4] This was no ordinary monk. Did the abbot perhaps deliberately send over a skilled man to win the king's attention and indulgence for the abbey? It is strange that a previous prior of Coggs had also won the patronage of the king.[5] The abbots must have been glad to have dependents in royal favour.

The war was nevertheless a trial to the monks. In August 1345 the abbot of Caen wanted to appropriate a church in the diocese of Coutances and sent a petition to Clement VI, lately abbot of Fécamp, 'quodque a dicto tempore occasione earundem guerrarum habuit monasterium plura dampna sumptus et expensas subire et quod ad obviandum inimicis regni Francie de novo fiunt in prefato monasterio fortalicie et clausurie murorum que omnia in multis depauperant monasterium prelibatum'.[6] There is no mention here of the specific grievance of not receiving rents from England.

---

[1] See above, pp. 51, 55. *C.Cl.R. 1333–37*, p. 643.

[2] *C.Cl.R. 1339–41*, pp. 55, 552–3. The lawful men of Sussex were to give evidence and send a report to Chancery.

[3] *C.Cl.R. 1341–3*, p. 128: 29 April 1341. A year later this bailiff went to the court of Rome over causes concerning him and the custody of spiritualities; when he returned he brought a commission touching the king's rights of patronage and imprisonment and the king threatened forfeiture if the ecclesiastics concerned proceeded to enforce the papal authority: *C.P.R. 1340–3*, p. 430; *C.P.R. 1343–5*, p. 22.

[4] See p. 106, n. C.   [5] *C.Cl.R. 1247–51*, p. 428.

[6] Calvados H 1841.

When Saint-Evroul made a similar plea for appropriation four years later, the monks claimed that they had missed more than £1,000 a year from England for the previous thirteen years, and asked that permission for the appropriation of Thurcaston church, originally granted by Celestine III but not used, be renewed.[1] Yet appropriation would in this case have not benefited the Norman monks directly, if money could not be exported from England. Only one document from these years proves that some money did go to France, but the prior of Longueville Giffard, who acknowledged receipt of arrears of apports, not current dues, did so at Avignon and papal influence was probably responsible for securing this payment.[2]

The priors were really at the king's mercy and the abbots and the popes powerless to help. They were called upon by the king to provide men-at-arms, sailors, provisions for the fleet, wool, trees for the navy, clerical tenths, and subsidies.[3] The king paid his debts from priory revenues and appointed to vacant benefices without consulting the monks.[4] The priors were summoned to his council and probably paid to get away.[5] Where the priors did not manage their own priories, the king's officers doled out an allowance of 1s. 6d. a week to each monk and 3s. a week to priors, with an additional 10s. a year for clothing and footwear: rates that were increased later.[6] The king enjoyed his unchallengeable

---

[1] See p. 106, n. D.

[2] *Newington Longueville Charters*, nos. 132, 6 May 1342, and 133, 16 August 1344.

[3] *C.Cl.R. 1337–9*, pp. 580–1; *C.Cl.R. 1339–41*, p. 217; *C.P.R. 1343–5*, pp. 151–2; *C.Cl.R. 1337–9*, p. 565; *C.P.R. 1340–3*, p. 357; *C.P.R. 1381–5*, p. 532; *Acts of the Privy Council*, ii. 357: 1414: this felling of trees for the navy may be only a later development of exploitation; *C.F.R. 1337–47*, p. 449, P.R.O. E 106/9/19: at least eighty-five priors paid the tenth on 13 December 1345. *C.Cl.R. 1346–9*, p. 339: 18 November 1347: the aliens who did not attend when the king ordered, or who had subsequently withdrawn, were summoned again to pay the subsidy.

[4] *C.P.R. 1334–8*, p. 466: ten days after ordering the confiscation in 1337 the king gave the sheriff and escheator, William Trissel, £1,000 to be paid partly from the farms of Beckford (£40 and 10 marks fine), Newent (£65 and 10 marks fine), Ware (£115), and Lire (£125). For appointment to benefices see *Year Books of Edward III: 13–14*, pp. 286–90.

[5] *C.Cl.R. 1341–3*, pp. 358–62; *C.Cl.R. 1343–6*, pp. 636–7; *C.Cl.R. 1346–9*, pp. 284–8. The purpose of these summons is not given but after one of them the priors paid the tenth: *C.F.R. 1337–47*, p. 449.

[6] *C.P.R. 1339–41*, p. 600; *C.F.R. 1356–69*, p. 69; *C.F.R. 1369–77*, pp. 255, 249;

position and brooked no interference from outside. When the commons asked for the expulsion of all alien monks in 1346 so that Englishmen could be put in their stead, the king replied that he knew how to look after his own interests without prompting by parliament. Parliament was not quickly silenced. The commons complained that the monks sent money oversea and demanded that no one, English or otherwise, be allowed to farm the monks' property or buy their lands, probably in the hope that direct royal administration would spare the English some taxation. The king replied that 'quant a cest point ce serroit contre notre Seigneur le Roi qar il prent per les mayns des fermers touz les profitz des tieux benefices et touz les plus des fermers sont Engleys'. Parliament then defended its point of view by saying that the 'les Aliens Moignes ne sont que lays gentz'. This was the crux of the question. Should the aliens, without the regular life of the convent, continue to enjoy the privilege of clerical status, once it was clearly in the lay interest to disappropriate them? In 1346 the king was strong enough to tell parliament that the monks were spiritual, not laymen 'quels chose ne poet estre trie en Parlement'.[1] Edward III held the aliens in his own hands and defended clerical privilege because he himself could disregard it when he chose. The commons' theories and solution were summarily repudiated. Weaker kings and stronger parliaments later deprived the alien monks of the protection of the monarchy and of clerical privilege.

III. *The Monks' Reactions* 1204–1360

The changed conditions of Anglo-Norman relations after 1204 did not apparently cause the monks to reconsider their position in England. At first the French annexation did not look irreversible, and until Henry III came of age and attempted to recover his patrimony the monks provided a spiritual link between members of families sundered by

---

C.F.R. 1377–83, pp. 37, 255. These rates compare favourably with those allowed fellows of Oxford Colleges: at Oriel, 15*d.* a week in addition to board and lodging, at New College, 12*d.*–18*d.* a week according to the price of corn, which shows they had to buy food with the money: E. F. Jacob, 'English University Clerks', p. 315.

[1] *Rot. Parlt.* ii. 162: September 1346.

political allegiance. There was only one alternative to holding their own in England, and that was to leave altogether. They were not only reluctant to do this; they thought it a sin to change the dispositions of their founders, who had given them property in England in perpetuity to have their name preserved in the monks' memories. Very few monasteries did sell their property. The nuns of Montivilliers sold their single English manor, Waddon in Dorset, probably because they had lost effective control of it in John's reign.[1] The cathedral canons of Lisieux[2] and Evreux[3] also disposed of their slight English assets before the middle of the thirteenth century. The confiscation of the counts of Eu's English property in 1244, willynilly disposed of Foucarmont's English revenues, completely derived from the tithes of the property, and for which the monks presumably received no compensation from the monks of Netley, the gainers.[4] The monks of Le Tréport were luckier. About 1195 they leased all their English tithes to the monks of Robertsbridge (both houses had been founded by the counts of Eu) for an annual payment of 9 marks, but agreed to sell them outright thirty years later for 100 marks. For nearly thirty years Robertsbridge tried to find the money and finally renewed the lease at the old rate. In Edward I's reign the projected sale was completed.[5] The willingness of the Norman monks to sell was in this case frustrated by the insolvency of the would-be purchasers.

An alternative to selling was exchange, but the Norman monks were far more generously endowed in England than

---

[1] *C.P.R. 1232–47*, p. 333: 18 October 1242. The king confirmed to Netley abbey the 'gift' of Abbess Margaret, appointed 1237. A William de Witefeld had possession in 1206 and still held about 1235: *Rot. Pat.* I. i. 67b; *Rot. Claus. Litt.* i. 74b, 80b; *Book of Fees*, i. 93.

[2] *C.P.R. 1232–47*, p. 455. For Séez see *C.Cl.R. 1227–31*, p. 578, and below, p. 103, n. 1.   [3] See p. 106, n. E.

[4] See below, p. 105, n. A. *C.Cl.R. 1242–7*, pp. 183, 190: May 1244.

[5] *H.M.C. Lord de l'Isle and Dudley*, i. 45, 1195; ibid., p. 128, a record of 9 November 1299 proves that William de St. Neot, abbot of Robertsbridge, paid a rent of 9 marks after purchasing the tithes from Arthur, abbot of Le Tréport in Henry III's seventh year: this was confirmed by Countess Alice, ibid., p. 83; ibid., p. 105, 1252: the abbot of Le Tréport was to be entertained at Robertsbridge when he came to England on business: payments were to be made alternate years in England and Normandy, so Norman monks must have come to England regularly during the century. The final sale occurred about 1291: ibid., pp. 125–6.

the English monks were in Normandy and possibilities were therefore limited. The monks of Cormeilles exchanged their Wiltshire church of Knoyle for Richard of Ilchester's church of Le Bois Hellain (Orne) probably at Richard's request as early as 1172/3.[1] A few years later the priors of Merton and Saint-Fromond negotiated an exchange: 'sicut permutatio illa rationabiliter et secundum Deum facta est ex indulgentia Lucii pape tertii et sicut carta episcoporum diocesanorum Hugonis Lincolniensis et Henrici Baiocensis et patronorum earundem ecclesiarum et decimarum rationabiliter testantur'. Merton had one Norman church to exchange against Saint-Fromond's six English churches, a pension from a seventh, and the tithes of Stamford castle.[2] In spite of this document Saint-Fromond still retained pensions from these churches in the late thirteenth century[3] so it cannot have become effective.

Immediately after Henry III accepted the loss of Normandy as permanent, by the treaty of Paris, the monks of Troarn and the canons of Bruton concluded the best documented of all Anglo-Norman exchanges. The houses were Norman neighbours, for the monks' parish of Langrune was adjacent to the canons' at Lion-sur-Mer.[4] They had no common benefactors but the documents explain that the original negotiations took place *amicis quibus intervenientibus*. The motives of the exchange were stated specifically: 'incommoditate non minima' and 'nos fructus et profectus seu proventus ecclesiarum . . . non possumus habere sine difficultate maxima periculis dampnis non modicis et expensis'. Bruton surrendered all its Norman interests; Troarn reserved only its rights in Hayling island. The prior of Bruton went to Normandy in the summer of 1260 and a draft proposal was agreed on 11 August, definite enough to impose a fine of 100 marks if either side defaulted.[5] Ratification

---

[1] *Delisle-Berger*, ii, no. DLXIX; *C.Ch.R. 1300–26*, p. 355.

[2] *Rot. Chart.*, p. 36: 27 February 1200: royal confirmation. Lucius's authority belongs to the years 1181–5. The churches were Cahagnes in Normandy, and Saxby, Bonby, and SS. John, Paul, Michael and George, with 2 silver marks at All Saints, Stamford. See below, p. 102, n. 5.

[3] *Taxatio*, pp. 57b, 62a, 74a. Bonby church was not sold until 1403: *C.P.R. 1401–5*, p. 217.

[4] Troarn's church of Campagnolles was about twenty miles from Bruton's church of Moion, in the Vire valley (Manche).

[5] B.N. MS. Lat. 10087, f. 19: morrow of St. Lawrence's day: this must be the

of the transfer then had to be sought from the bishops, chapters, and kings concerned, and this proved less easy. The chapter of Bayeux and the bishop of Coutances referred to decisions to be reached by the dean of Wells and the bishops of Winchester and Chichester and deferred their approval until later.[1] What these decisions were is not known. But the delays were not to be from the English end. Stephen, canon of Bruton, was admitted as prior of Horsley in the summer of 1262,[2] after returning from Normandy, where he had handed over Bruton's possessions to Troarn.[3] The chapter of Bayeux accepted the change without demur,[4] but at Coutances there was a complication: Bruton's churches in that diocese had been converted into a cathedral prebend.[5] In August 1260 Bishop Jean had not foreseen the canon's objections to the monk-canon,[6] but a year later he had to renew his order requiring the rural deans of Saint-Lô and Les Pieux to give the monks corporal possession of the churches of Moion and Pierreville in the presence of Canon Stephen[7] and insist that 'in canonicum et fratrem recipere nullatenus omittatis'.[8] The canons defied the bishop and persisted in their refusal for nearly ten years. Their real motive is not easily guessed at. Their final conditions allow only for a payment of money and a guarantee that the monks would not allow their prebendary to vote in episcopal elections: this condition had been imposed on the canons' prebend also. Part of the explanation is probably the chapter's bad relations with the bishop. It is true that when the archdeacon of Bayeux at last succeeded in composing the differences between the bishop and his chapter in 1263, this matter of Troarn's prebend was the first point at issue for

August, not the October, festival. Copies of many of the relevant documents may be found in P.R.O. 31/8/140 B, iii, pp. 361–2, 378–87.

   1 B.N. MS. Lat. 10087, f. 20–20ᵛ: 12 and 20 January 1261.
   2 *Bruton Cartulary*, no. 317.   3 Calvados H 7780.
   4 B.N. MS. Lat. 10087, f. 138: 9 May 1262. The monks were allowed to put vicars in the church of Lion and its chapel: the canons may have served in person. See also *Bruton Cartulary*, no. 312: September 1260.
   5 Calvados H 7781: 1222.
   6 Calvados H 7780, no. 156 = B.N. MS. Lat. 10087, f. 28 = *Bruton Cartulary*, no. 311: 31 August 1260.
   7 Calvados H 7780, nos. 161–2: 2–3 September 1261.
   8 Calvados H 7780, no. 158 = B.N. MS. Lat. 10087, f. 21ᵛ: 30 December 1261.

the chapter wrung from the bishop a promise that he would
give up pressing for the abbot's admission: 'ne ipse procedat
ulterius super facto prebende ... compellendo capitulum ...
ad receptionem abbatis de troarno ...'. Other complaints
against the bishop were that he had consecrated abbots
elsewhere than in his cathedral, so that the canons may have
been suspicious of the bishop's indulgence to monks in
general. Furthermore, the bishop's nephew, William de
Troarno, was the subject of other charges. His name suggests that the bishop had local connexions at Troarn which
made him partial to the monks there.[1] With the bishop
forced to abandon the monks' cause, the chapter continued
to defy the monks for another six years, until the papal
legate, formerly bishop of Evreux, persuaded the canons to
give way in return for 200 pounds paris to cover their expenses: 'non levia ut asseritis expensarum onera subiistis',
to endow a fund for cathedral lamps. The money was to be
paid in two instalments at Easter 1270 and 1271.[2] The
cardinal, in two otherwise identical letters, informed the
chapter, but curiously enough not the abbot, of this clause.
The first instalment was paid promptly,[3] but the monks
probably could not afford to pay it out of their revenues.
They looked around for someone to purchase their remaining English estate, on Hayling island, and the sale to John
le Faukoner was confirmed by Henry III in January 1271,[4]
neatly timed to provide the ready money for the next payment to the chapter in the spring. The abbot did not stop
there, however. He also hoped to recover the £200 from
the canons of Bruton who had caused him this trouble. The
prior wrote back a plaintive letter asking for the abbot to
have patience because the civil disorder in England prevented him helping the monks.[5] There the matter rested.

[1] Bayeux Chapter MS. 124, ff. 81–93: *Gallia Christiana XI*, Instrumenta 263–
70: 16 August 1263. Previous attempts to compose their differences had failed.
[2] Calvados H 7780, nos. 184–5 = B.N. MS. Lat. 10087, f. 21ᵛ: Ralph, cardinal
bishop of Alban. Gregory X confirmed the settlement: B.N. MS. Lat. 10087,
f. 21ᵛ: 7 May 1273. The bishop of Lisieux had inspected the original grant of the
prebend 1261/7, but the significance of this is not known: Calvados H 7781.
[3] Calvados H 7780: May 1270.   [4] *C.Ch.R. 1257–1300*, p. 161.
[5] *Bruton Cartulary*, no. 389. Calvados H 7780: 'Scripsistis nobis per mag.
Nicholaum quod vos ducentas libras par' capitulo Constant' loco nostro solvistis
vestra gratia quod vobis onerosum est et grave et nobis minus utile; veruntamen quia

The monks of Saint-Wandrille lost possession of the advowson of Towcester church in 1266,[1] and twenty years later decided to dispose of what lands they held in the parish by exchanging them with St. Mary, Bradenstoke, for the church of Rogerville (near Le Havre).[2] The last midland property of the monks, Countess Judith's gift of 110s. at Multon, was sold to a layman, John de Boughton, at the turn of the century.[3] A later abbot tried to recover this rent,[4] but the sale represented a purposeful step towards concentrating the monks' assets in Wiltshire and Yorkshire and the abandonment of outlying properties. The exchange and the sale both promoted an 'estates' policy and do not reflect a desire to quit England altogether. There are few examples of exchanges on the Troarn–Bruton model.[5] But Lessay,[6] Cérisy,[7] Fécamp,[8] Mont Saint-Michel,[9] Saint-Evroul,[10] and

nos tenemur et volumus conservare indempnes cum facultas se optulerit secundum tenorem mandati vobis per nuncium nostrum et dicto capitulo prius directi vobis supplicamus attentius quatinus hoc adhuc modicum patienter sustinere velitis quousque deus omnipotens rabiem et discordiam a regno Anglie auferat et pacem et tranquillitatem infundat. Conserva vos deus per tempora longiora'. No date, but it must be later than Easter 1271 if the monks had paid the £200 paris (solvistis).

[1] C.P.R. 1256–66, p. 621: by possessory assize.

[2] C.Ch.R. 1257–1300, p. 329: 1286; F. Lot, op. cit., p. lxxvi, n. 6; C. de Beaurepaire, 'Les Pouillés'; B.É.C. lxiv (1903), 614.

[3] Abbot William de Norville, who negotiated it, died in 1304. It was still the monks' property in 1291: Taxatio, p. 55.

[4] C.Pap.L. ii, p. 536.

[5] The priory of Tregoney, a cell of Notre Dame du Val, was exchanged by the abbey for the priory of Cahagnes, belonging to Merton priory in Normandy: Exeter Registers: Bronscombe, p. 275; ibid., Quivil, p. 379. A. Longnon, Les Pouillés de la Province de Rouen, p. 96. See above, p. 99, n. 2.

[6] Jean d'Essey, bishop of Coutances, allowed Lessay to dispose of its English property 'tam propter locorum distanciam quam viarum discrimina et pericula' in 1271 and the monks presumably used this authority to sell their Lincolnshire churches: see above, p. 46, n. 2: Inventaire-Sommaire, Manche H 7753.

[7] Cérisy's Norman priory, Deux Jumeaux, gave up to Cérisy's English priory, Monks Sherborne, a rent of 10s. for tithes paid by the bishop of Salisbury: Sarum Charters, no. CCXI, pp. 250–1; V.C.H. Hampshire, ii. 227.

[8] The monks of Fécamp sold Navenby manor in Lincolnshire to the canons of Lincoln, who persuaded Edward I to allow the sale by offering prayers for Queen Eleanor's soul: C.P.R. 1281–92, pp. 375, 487; C.P.R. 1292–1301, p. 11; Seine-Maritime 7 H 12, 7 H 57. See above, p. 76.

[9] Several churches were sold to the bishop of Exeter and the priory of Selborne: Otterton Charters v: c. 1206; Fines sive Pedes Finium, p. 64: 1195–1204; C.Ch.R. 1226–57, p. 182; C.Cl.R. 1296–1302, p. 450: 1233–4; Selborne Priory Charters, ii. 1–4.

[10] C.P.R. 1317–21, pp. 121, 322. The manor and church of Rowell were sold to Winchcomb abbey for a rent of £20 p.a. which was still paid in the fifteenth century: B.M. Cotton MS. Otho B xiv, f. 110ᵛ.

the canons of Séez[1] all abandoned isolated properties to eager purchasers. Just as the monks sold lands, so they also bought lands, even after 1337, as may be seen from licences to acquire lands in mortmain. The value of these purchases may be slight, but the days of extensive buying were over in the twelfth century, and the important point here is that the monks thought it worth paying the fine to improve their estates. The war did not fill them with foreboding or make them less optimistic that they would enjoy their English property for ever. Blanchelande bought lands worth 10 marks,[2] Saint-Martin of Séez lands worth £10,[3] Jumièges the advowson of a church,[4] and there are many other cases.[5]

It was the canons of Rouen who first, after Troarn, liquidated their English assets. A desire to do so may be detected in Edward I's reign. The king confiscated the manor of Ottery in 1277 on the ground that it had been alienated without permission to the monks of Ford,[6] but this was due to a misunderstanding: the canons had farmed the manor to the monks.[7] A little later the archbishop of Rouen sent master John Lalce to England to discuss with the king 'super quadam permutatione seu venditione bonorum immobilium qui in vestro regno possident facienda' and to complain of the depredations of the bishop of Exeter, who may already have cast covetous eyes on the canons' property.[8] The canons had farmed most of their manors during the

---

[1] C.Ch.R. 1226–57, p. 285. See above, p. 98, n. 2.

[2] C.P.R. 1317–21, p. 21.   [3] C.Pap.Pet., p. 102.

[4] C.Cl.R. 1330–3, p. 130.

[5] C.P.R. 1282–92, p. 420; C.P.R. 1301–7, p. 385; C.P.R. 1307–13, pp. 504, 589; C.P.R. 1313–17, p. 294; C.P.R. 1317–21, pp. 37, 343; not surprisingly there were no buyers 1321–7; C.P.R. 1327–30, pp. 393, 441; C.P.R. 1330–4, p. 245; ibid. 1338–40, p. 541; C.P.R. 1343–5, p. 120; C.P.R. 1348–50, p. 290.

[6] C.F.R. 1272–1307, p. 78: 26 April 1277.

[7] C.P.R. 1272–81, p. 123: 5 November 1276.

[8] P.R.O. Ancient Correspondence xx. 53: 3 September 1279: '. . . Reverendus pater episcopus Exon. et Johannes Clarelli clericus bona dicte ecclesie q' rabie rapina dilacerant et velut instructi ferali sevicia membra eius impiis diripunt morsibus fructus eius redditus maneria et decimas occupant minus juste et detinent et invadunt et destruunt contra nostram et dicte nostre Rothom. ecclesie voluntatem et canonicorum ex vestrorum autem liberalitate sincere progenitorum cotidiana percipientium stipendia pro eorum commemoratione piissima et anniversariis faciendis in ea quibus stipendiis sine causa rationabili, sed non sine dictorum episcopi et Johannis et etiam aliorum quorundam fraudibus sunt fraudati. Propter quod vestram regiam celsitudinem sollicitandum duximus . . .'.

thirteenth century and reduced their direct responsibilities in England to a minimum and the proposal to leave England altogether was soon revived. When Pierre Roger went from the abbacy of Fécamp, where he had tried to sell the abbey's English woodlands,[1] to the archbishopric of Rouen, he obtained John XXII's authority to sell or exchange the English lands of the cathedral.[2] The archbishop of York was enfeoffed with the Yorkshire manor of Kilham and the Hampshire manors of Kingsclere and Bentworth.[3] In June 1334 John Grandisson, bishop of Exeter, offered to buy the remaining manor of Ottery, situated less than two miles from his own country-house[4] and just over three months later the king allowed the dean of Rouen to complete the transfer.[5] Here Grandisson established his collegiate church of St. Mary Ottery, jointly dedicated to the Virgin and to Edward the Confessor, the first English benefactor of the canons of Rouen, whose name had presumably been venerated in the church of Ottery which he had given them, for nearly three hundred years.[6] At the same time the canons of Coutances sold the manor and advowson of Winterbourne Strickland, their sole English property, to the monks of Milton Abbas, who obtained the king's consent by setting up chantries for the royal house.[7]

These two sales are the only signs that the Normans may seriously have reconsidered their position in the light of the French wars of 1294 and 1324–6. From their contact with the king's escheators they had reason to doubt the king's good faith, and they may have sensed impending disaster in the insincere negotiations over homage during Edward III's early years. Wisely they surrendered property of doubtful value. When the war was resumed in 1337, sales and ex-

---

[1] See above, p. 70.

[2] Seine-Maritime G 4706: 17 March 1333 = P.R.O. 31/8/140 A, no. 307.

[3] *C.F.R. 1327–37*, pp. 391, 432, 451; *C.Cl.R. 1333–7*, pp. 331–2; March-May 1334, 1335. [4] *Exeter Registers: Grandisson*, i. 273: 10 June 1334.

[5] *C.P.R. 1334–7*, p. 20: 25 September 1334; *M.A.* iii. 59–61: Collegiate Churches.

[6] *C.P.R. 1334–8*, pp. 562, 569; *M.A.* i. 549. No details of how much money the canons received for their manors are given. Ottery was said to be worth £160. The canons of Ottery St. Mary had permission to buy the abbot of Caen's manor of Northam, but this sale was not concluded: *C.P.R. 1350–4*, pp. 53, 62; *C.P.R. 1358–61*, p. 296; *C.P.R. 1361–4*, p. 401; *C.P.R. 1401–5*, p. 192.

[7] *C.P.R. 1334–7*, p. 344: 26 September 1336.

changes were more difficult to negotiate. As the war continued a new class of would-be buyers emerged, the English lay lords. The monks were reluctant to part with all their rights, which if of slight immediate value might yet one day again bring in the profits of those fabulous post-Conquest days if nursed through troubled times. The buyers were not to be put off by these foolish dreams, and what the monks would not part with willingly at market prices they took. Under cover of war-time suspicions they ignored clerical privilege. In less than a century the monks' eternal titles were surrendered and the laity, by the dissolution of the alien priories, had stormed the outer defences of medieval monastic privilege.

NOTES

A. The widowed countess of Eu, Alice, confirmed the monks' land at 'Tuffort' to Foucarmont and four pounds from her demesne at Blyth and all her English tithes, 17 May 1219; in return the monks 'concesserunt se constituturos decem sacerdotes qui deo in perpetuum deservirent in eadem abbatia pro salute anime domini mei et in remissione delictorum meorum et peccatorum heredum et parentum meorum': Rouen MS. Y 13, ff. 55ᵛ-56. Six months later she made another grant not referring to tithes but to rents of seven pounds ten pence and sixty shillings nine pence in different places, together with 'Tukefort': Seine-Maritime 8 H 9, 9 November 1219. Twelve years later these sums have been increased: possibly another six shillings from two manors, but a certain fifty-six or a hundred, the manuscripts differ, in another: 'et hic redditus totus sterlingorum et assignatus pro decima reddituum meorum ita tamen quod firmiter promisi me diligenter et bona fide inquisituram valorem totius terre mee de anglia quam modo teneo'. If at any time she increased her holdings the tithe would be increased proportionately: Seine-Maritime 8 H 9 = Rouen MS. Y 13, f. 54-54ᵛ: 1231. Two years later her clerk did make a survey as she had promised and the archbishop of Rouen witnessed that the countess had kept her word: Rouen MS Y 13, f. 62ᵛ: 1233. Nevertheless in 1238 all payments were revoked and the countess conceded instead certain tenants with services elaborately specified: M.A. ii. 976. This series of deeds shows how determined the monks were after 1204 to be certain that they were getting all that they were entitled to out of England.

B. The prior of Sherborne protested his inability to pay a farm of £80 from revenues not worth £60 and asked that the farm be reduced or that he be given a respite from paying, or that the king take the custody and pay the prior and monks an allowance from the revenues: C.Cl.R. 1339-41, pp. 240, 330: 22 August and 22 November 1339. Overseers were appointed to act according to the prior's advice for the relief of the house: C.P.R. 1340-3, p. 12: 28 July 1340. At Eye the prior discreetly pleaded that he could not pay £160 because his pensions and portions were withheld. Two exchequer clerks eleven months later took the farm, promising to pay the full £160 and to allow the monks something, but after three years they found it was impossible and asked for a reduction of the farm to £140: C.F.R. 1337-47, p. 88, 3 August 1338; ibid., pp. 133-4, 24 June 1339; ibid., p. 258, 18 February 1342; C.Cl.R. 1339-41, pp. 25, 93, 160, 167. The prior of Harmondsworth asked for a reduction of his farm and an inquiry was ordered: Winchester College, Harmondsworth Charter no. 73, f. 3. The prior of Arundel used his patron, the earl of Arundel, to obtain a reduction of his farm from £35 to £27, the assessment of 1295, because the revenues would not otherwise suffice for the support of the monks: *C. Cl.R. 1339–41*, p. 535; *C.F.R. 1337–47*, pp. 172–3: 15 May 1340. Some houses simply failed to pay. Stogursey was pardoned its arrears as early as 1340: *C.F.R. 1337–47*, p. 191, 9 September 1340.

C. Seine-Maritime 7 H 43: Abbot William wrote to the bailiff 28 July 1341 about the new appointment: 'Cum dilectus noster in christo frater Radulfus le frison commonachus noster prior in prioratus curato de Cogges Lincolniensis diocesis, cuius ius patronatus et presentandi ad nos pertinet et noscitur pertinere ex certis et legitimis causis, bonum sue conscientie attendens dicto prioratui curato renunciare desideret ac etiam pure et simpliciter resignare eundem cum ipsius iuribus et pertinentiis in manibus reverendi in christo patris ac domini episcopi Lincolniensis vel cuiuslibet alterius dictas renunciationem et resignationem recipiendi potestatem habentis, vobis quo ad presentandum vice et nomine nostri dicto reverendo patri seu aliis quibus fuit faciendum dilectum nobis in christo fratrem Guillelmum Hamonis commonachum nostrum professum presbyterum ad dictum prioratum curatum, cum nuper per resignationem dicti fratris Radulfi vel eius procuratoris ad hec sufficienter constituti vacare contigerit et ad supplicandum nomine quo supra eidem reverendo **patri** vel aliis quibus faciendum fuerit, quod dictum fratrem Guillelmum tunc sic presentatum ad dictum prioratum velit favorabiliter admittere, et eidem presentato dictum prioratum sic vacantem cum ipsius iuribus et pertinentiis universis caritatis intuitu et dicte presentationis obtentu conferit, et ipsum instituere in eodem et in possessionem eiusdem prioratus iuriumque et pertinentiarum ipsius iudici facere corporalem, et ad omnia alia et singula faciendum que circa ea et in hiis quolibet fuerint facienda, tenore presentium concedimus potestatem ad hec vobis vices nostras plenarie committentes . . . .': *C.P.R. 1345–8*, p. 447; *C.P.R. 1348–50*, pp. 394, 407; *C.P.R. 1354–8*, p. 44; *C.P.R. 1361–4*, p. 244; *C.P.R. 1364–7*, p. 39; Lincoln Register: Burghersh, f. 289.

D. B.N. MS. Lat. 11056, f. 200ᵛ: petition of May 1349. Permission was granted 4 October 1349: Orne H 898: *inspeximus* by Guillaume, bishop of Lisieux, 27 January 1350/1: 'quod prefatum monasterium certis ecclesiis et redditibus in regno Anglie constitutis pro magna parte ab initio fundatum extitit et dotatum ex quibus fere a tresdecim annis circa quibus guerrarum turbines uiguerunt in partibus illis dicti abbas et conventus nichil percipere potuerunt quodque propter mortalitatem gentium illarum partium terris incultis remanentibus redditus et proventus ipsius monasterii diminuuntur in maxima quantitate maneria quoque eidem monasterio subiecta tempore dicte guerre combusta fuerunt et bona ipsorum plurima devastata multa etiam prefatum abbatem in novitate provisionis ipsius oportuit subire onera expensarum ipsumque monasterium hospitalitate non modicum oneratur ac premissorum occasione ad paupertatis et desolationis opprobrium quodam modo est redactum . . .'.

E. *C.P.R. 1247–58*, p. 46. There is an extraordinary petition from some canons of Evreux to Henry III protesting against their dean and fellow canons for forcing through the sale of the English manor: P.R.O. Ancient Correspondence, iii. 86: Excellentissimo domino Henrico dei gratia illustrissimo regi Anglie Devoti et humiles mag. Petrus de Husseia, archid. W. de Butell. Ric. de Malavilla, Angerus de Rothom, Galfrid. de Corcell., canonici Ebroicenses Salutem et regni gubernacula domini feliciter possidere. Celsitudini regie maiestatis lacrimabiliter intimamus quod Decanus et quidam concanonici nostri manerium de Braunfort quod felicissime memorie Henricus quondam rex Anglie ob sui et predecessorum suorum ac etiam successorum veniam peccatorum nostre ecclesie piissima largitate concessit ut in sui et regno Anglie perpetuam memoriam divinum pro ipsis apud nos celebraretur officium annuatim nobis et multis aliis reclamantibus et invitis contra deum et iura vendere presumpserunt; unde timendum est ne processu temporis predicti inclitissimi principis benefactoris memoria in nostra pereat ecclesia et recedat. Quod cum gravi cordis amaritudine sustinemus, ut tanti principis piissimum propositum qui sui et suorum in divinis officiis voluit perpetuam apud nos habere memoriam in futurum immutetur non absque ingratitudinis vicio et piissimi defuncti principis et vestra iniuria et contemptu. Quare vestre maiestati humiliter supplicimus ut alienatio elemosine predecessoris vestri in defuncti principis et vestram iniuriam contra deum et iura presumpta vobis displiceat, nec velitis ut in nostra depereat ecclesia predecessorum vestri et vestrorum memoria successorum. Bene et diu valeat regia celsitudo.

IV

THE DISSOLUTION OF THE NORMAN PRIORIES

1. *The Expulsion of Monks in* 1378

EFORE 1360, while the English had the best of the war,
Edward III showed no sign of allowing others to interfere in the affairs of the alien monks, and the aliens did
not regard their possessions as good as lost because of the
king's policy. When the war began again in 1369, the aliens
received their lands at farm from the king and promised not
to leave the country, send gold or silver abroad, or reveal
the secrets of the kingdom, as they had done in 1337.[1]
Events did not, however, duplicate those of Edward's
earlier, more successful years. Defeatism roused the vin-
dictiveness of the English and the aliens fell victims to other
passions.[2] In the same year as parliament petitioned for the
removal of priors from the coasts 'eiannt regard q'il sount
Fraunceys en lours corps et espiont les Secretz et Ordyn-
ancez' and because they sent gold and silver *et autres artelries*
oversea,[3] two Essex alien priories were farmed to laymen:
West Mersea to a citizen of London, Richard Lyons, Panfield (with its companion Well Hall in Norfolk) to Hugh
Fastolf.[4] Even if in these cases the priors had been removed
because of the priories' proximity to the coasts, lay farmers
cannot easily be accounted for in this way at Minster Lovell,
Astley, Haugh, Beckford, Ecclesfield, or the priory of Pont
Audemer.[5] Edward III's last parliaments heard a lot about

---

[1] *Rot. Parlt.* ii. 302, n. 26; *Rymer*, vi. 629: 1369. The priors had been restored to
their priories in 1361: *C.P.R. 1358-61*, pp. 558-61.

[2] *C.Cl.R. 1369-74*, p. 63: 12 November 1369: The prior of Hayling with a groom
and a companion was taken to Southwick priory on suspicion of having received
letters to the king's prejudice and of having revealed secrets.

[3] *Rot. Parlt.* ii. 320: 1373.

[4] *C.F.R. 1369-77*, pp. 222-3, 232. For the case of a secular 'occupier' at Wootton Wawen in 1374, see Worcester Episcopal Registers: *Sede Vacante* (Worcester
Historical Society f. 169). [5] Ibid., pp. 225, 246, 255, 304, 317, 374.

such farms, and divine service, almsgiving, and charitable works not surprisingly suffered as a result.[1]

In the past priors had normally taken custody of their own estates. Very occasionally other monks,[2] not exchequer clerks, had been given responsibility; laymen are rarely found: mainprisors occur[3] and the military installations at St. Michael's Mount excuse the presence of lay custodians.[4] Other instances are not so easily explained away.[5] The countess of Ulster acquired the lands of the nuns of Caen[6] from the king; the monks of Caen themselves farmed two manors to Walter de Frampton in 1362, but this was during the peace and the monks needed the money.[7] More common than physical possession was probably the king's assignment of expected alien revenues to his creditors. The continuation of the war and the custody was the guarantee of their income. The king's daughter, Isabel, had £140 from the farmers of Eye, £200 from those of the nuns of Caen and 64 marks from those of Ivry.[8] Robert of Artois was subsidized by his fellow Frenchmen;[9] John Darcy of Knayth received part of his annuity from the proctor of Lire.[10] A few clerks openly took the farms as part of their salary or as personal recompense for their services.[11]

In Edward's earlier years grants to lay farmers were the exception: they became the rule. When the old king was

[1] *Rot. Parlt.* ii. 342, petition 65: 1376. The last parliament of Edward's reign complained of aliens going to the court of Rome for remedies for their grievances: ibid., p. 333a: 1377. Lord Latimer's chaplain forced the prior of Ecclesfield to leave his church in 1376, and the prior hid his treasure there: ibid., p. 329.

[2] *C.F.R. 1347–56*, pp. 47, 54: Ellingham; ibid., pp. 146, 149, 152 and *C.F.R. 1356–69*, pp. 2–3: Ecclesfield: in this case a monk of Saint-Wandrille shared the custody with the prior of Monk Bretton. See also M. Chibnall, *The English Lands of the Abbey of Bec*, p. 125.

[3] *C.F.R. 1337–47*, p. 126: this may also be the explanation for the appearance of laymen at Otterton: *C.F.R. 1347–56*, p. 322.

[4] *C.F.R. 1337–47*, pp. 46, 84, 88, 91, 96, 177. For an earlier example of lay interference at St. Michael's Mount see Hoveden (R.S.), iii. 238; P.R. 6 John, p. 40.

[5] *C.F.R. 1347–56*, pp. 141, 339, 350, 367; *C.F.R. 1356–69*, p. 390; *C.F.R. 1369–77*, p. 135.

[6] *C.F.R. 1337–47*, p. 146; *C.P.R. 1345–8*, p. 372; *C.P.R. 1348–50*, p. 97: she was Edward's daughter-in-law.

[7] *C.P.R. 1361–4*, p. 260; because of his abuses he was removed by the king, and the manors granted to others: *C.F.R. 1377–83*, p. 180; *C.P.R. 1374–7*, p. 160.

[8] *C.P.R. 1354–8*, p. 518; *C.P.R. 1358–61*, p. 474.   [9] *C.F.R. 1337–47*, p. 88.

[10] *C.P.R. 1338–40*, p. 305; *C.P.R. 1343–5*, p. 426.

[11] *C.F.R. 1337–47*, p. 165, cf. pp. 176, 178; ibid., p. 168.

dead and the kingship too weak to defend its monopoly to exploit the aliens, parliament met and demanded the expulsion of all aliens during war-time.[1] Their profits would help the war effort; their founders' kin and patrons would gladly pay the king as much as any prior or farmer; Englishmen would perform the divine offices and deprive the aliens of their last excuse for staying.[2] The government accepted this but made exceptions for 'les Priours conventuell et autres persones q'ount title a terme de vie en lour Benefices ou offices et conuz pur bones persones et loiaulx et nyent suspectes d'espiaill ne d'autre prejudice au Roi ne au Roialme'. The expulsion was fixed for Candlemas 1378. All communications with France would be censored. Those monks who had to leave would depart through Dover, where they could be searched; those found in the country after Candlemas were to be held for ransom and those who denounced them were to be offered one-third of their goods. Englishmen would replace the exiles, spiritualities would be farmed to churchmen, and temporalities offered to anyone 'suffisant les vorra prendre a ferme de nostre Seigneur le Roi a pluis haut pris'; the new farmers were to accept responsibility for maintaining religious services in the priories.[3]

The order was proclaimed on 20 December[4] and a large number of monks did leave England in February 1378. The treaty rolls give the names of more than a hundred monks who received permission to go and of about forty who subsequently obtained permission to remain.[5] The lists cannot be complete because several monasteries are not represented on the lists. The abbot of Séez said two years later that eighteen of his monks had been violently expelled,[6] but only seven names appear on the rolls. The numbers of monks who remained is probably more certain than the number who left,

---

[1] An alien, Stephen Philip, accused of spying, was imprisoned in 1375; he claimed to have been visiting his friend, a monk at Long Bennington: C.Cl.R. 1374-7, p. 139. The abbot of Saint-Pierre-sur-Dives excused his prior of Modbury in 1376 the customary payment of 3 silver marks because he had not the wherewithal: Eton College, Modbury Charter no. 40. Does this imply that all payments had not automatically ceased in 1369 ?

[2] 'La ou les dite Enemys a ore fount colour pur lour demure par divine service.'

[3] Rot. Parlt. iii. 22-23, petition 50: 1377. See also petition 28, p. 19.

[4] P.R.O. C 76, no. 61, m. 11.

[5] Appendix III.   [6] C.Pap.L. iv. 239-40.

simply because it was more difficult to stay without express permission.

The first effect of the expulsion was to bring to an end all conventual life in the priories; it was the priors not the priories that were saved by the 'conventual' clause, for the prior's legal status was unassailable. Of the twenty-seven named inmates of Bec's cells only seven subsequently obtained permission to stay; only two of Séez's seven named monks and only two of the nine named inmates of Blyth priory. At Eye there were four survivors out of eight: one had been a monk there for forty-eight years and was presumably too old to be moved. The prior himself was blind, weak, and incompetent, the buildings in ruins and the convent burdened with corrodies. The farm was given to the prior of Thetford, and the priory's patron, William de Ufford, earl of Suffolk, supervised the spending of money on the repair of the church and fabric.[1] Eye was saved as a priory through the influence of its patron. As soon as this support was removed by death, the prior applied for letters of 'naturalization' as the only way to secure its survival.[2] The only other priory to take this step was Stoke by Clare, which lost most of its monks in 1378, because they were French, and this priory had to pay dearly for the privilege in 1395.[3] Elsewhere priories ceased to exist, unless the monks were English. This was not often the case.

Most of the monks who remained in England after 1378 were single representatives of their monasteries. According to law they should have been conventual priors or at least priors with a life title, but there were a number of monks who obtained letters permitting them to stay, although they lacked this justification. Even when they were allowed to stay, they rarely farmed the monastery's lands as their predecessors had. A handful of priories were farmed by monks,[4]

---

[1] C.F.R. 1377–83, pp. 129–30.

[2] C.P.R. 1381–5, p. 491. A new prior had been appointed in 1382: C.F.R. 1377–83, pp. 329–30.

[3] M. Chibnall, The English Lands of the Abbey of Bec, p. 127. Thomas of Woodstock, as earl of Buckingham, received £60 p.a. from Stoke to keep up his rank in 1379: C.P.R. 1377–81, p. 224. As duke of Gloucester, by 1392 his total revenues from alien property were £1,000: C.Ch.R. 1341–1417, pp. 328–30; C.F.R. 1399–1405, p. 224.

[4] C.F.R. 1377–83, p. 274; C.F.R. 1383–91, p. 209; C.F.R. 1391–9, pp. 204, 218, 240.

exchequer clerks,[1] or other clergy.[2] Most passed into the
hands of the laity—not patrons or protectors of the monks
stepping between them and an oppressive government, but
transient despoilers on whose behalf the expulsion had been
decided. A petition against them was presented in the parliament of 1385, asking for a return to the earlier system of
administration: 'pur l'onour de Dieu et augmentation de
divines services et en eide del almes pur queux les ditz
priories estoient fonduz en oevre de charite'. Such complaints became general,[3] but although one petition became
an ordinance there was no end to the abuse.[4] Almost nothing
is known about these farmers, except if they negotiated with
the monks for a more permanent claim to the lands than the
government grant of the farm *guerra durante* could give
them. The farmers either rarely approached the monks for
this purpose, or, as is more likely, the monks refused to do
business with these temporary enemies.

Sir John Devereux tried to negotiate with the monks of
Caen for a lease to him and his heirs for four lives of the
priory of Frampton, which he already farmed for the king.[5]
The monks of Caen ignored or refused his proposal. Yet
Devereux was in such favour at court that the whole farm
was remitted in 1385[6] and in the same year he acquired
another priory, Newent, at farm.[7] After his death these
priories fell to Sir John Cheyne, a member of Henry IV's
privy council.[8] Devereux's son-in-law, Walter fitz Walter,
successfully challenged Cheyne's rights in 1400 and the
priory of Frampton at least reverted to him.[9]

Parliament continued to worry about the monks' possible treason, but the government dismissed these fears as unreal: *Rot. Parlt.* iii. 64, par. 40, petition XIV; ibid.,
p. 96, petition XX.

[1] *C.F.R. 1377–83*, pp. 74, 83, 86–89, 105–6, 158, 248; *C.F.R. 1383–91*, pp. 129,
131–2, 137, 161, 183; *C.F.R. 1391–9*, p. 31; *C.F.R. 1399–1405*, pp. 27, 64. The
priories were amongst the smallest; they may have been farmed for the king or for the
clerks' own profit.

[2] *C.F.R. 1383–91*, pp. 121, 331; *C.P.R. 1370–4*, p. 30; *C.P.R. 1396–9*, p. 419.

[3] *Rot. Parlt.* iii. 213, par. 39: 1385–6; ibid., p. 256, no. 18: 1387–8; ibid., p. 262,
no. 19; p. 276, no. 12: 1389.   [4] Ibid., p. 301, par. 7: 1392–3.

[5] *C.P.R. 1381–5*, p. 111: 1382. For Devereux see *Complete Peerage*, iv. 296–302.

[6] *C.P.R. 1385–9*, p. 13.

[7] *C.F.R. 1396–9*, pp. 559–60; *C.F.R. 1381–9*, pp. 88, 177, 225.

[8] *Proceedings of the Privy Council*, i. 122.

[9] *C.F.R. 1399–1405*, pp. 12, 105–6; *C.P.R. 1399–1401*, pp. 399, 431.

Cheyne himself had acquired his first alien priory, the priory of Beckford, in 1379. Exchequer clerks had farmed it since 1378 and Cheyne's possession was at first so temporary that the clerks even recovered it for a fortnight; but Cheyne then received a life interest in it.[1] Since he offered no greater farm than the clerks, he presumably owed his success to his influence. Like Devereux, he negotiated with the Norman owners. He may have tried immediately, but it was not until 1389 that the terms were agreed. It is quite likely that it was the pressing needs of the prior of Sainte-Barbe-en-Auge which made him willing to sell property, not acceptance of Cheyne's position as permanent. The prior, Louis Vigorosi, owed the Avignonese curia of Clement VII 400 francs d'or for his collation to the priory in 1385. As late as 1388 only 100 francs had been paid[2] so that this outstanding debt may have given Cheyne his chance. He sent his brother to Normandy the next year to assay the ground.[3]

The agreement transferring the priory of Beckford to Cheyne, his wife and his son for the longest of three lives in return for 1,800 francs or 660 gold nobles, to be paid in Normandy at Rouen, Harfleur, or Caen, was settled six months later. A canon was to be accepted in England, who should receive 12 marks a year or a lump sum of 100 gold francs. If the canon agreed to sell outright, Cheyne's offer of 3,000 gold francs *ou autre some d'or* would be taken up.[4] Richard II agreed to this[5] and Cheyne himself declared that he had received the lands for 1,500 francs *per nos ipsis religiosis persoluta* and agreed to pay a canon 6 marks when he first arrived in England, and 6 marks half a year later, provided the king allowed French religious to enter England, an important condition.[6] The only record of a canon going to England, in 1401,[7] may indicate that the implementation

[1] C.F.R. *1377–83*, pp. 77–78, 167, 238, 240. He acquired the neighbouring priory of Newent in 1400: C.P.R. *1399–1401*, pp. 200, 205.

[2] Calvados 2 D 184: possession given 16 April 1385; 100 francs paid 21 April 1386; inspeximus dated 1 April 1388.

[3] Calvados 2 D 170: 21 March 1389.

[4] Calvados 2 D 170: 9 September 1389.

[5] C.P.R. *1388–92*, p. 118: 15 October 1389.

[6] Calvados 2 D 170: 20 November 1389. The agreement was approved by Boniface IX, although the priory was in the obedience of Clement VII: C.Pap.L. ii. 328.

[7] Calvados 2 D 170. All the previous documents were inspected by the vicomte of

of this clause depended upon the royal rescission of the order of 1378. A later memoir prepared in 1421, when only Cheyne's wife of the three survived, claimed that no money had ever been received by the priory or the canons of Sainte-Barbe,[1] but it seems implausible to suggest that Cheyne did not in fact pay for the documents he obtained or that the prior would have committed himself to writing without ready cash first being paid. Cheyne held other lands[2] and is probably representative of other farmers of whom less is known.

Grants of leases, even sales, waited upon the monks' pleasure and there is no evidence that they were stampeded by events. In a few cases they accepted proposals for one or the other, perhaps because they trusted the men concerned. Most agreements of this kind[3] specify that the lessee will accept a monk on the manors and will undertake to provide him with necessities. Mont Saint-Michel leased Otterton priory to Sir Peter Courtenay and others (who included Lonlay's alien prior of Stogursey, Richard Amys) for Courtenay's life and one year[4] and the priors continued to live there as carefree pensioners.[5] Yet this marked the end of the monks' control over the priory. After Courtenay's death it passed to the king and the monks probably never received any money 'a cause et pour raison de la dicte baille a ferme' which should have been paid at the end of the war. Cormeilles actually recovered the priory of Chepstow, leased on similar terms to Sir Benedict Cely,[6] unless Cely was never given seisin. Only the conditions of Saint-Wandrille's proposed lease of Ecclesfield priory to Sir John Luvetot survive, but even if the proposals fell through they show the monks

Caen; Brother Geoffrey Legascoing was to choose a suitable confessor at Beckford: he had no other companion. See P.R.O. 31/8/140 B, i, pp. 36–45.

[1] Calvados 2 D 170. Margaret had remarried and took the lands to her new husband, William Herle: *C.Cl.R. 1419–22*, pp. 178–9: 21 November 1421.

[2] He held lands of Beaubec in Gloucestershire: *C.F.R. 1391–9*, p. 175.

[3] The prior of Harmondsworth farmed the manor of Tingewick for six years to laymen in 1380 with no special clauses: New College, Oxford, Cartulary, ii. 270. See also *C.P.R. 1354–8*, p. 4.

[4] *Otterton Charters*, nos. XXXII and XXXIII: 1389.

[5] *C.P.R. 1396–9*, p. 148: 10 June 1397. See M. Chibnall, *The English Lands of the Abbey of Bec*, p. 125.

[6] *C.P.R. 1396–9*, p. 469; *C.P.R. 1399–1401*, pp. 163, 179.

determined to lose nothing by their temporary weakness.[1] Outright sales to laymen were Beaulieu's sale of Patricksbourne priory[2] and Saint-Evroul's sale of its Gloucestershire manor of Wilcote to three gentlemen 'pro commodo monasterii nostri magnam et notabilem pecunie summam nobis pre manibus persolvit'. The monks still held out for good terms and did not accept their weakness as permanent.[3]

Probably most of the other lay farmers made similar attempts to secure concessions from the owners. The earl of Arundel, for example, had been given the lordship and services of the manors of Bury and West Burton, belonging to Fécamp, which are adjacent to Arundel, and also permission to hunt in the abbot's park of Warminghurst, ten miles away, by Edward III.[4] He wrote to the abbot suggesting that the monks should sell their manors to him[5] and thirty years later the king believed that the monks had enfeoffed the earl with the property;[6] however, in 1393 the earl's son left money for his heir to purchase the manor of Bury: 'et nomement al abbe et covent de Fyscamp pur le purchase del manoir de Bury par tiele manere qe soit resonablement greable a eux en descharge de l'alme mon treshonoure seigneur et pier . . . si jeo ne le fac en ma vie.'[7] After nearly fifty years of effort the monks still resisted the earls' blandishments.

If laymen could enjoy only a temporary title in the Normans' lands, the case of religious who acquired alien property was more serious and the Norman monks negotiated with them in order to salve something from the wreck. Richard II's favourite, the earl of Arundel, was more successful than his father with Fécamp, in buying Arundel priory from the monks of Séez with the money his father had left for the foundation of a chantry. Only the prior was left in the priory after 1378 and Clement VII made no difficulties,

[1] Appendix V A. *C.F.R. 1369–77*, pp. 17, 24, 362, 374; the priory was given by Richard II to the Carthusians: *C.P.R. 1385–9*, p. 112.

[2] *C.P.R. 1388–92*, p. 258; *C.F.R. 1383–91*, p. 331.

[3] B.N. MS. Lat. 11056, f. 190, nos. 1146–7; Orne H 3340: 8 June 1397. P.R.O. 31/8/140 B, I, pp. 330–1, no. 158. There is a summary of the deed in the *Inventaire-Sommaire*. [4] *C.P.R. 1338–44*, p. 431; *C.P.R. 1343–5*, p. 557.

[5] See p. 142, n. A. [6] *C.Cl.R. 1368–74*, p. 329: 26 April 1372.

[7] J. Nichols, *Royal Wills*, p. 128: the will is dated 4 March 1392/3. The *Complete Peerage* wrongly gives the date as 1382/3: a printing error.

provided the money was devoted to repairing the Norman monastery and to the purchase of *rentes* in France.[1] The earl had left 1,000 marks for this purchase, but it is not certain that the monks received all this money. A few years later when the same earl tried to buy out the nuns of Almenesches settled at Lyminster, with the advantage of being lay farmer of the priory, he was foiled:[2] this time he had no religious justification for his action.[3]

The disposal of alien priories in the fifteenth century enabled Henry V to endow two religious houses and Henry VI two colleges. Similarly, in the fourteenth century the endowment of New College, Oxford, and Winchester College by William Wykeham and the foundation of some Carthusian priories was made easier by the availability of alien lands. Wykeham's dealings with aliens were extensive, but the only Norman monastery affected was Sainte-Cathérine-du-Mont at Rouen. From Urban VI the bishop of Winchester obtained permission to buy lands to the value of 500 marks; from the king, lands worth 200 marks; before the end of November 1390 the substance of his agreement with the monks of Rouen was already settled. The monks sold the lands of Harmondsworth priory, including scattered rights,[4] for 8,400 francs 'du bon or de bon aley de bon pois et du coing du Roy de France'. The 400 francs were to be used for the purchase of 'rentes . . . a ce que ledit monsire levesque soit perpetuellement mis en prieres dudit covent' and for the abbot's 'chambre . . . pour emploier au prousfit et gouvernement dudit lieu'. Wykeham also promised to send 'une bonne chapelle fournie de ce qui y'appartient a tel Seigneur come il est' for the great altar of the monastery,

[1] *C.P.R. 1377–81*, p. 402; *C.Pap.L.* iv. 239–40; Denifle, *La Désolation des Églises*, ii (1899), 758, n. 1; *C.P.R. 1377–81*, p. 494; *M.A.* iii. 101–4. As early as 1353 the priory was said to be of no profit to the monks although this was admittedly an excuse offered to justify the appropriation of a church: *Chichester Cartulary*, nos. 922–3.

[2] P.R.O. C 76, no. 68, m. 19: the earl had the king's permission *ad opus ipsius comitis faciendum*: 18 September 1383. He had been joint farmer with the prioress and his new prior of the Holy Trinity, Arundel, for one week: *C.F.R. 1383–91*, p. 4: 11 September 1383. The nuns recovered possession in 1399: *C.F.R. 1399–1405*, pp. 97–98.   [3] See p. 142, n. B.

[4] Manors and churches of Harmondsworth, Tingewick (Buckinghamshire), and Saham Tony (Norfolk) and the church of St. Leonard's, Hastings (Sussex).

and to provide the prior of Harmondsworth and his companion Jehan le Cellier with food, drink, clothes, and lodging for life 'comme il appartient a avoir aus religieux de leur estat'.[1] This last provision is similar to those written into leases to laymen and shows that in spite of the sale the monks intended to keep two of their number in England. During the succeeding eleven months both sides took the steps necessary to complete the transfer.[2] In October the abbot announced his intention of selling his English lands because they were 'quasi inutilia et pro necessitatibus et utilitatibus nostris . . . relevandis'. The war was chiefly to blame, he said, for the slight value of the lands but even in peace-time they were an encumbrance: 'propter locorum distanciam linguae ignorantiam maris intermedii difficilem et periculosum transitum et alia viarum discrimina'.[3] It is interesting that the abbot speaks as though the money had been paid ('pro quadam summa pecunie notabili nobis prae manibus habita et soluta et ad perpetuam utilitatem dicti monasterii nostri conversa')[4] whereas Wykeham's agent, Richard Altrincham, received a quittance from the abbot only ten days later, acknowledging receipt of 8,600 francs and 40 pounds tours more, 'pro viagio fratris Johannis Fecourt monachi nostri ac Prioris Prioratus de Biriaco in Anglia facto' with another 60 pounds tours for the expenses of the prior of Sainte-Catherine-du-Mont.[5] The following month the prior of Harmondsworth handed over to Wykeham's agents the possession of the property[6] and in January Wykeham endowed New College with it.[7]

[1] T. Kirby, 'Charters of Harmondsworth, etc.', Archaeologia, lviii (1902), 341–58. Winchester College, Harmondsworth Charters. This agreement is dated 30 November 1390.

[2] In March the agreement was exemplified in the great court of Rouen: Winchester College, Harmondsworth Charters, no. 23; Richard II confirmed it the same month: C.P.R. 1391–6, pp. 60, 434; in May the prior and his fellow Jehan d'Anseuyll went to Normandy: P.R.O. C 76, no. 74, 14; an extent was made at Tingewick the same month: Winchester College, Harmondsworth Charters, no. 73, f. 2; in June Wykeham sent the money through his financiers, agents of the societies of Cathanin, Grylle, Guynirs, and Lomelyn—all Italians: ibid., no. 24. Kirby mistakenly has 9 June 1392. The archbishop's licence was given 26 July 1391.

[3] Winchester College, Harmondsworth Charters, no. 25.

[4] Ibid., no. 29. [5] Ibid., nos. 27, 28, 30.

[6] Ibid., Titley Charters, nos. 20/20, 23, 24, 21, Hamble Charters, nos. 45, 45a, Harmondsworth Charters, nos. 22a, 26. Marquis of Anglesey's Muniment Catalogue, nos. 783, a, b. [7] Winchester College, Harmondsworth Charters, no. 26.

The Carthusians were the only other religious purchasers of aliens' lands on a wide scale. In spite of several Norman concessions it seems doubtful if any money actually changed hands. Richard II granted some priories to St. Anne's, Coventry, in 1385[1] and some to Mountgrace priory in 1399.[2] Saint-Pierre-sur-Dives had permission to sell the manor and advowson of Wolston priory to Coventry for 2,400 gold francs[3] and Boscherville expected the Carthusians to pay 1,000 gold French florins for Edith Weston, as well as a pension of 4 pounds tours.[4] In a very elaborate document the abbot of Aunay formally leased his manors and churches of Great Limber, Kirtlington, and Ashby Mears at perpetual farm to Coventry in 1392, reserving a payment of 100 pounds tours or its value in goods when firm peace should be concluded between the kings of France and England.[5] The conclusion of peace was perhaps the unwritten condition of all these payments.[6]

Apart from the Carthusians there were a few other religious purchasers, usually taking advantage of the Normans' wish to sell, rather than urging sales because of their position as occupiers of alien property. After a devastating fire at Aumâle, the monks decided to raise the money they needed by selling their already ruined priory of Birstall (since disappeared altogether into the Humber) to Kirkstall abbey in 1395 for 10,000 pounds tours.[7] The negotiations were made through John of Gaunt.[8] The canons of Blanchelande were authorized by the abbot and chapter-general of Prémontré to sell the priory of Cammeringham, when the king forced the prior's companion to leave England, because certain

---

[1] C.P.R. 1385-9, p. 112.   [2] C.P.R. 1396-9, pp. 497, 570.
[3] C.P.R. 1396-9, p. 352; V.C.H. Warwickshire, ii. 132-3.
[4] C.P.R. 1388-92, p. 317; the archbishop of Rouen allowed the sale in June 1390 because the manor was dampnosum and useless because of the war and its distance from Normandy: Seine-Maritime 13 H 13.
[5] C.P.R. 1391-6, p. 242: 15 October 1392. Calvados H 1251: 24 June 1393, an inspeximus of 1511.
[6] Mountgrace paid £1,000 to the king, not to Saint-Evroul, for the priory of Ware: C.P.R. 1396-9, p. 348; C.P.R. 1399-1401, p. 532; C.P.R. 1416-22, p. 395.
[7] M.A. i. 589-90.
[8] Bodleian MS. Dodsworth, vol. 7, p. 239: 1 October 1395. Charles VI refers to the lease of Birstall to 'our cousin' the duke of Lancaster; ibid., p. 237, 21 February 1396: the abbot of Kirkstall appointed his proctors.

English clergy had offered 700 marks or 2,800 francs d'or for the purchase of tithes of lay fee in France and the Norman canons 'mènent une vie malheureuse et se voient enlever journellement par les Anglais leur pain, leur cervoise et leur viande'.[1] This was in 1371. The priory fell into arrears with its royal farm and the abbot of Barlings took the custody for a while. Later it was in the hands of royal clerks until the prior was restored in 1387.[2] Perhaps would-be purchasers having seen the priory's condition were less anxious to buy; perhaps the settlement of a new fellow with the prior in 1374[3] made the canons less willing to sell. Not until 1396 did the canons actually dispose of it, to the abbey of Hulton.[4] In this case they may have received the money for the priory, for in 1411 Charles VI allowed them to buy 60 livres of rente in mortmain and to spend more on repairs to the abbey and to buy ornaments and jewels 'pour l'église qui en était moult denuée'.[5]

These sales to laymen and religious are significant, but not numerous; only the expulsion of 1378 had weakened the monks; they were not in general inclined to abject surrender, as many of the terms of sale prove. Why were the monks expelled? The excuses of the government, to the admittedly anti-French Roman papacy, blamed the monks for disloyalty, but no evidence for this was ever produced. Mrs. Chibnall in 1942 suggested that popular discontent with the conduct of the war produced an anti-French feeling that was irrational and needed no evidence to justify it.[6] Professor Perroy has shown how the schism, which broke out after the expulsion, influenced events.[7] These factors are, however, less important

---

[1] Manche H 183: from the *Inventaire-Sommaire*.

[2] *C.F.R. 1369–77*, pp. 16, 75, 249; *C.F.R. 1377–83*, p. 30; *C.F.R. 1383–91*, p. 209; *C.F.R. 1391–9*, p. 137; *C.P.R. 1381–5*, p. 357; *C.P.R. 1385–9*, p. 314.

[3] *C.F.R. 1369–77*, p. 249.

[4] *C.P.R. 1391–6*, p. 579.

[5] Manche H 183, from *Inventaire-Sommaire*.

[6] M. Chibnall, 'The Suppression of the Alien Priories', Historical Revision XCIX, *History*, xxvi (1942), 204–12.

[7] E. Perroy, *L'Angleterre et le Grand Schisme d'Occident*, pp. 392–401: 'prefati monachi Gallici venientes ad regnum pro libito et deinde ad propria redeuntes archana regni detegant et quamplures prodiciones faciant continue in maximum regni periculum prout cotidiana experiencia manifestat'. *C.Pap.L.* iv. 283. Four monks of Saint-Pierre-sur-Dives renounced Benedict XIII in 1395, and one of them, John Roger, gave his allegiance to Boniface IX on becoming prior of Modbury: Eton

than the fact that the demand for expulsion was made
not to Edward III but to the council that governed in the
name of a minor. The council was not interested in royal
profits from aliens or royal protection of a privileged group,
but in the profits that they and their friends (Devereux was
a member of the council) could make by their own direct
exploitation of the property.[1]

ii. *The Suppression*

Richard II's pro-French policy affected the alien priories
for two reasons. First, it marks the reassertion of royal
power as against the aristocracy, and therefore a reaction
against lay farmers of alien property; second, Richard's
father-in-law, Charles VI, asked for, and received, certain
concessions in favour of the alien monks. The royal abbeys
of Saint-Denis and Fécamp were allowed half their traditional English revenues: 'non contestans les causes que
l'on pourroit alléguer et a esté en partie allégué'.[2] Richard
went even further and admitted a French prior at Monks
Sherborne, to please Charles VI, in spite of Wykeham's
doubts.[3] What is more difficult to explain is Henry IV's
rescission of the order of expulsion and the granting of
priories to the priors' custodies, which the king ordered
immediately after his coronation.[4] Although Henry did not
persist in this course, the step probably marks a desire on his
part to recover the royal monopoly of taxing the aliens and
the full exercise of royal power as under Edward III in his
heyday.

For the moment at least some monks enjoyed a respite
under the new government. Particularly the so-called conventual priories began to recover and to assume a separate
existence from other aliens. The commons exempted them
from its call for a resumption of alien lands in February

College, Modbury Charters, nos. 43, 44. The schism did not break out until after
the aliens' expulsion.

[1] Wycliffe used the example of alien priories to show what power the secular ruler
already exercised over the church: *De ecclesia*, p. 332; *De eucharistia*, p. 320; *De
blasphemia*, p. 156.

[2] *C.Cl.R. 1396–9*, p. 370; *C.P.R., 1396–9*, pp. 148, 322.

[3] *C.P.R. 1392–6*, pp. 625, 632.

[4] *C.P.R. 1399–1401*, pp. 70–72: 13 November 1399: this restoration affected the
priories granted to Mountgrace priory in May 1399, but not those that had been sold.

1401[1] and the king allowed them their full revenues, reserving only the apport they had paid to France.[2] Although conventual priors had been allowed to live in England after 1378, these were the first signs that the conventual character of the priories was considered.

Nevertheless other priories also benefited and there were probably many monks coming into England in Henry IV's early years, to resume their old manner of life. The bishop of Lincoln admitted a new prior of Coggs in April 1402, when he was sent over by the abbot of Fécamp,[3] and William Heberd, a monk of Saint-Evroul, recovered possession of the priory of Ware from the Carthusians who claimed the priory, unsuccessfully, from Henry IV:[4] the king gave them a pension of £100 as compensation.[5] A later prior of Ware, Nicholaus Champyny, even received a fellow from Saint-Evroul in 1410,[6] but by this date the only mention of the arrival of other monks is in connexion with 'conventual' priories, like Cowick[7] and Tutbury.[8] It may be presumed that the Norman monks took advantage of the king's benevolence to come to England, but the extent of immigration is unknown.

By the autumn of 1402 Henry's early popularity had waned and the commons had become restive. He was unsuccessful and in financial difficulties, but the commons cannot have renewed their demands for the seizure of alien lands and the expulsion of the monks in order to help the king's exchequer, because their chief concern was that lay occupiers should lose nothing by such an ordinance: 'purveux et sauvez tout foitz que toutz ceux de voz lieges quelx ount Estate per grante relesse ratification ac confirmation de ceux de par delea ou par faitz a autres que estate ils ount des terres tenementz ou possessions des aliens avantz ditz per

---

[1] *Rot. Parlt.* iii. 457: 'purveuz toutes foiz que les priories aliens conventuelx demourgent en leur estat et liberte solonc les grantes de notre dit seigneur le Roi ...'.

[2] Ibid., p. 469a, par. 56: before November 1401.

[3] *C.P.R. 1401–5*, p. 87; Seine-Maritime 7 H 57: 19 April 1402.

[4] P.R.O. S.C. 8, file 128, no. 6368.

[5] *C.P.R. 1399–1401*, p. 532: 16 July 1401: the history of this pension is obscure. In 1415 the Carthusians of Shene who received Ware had to pay the £100 to Mountgrace. See below, p. 127.

[6] *C.P.R. 1408–13*, p. 157: 5 February 1410.

[7] Ibid., p. 193: 28 April 1410.   [8] P.R.O. C 81, 649/6647: Privy Seal.

purchase en fee ou pur terme de vie ou pur terme des ans . . .
ne soient mye oustez de lour droitz terres tenementz ou
possessions par cest Estatut'.[1] Whether Henry approved the
proposal because he thought that he might make more
money out of the priories by this means or because he could
not resist the appropriators' pressure any longer is not clear.
Once again conventual priories were excepted[2] and the royal
council appointed a commission to examine what houses
could claim exemption for this reason: *ceux qui vuillent entrer
en traitie* were asked to appear before the treasurer; *les autres
qui ne veullent treter* were to show their charters or other evidence direct to the council.[3] Local inquiries may also have
been made.[4] The parliament that met a year later, after Hot-
spur's rebellion, made the order of expulsion more precise:
all conventual priors and priors who had *institution et induction*,
the prior of Ogbourne and the bailiff of Warminghurst (to
whom this clause did not apply) and French-born monks who
were blind and old *q'ils ne purront travailler* were exempted
'par ainsi q'ils soient Catholiks et q'ils facent seuretee q'ils ne
discoeveront ne ferront discoevrer le conseil et les secretes
du Roialme'.[5]

The history of alien priories after the parliament of January 1404 is a mosaic of case histories. The aliens do not re-
appear in the records in numbers; the very date of their
expulsion, if it resembled that of 1378, is unknown. What
is certain is that the lay farmers loom larger than ever in
the affairs of every house. At Frampton, the clerk, Nicholas
Bubbewyth, and the prior, Ralph de Nubibus, accepted the
farm for £83. 6s. 8d. in February 1403;[6] in July, presumably
after the inquiry, the prior took sole charge, without payments, because his priory was conventual.[7] If this were the
case, the prior had nothing to fear from parliament's decision
in 1404, yet in March 1404 the priory was entrusted to the
king's son John, later duke of Bedford, and the clerk,

[1] *Rot. Parlt.* iii. 499, no. 11: September 1402.   [2] *Rot. Parlt.* iii. 491, no. 23.
[3] *Proceedings of the Privy Council*, i. 190–9: January 1403.
[4] *C.Cl.R. 1402–5*, p. 25.
[5] *Rot. Parlt.* iii. 529. The bailiff of Warminghurst had made a ship for his own
use from local timber; this was confiscated because of the war, *C.P.R. 1391–1401*,
p. 398.   [6] *C.F.R. 1399–1405*, p. 199: 4 February 1403.
[7] *C.P.R. 1401–5*, p. 88: 3 July 1403.

Thomas Langley, later bishop of Durham, at £93. 6s. 8d.,[1] a farm £10 more than that of 1403. The prior is never heard of again. In effect the monks lost control of the priory, conventual or not, between the summer of 1403 and the spring of 1404, and the extra £10 may represent the increased value of the priory once the monks had left. Similarly the priors of Panfield and Well[2] Hall and Loders[3] last occur in the records at the beginning of 1403.[4] It is almost certain that a second expulsion of monks about this time dissolved the barely revived alien priories.

After providing for his son and queen Henry was allowed by parliament to appropriate alien revenues for household expenses,[5] but the commons were not satisfied with the effective disappearance of the monks: they wanted legal guarantees that peace would not restore the monks to their lands. Their proposal was not really calculated to help the king, but to perpetuate the position of those who enjoyed possession. The chancellor was asked to give 'chescune de vos lieges que voudrait purchacer des ditz manoirs' licence to bargain with the monks for the purchase of them for life, for a period of years or in fee for ever, and the king would obtain 'une resonable fine apres un tiel purchase fait pur la confirmatione d'icelle a vous a faire et a paier come purra estre accordez par entre votre Chaunceller et voz ditz lieges' and also feudal dues: 'Et adonques notre dit Seigneur le Roi avera Gardes, Mariages Fynes pur alienations et plusours diverses autres profitz des ditz manoirs'.[6] The motive of this petition is related more to the wishes of occupiers of alien lands than to concern for the king's financial embarrassment.

One of these occupiers was the king's own brother-in-law, Sir John Cornewaile. In 1403, when the inquiry into conventual status had already begun, Cornewaile with the

---

[1] *C.F.R. 1399–1405*, p. 250: 2 March 1404. See M. Chibnall, *The English Lands of the Abbey of Bec*, p. 128, for other grants to the duke of Bedford.

[2] *C.F.R. 1399–1405*, p. 195: the prior John Moryn last appears 4 February 1403. William Bourgchier and his wife Anne, countess of Stafford, accepted the farm in 1409, not for £43. 6s. 8d. like Moryn, but for £55 and £56: *C.F.R. 1405–13*, pp. 148, 152, 177.   [3] *C.F.R. 1399–1405*, p. 194: 28 January 1403.

[4] *C.P.R. 1401–5*, p. 454: 12 February 1405; *C.P.R. 1408–13*, p. 86: 1 July 1409.

[5] *Rot. Parlt.* iii. 586; *C.P.R. 1408–13*, p. 459; *C.P.R. 1416–22*, p. 40.

[6] *Rot. Parlt.* iii. 617: 1408: conventual priories were not to be affected.

monks' bailiff secured the joint farm of all Fécamp's English lands.[1] This was a revival of the system prevailing under Richard II which gave the laymen control over the priory while they appeared to share the privilege with a monk. When parliament approved the spending of alien revenues for the household, Cornewaile was excused all rent from the property.[2] The bailiff died in April 1409[3] and Cornewaile wrote and urged the abbot of Fécamp to lease his lands to him for 100 or 120 years, 'vous donnant une certaine somme de monoie come nous pourions acorder'. Cornewaile was eager for the lease and had already written once to the abbot without receiving a reply. He advised the abbot to settle for a sum of money rather than to 'les lesser en le manere come il est maintenant, qar durant nos vies nous sumez surez assys', but the abbot had no intention of accepting the intolerable alternatives Cornewaile proposed.

A little later in the same year the lieutenant of the Tower of London, Richard Newport, negotiated with the monks of Lire for the church of Newchurch, in the Isle of Wight, which he wished to give to the 'collegiate church of Beaulieu in the New Forest'. He offered £500 for the purchase of a pension of £50 a year in France or in the *pais Boulonais* or elsewhere and also to pay the *amortissement* fine to the king of France, but the monks of Lire believed him influential and asked services of him, as well as money. He had to promise to have the monks' proctors instituted in the priories of Carisbrooke, Liver's Ocle, and Hinckley *qui étoit déjà en mains séculières* where they should once more pay the king's farm during the war; to aid and succour the monks *en leurs lieux et hotels*; to pay the king's *droit de douane ou de sortie* so that monks of Lire still in England could bring out with them gold, silver, fabrics, jewels, or indeed anything except armaments; to provide expenses for monks sent from Normandy and safe-conducts from Boulogne to Calais and from

[1] *C.P.R. 1401–5*, pp. 205, 240; Cornewaile's influence may have obtained for the abbey's agent the exemption from the order of expulsion: see above, p. 110.

[2] *C.Cl.R. 1402–9*, p. 343; *C.P.R. 1401–5*, p. 396; *Rot. Parlt.* iii. 528, 550.

[3] Appendix V: Cornewaile was to have fought *à outrance* with the steward of Hainault, Jean de Werchin, on 1 June 1409, before the duke of Burgundy. This would explain why he wrote to the abbot from Lille on 2 June. In fact the tournament was summoned to Paris by Charles VI for 19 June.

Calais to England, and back; and finally to send to Normandy the proctor of the priory of Carisbrooke, Odo des Ormes, with a safe-conduct from Calais to Boulogne.[1] Newport cannot have seriously expected that he could perform these services for the monks, but the weakness of the monks in England and their need of powerful assistance are easily perceived in this pathetic bid for help.[2]

In 1411 the duke of York founded the collegiate church of Fotheringhay[3] and five or six monks of Cormeilles and Boscherville with servants and horses came quickly to England[4] to see what they could obtain from the duke for their lands, which had been granted to him for the foundation. Once more property was passing to the religious and the aliens lost hope of its ultimate recovery. It is not known if they did get something from the duke.

In spite of the fact that many monks had left England and had lost control of their property, the commons of Henry V's first parliament were not satisfied that the statute of 1404 was being properly enforced. To this the king replied that 'le Roy le veut sauvant a luy sa prerogatif et q'il purra dispenser ovesq ceuz quex luy plerra'.[5] The commons also asked for strict enforcement of the ordinance of Richard's reign, depriving aliens of English benefices; some Frenchmen had bought letters patent *d'estre Denizeins et lieges du Roy*, whereby 'les Aliens Fraunceys sont encrescez en arrerisement des lieges du Roy' and treasure and secrets of the realm carried to the king's enemies. Once again the king accepted the petition, except in so far as it might affect conventual priories and priors having institution and induction,

---

[1] Eure H 590, chapter 97, no. 102: 25 October 1409. The bailiff of Boulogne obliged himself to execute these orders: 6 November; Henry Beaufort confirmed the grant to Beaulieu: ibid., no. 49; Henry IV received £20 from his kinswoman the Countess Lucy for allowing it: ibid., no. 11. *C.P.R. 1408–13*, pp. 80, 266. Arreton church, formerly part of the priory of Carisbrooke, was annexed to Quarr abbey *in proprios usus* in 1405: R. Worsley, *Isle of Wight*, Appendix 78. The priory was being dismembered. Odo des Ormes did not return to Normandy but was allowed to end his days in England: *C.P.R. 1416–22*, p. 66: 11 November 1417; P.R.O. C 81, 665/794: Privy Seal.

[2] A new prioress of Lyminster was admitted this year, presumably because the priory was conventual: *Chichester Registers: Reade*, i. 38.

[3] *Rot. Parlt.* iii. 652–5, no. 18.

[4] P.R.O. C 76, no. 95, m. 15: 23 May 1412.

[5] *Rot. Parlt.* iv. 5: May 1413.

because they were 'Catholiks' and had given surety.[1] Since the petitioners could not move the king by playing on his fears of the French, they made their position quite clear by asking that all alien priories, conventual or not, should be resumed into the king's hand from Michaelmas 1413 'en reliefment et supportation de la communes'. The only exceptions were to be those priories already purchased or 'a purchasers de ceux de les soveraignes measons de par de la par les lieges nostre seigneur le Roy si bien spirituelx come temporelx' by the licences of the kings since Edward III 'en heritement ou a terme de vie ou a terme d'ans ou en perpetuel almoigne et durant les guerres'. The conclusion of the petition is concerned only with the farmers. After Michaelmas 'null fermer des ditz Priories serra ouste des ditz Priories ne de les Terres et Tenements as ditz Priories regardauntz saunz resonable garnisement. Et qe les fermers des ditz Priories soient preferrez pur les avoir a ferme devaunt autres paiant ataunt pur icelles comes autres vorroient paier. Et qe apres les ditz fermers eient covenable jour et temps pur encarier emporter et amener lour bien et chateux vifs et mortz ou lour plerra hors de les priories avauntz ditz ou des les possessions d'icelles.'[2] There could be no more revealing picture than this, of how the laity had taken possession of alien property in their capacity as farmers. It is not clear whether the farmers hoped to continue their farming even at increased rates; certainly the petitioners make no other proposals as to what the king should do with the lands when he resumed them for himself. In fact the king accepted the petition, but exempted conventual priories. Legally this order should have made little difference, for apart from those protected by royal prerogative, only conventual priories were left in England by this time. Perhaps Henry V intended not to allow any exceptions in the future; perhaps he aimed only at placating the commons. All past purchases of property were confirmed, but the king passed over in silence the purchases about to be made.[3] In August 1413 the order was acted

---

[1] *Rot. Parlt.* iv. 11: no. XIII, par. 32. See S. L. Thrupp, 'Survey of Alien Population', for the fear of aliens at this time.   [2] *Rot. Parlt.* iv. 13–15, no. XX, par. 38.
[3] Ibid., p. 15. When the denizens died, Englishmen were to replace them.

upon and all farmers were required to treat with the king, if they wished to continue in their offices after Michaelmas.[1] As a result of these measures the aliens had for the most part been expelled, and the lands of all but conventual priories taken into the king's hand as a preliminary to general lay farming.

All that remained to be done was to make the aliens' dissolution permanent. The parliament of Leicester in 1414 reminded the king that the English had been disinherited in France, and declared that even if peace were made to mutual satisfaction and the king recovered his French lands, he would be ill-advised to hand back alien property in England to the monks. The king was to remember what damage would be caused by the payment of money abroad 'par les graundes fermes et apportz ed monoye quel d'an en an toutz jours apres serroient renduz de memes les possessions a les chiefs maisons'. He was therefore advised to take the religious' lands himself, except those of conventual priories and of priors with institution and induction, those given to Fotheringhay and those purchased or to be purchased by Englishmen. Englishmen were to take the monks' place for divine service.[2] The remedy does not state that this resumption was different in kind from that recommended by the previous parliament, but the preamble makes it clear that this measure was intended to be a permanent disappropriation of the monks, and the dissolution of the alien priories is commonly attributed to this parliament.

The implementation of the last provision of the petition was immediate. The king founded the Carthusian priory of Shene on 25 September 1414, by giving the monks the reversion of the lands of Fécamp (then enjoyed by Sir John Cornewaile), which they had licence to acquire from the Normans and the lands of St. Peter's, Ghent, at Lewisham.[3] The following April the property of Saint-Evroul, Jumièges, and Lire (except Hinckley priory) was added to the endowment and the Carthusians were required to pay £100 a year to Mountgrace as compensation to them for the loss of Ware priory, and given licence to negotiate with the Normans.[4]

[1] *C.P.R. 1413–19*, p. 31: 26 August 1413.
[2] *Rot. Parlt.* iv. 22, petition IX: 26 June 1414.
[3] *C.Ch.R. 1341–1417*, pp. 469–70; *M.A.* i. 973–7.
[4] *C.Ch.R. 1341–1417*, pp. 479–80: 1 April 1415.

A month earlier a house for Brigittine nuns had been founded at Syon with the reversion of the lands of the abbeys of Séez, Mont Saint-Michel, La Trinité, Caen, and Fécamp.[1] The cathedral chapter of Chichester acquired the lands of its former canon, the prior of Wilmington.[2] These clergy did not actually enjoy possession of the lands, and were expected to acquire further, unspecified, rights to them from the Normans, but it is not certain that the king wanted the Normans to be compensated in this way for the surrender of their rights. Permission for negotiation was given, but the Normans had nothing to negotiate except legal rights, for which the new owners would not offer much.[3] The Norman monks certainly expected compensation, at least, for the loss of their property, but it is possible that they asked more than the English would pay. Henry IV had given the nuns minoresses of Aldgate Montebourg's priory of Appuldurcombe in 1399, and the Normans had royal permission to sell the priory,[4] but in 1429 the nuns were still trying to conclude a sale:[5] it was the Normans who were unwilling—presumably because they expected too much. Jumièges sent a new 'prior' to England when their expectations of compensation from Shene for the loss of Hayling priory were deceived:[6] here perhaps the Carthusians refused to bargain. Nevertheless, if the far from impartial abbot of Lire be believed, the Carthusians had been offered £400 a year by the king if they lost their revenues,[7] which can only refer to the possibility that the Normans might recover possession, or refuse to sign away their rights. The evidence is too scanty for generalization.

[1] *M.A.* ii. 360–2: 3 March 1415: Fécamp's lands reverted to Shene.
[2] *Rot. Parlt.* iv. 43.
[3] For permission to negotiate in Normandy see *C.P.R. 1413–16*, pp. 165, 257; and *Rot. Parlt.* iv. 43 and below, p. 133, n. 4.
[4] *C.P.R. 1399–1401*, p. 34. Other sales of this period which may have involved handing over money were Bourne abbey's purchase of Wilsford priory from Bec: *C.Pap.L.* v. 432; *C.P.R. 1399–1401*, p. 455; and Beauvale abbey's purchase of Bonby priory from Saint-Fromond: *C.P.R. 1401–5*, p. 217; P.R.O. Ancient Deeds B 480.
[5] *C.P.R. 1422–9*, p. 504; Edward IV confirmed it to them in mortmain: *C.P.R. 1461–7*, p. 88.   [6] *Histoire de Jumièges*, ed. J. Loth, ii. 215.
[7] Eure H 590, chapter 97, no. 103: 24 July 1417. According to *Gallia Christiana XI*, 648, the abbot did receive some of his temporalities when he did homage to Henry V in 1419.

Only in one case did the Normans certainly receive something for their surrender of their claims. The priory of West Mersea had been recovered by Saint-Ouen after 1399, and almost immediately farmed to Henry, bishop of Annaghdown, John Doreward and his wife Isabel for life. The most interesting provision of the lease was that the lessees 'infra tres annos concedunt facere rotulum novum in quo continebuntur nomina et cognomina tenentium ad dictum manerium sive prioratum spectantium in quo rotulo continebitur etiam summa pecuniarum et modus serviciorum pro singulis tenentium debitis et copiam de rotulo predicto in lingua latina infra quinque annos a data predicta . . . dandos eisdem abbati et conventui deliberabunt seu deliberare facient'.[1] Thus the monks looked forward to the day when they should once more take up direct administration of the priory. The bishop and his fellow occupiers were excused payment of the king's farm in 1401[2] and not surprisingly Doreward could show evidence of what amounted to 'purchase' in 1403.[3] In 1420, however, Archbishop Chichele and his brother William bought the property outright from the monks for their collegiate foundation at Higham Ferrers. The abbey had loaned its plate to the city of Rouen during Henry V's siege and was in desperate need of cash. Chichele offered them 5,000 francs: 'in relevationem necessitatum et ad convertendum in utilitatem eorundem', 3,500 francs; 'pro vestiario et aliis necessariis suis', 1,000 francs; and for the repair of the ruined cloister and making a stained-glass window, 500 francs. In the window 'ponentur duae imagines honestae una viz. de sancto Thoma dudum Cantuariensi Archiepiscopo et alia de dicto Henrico Archiepiscopo ante eum genuflectente ambae pontificalibus indutae'. Chichele received all the monks' deeds for the property and promised to send a copy of the papal bull 'super alienationibus prioratuum et possessionum alienigenarum in Anglia' and a copy of the royal statute of confiscation to the abbot within a

[1] C.P.R. 1399–1401, p. 308: 27 June 1401: royal approval of agreement dated 20 June 1400. Henry V inspected this in 1421: Seine-Maritime 14 H 910 = P.R.O. 31/8/140 A, no. 225. The bishop had previously farmed Ellingham priory: C.F.R. 1399–1405, p. 224.
[2] C.P.R. 1399–1401, p. 480: 28 March 1401.
[3] Proceedings of the Privy Council, i. 199: 25 January 1403.

year.¹ As soon as Chichele had bought out the surviving Isabel Doreward, then a widow,² he granted the priory to his college.³ If this sale brought the monks real advantages, it was probably exceptional.⁴

Most monks were not fortunate enough to find someone like Chichele and were reduced to making petitions to the king, the Carthusians, and the councils of the church. One of the earliest was presented by monks of Fécamp to the bishop of Norwich, presumably Richard Courtenay, who went on an embassy to France after May 1414. (He died in September 1415.) The monks do not mention the king's grant of their lands to his new foundation at Shene, but this does not help to date the document for even in later petitions the monks avoided mentioning it. All they ask in this case is permission to draw half their English revenues as granted by Richard II and confirmed by *illustrissimo rege Henrico ultimo*. The monks pleaded their long association with the kings of England, since the Confessor, who had given them *libertates pulcherrimas atque franchisias* for which the monks never ceased 'a missis orationibus ac devotionibus quas pro suffragiis animarum suarum predicti reges perpetuo celebrandas ordinarunt'. The monks asked for complete restoration *cum pristina libertate gubernandi*.⁵

Probably in the summer of 1416 the same monks sent to England an agent 'qui ira a saint thomas en Angleterre', thus posing as a pilgrim, to gather information and money. He was to find out 'qui a eu les lettres tiltres et autres choses

¹ F. Pommeraye, *Histoire de St. Ouen*, pp. 486–8; *C.P.R. 1416–22*, p. 441, P.R.O. 31/8/140 A, no. 325. Pommeraye, op. cit., p. 317, thought that there were two records of this, but he misunderstood a grant of the priory at farm made to William, bishop of London, in 1202: *C.D.F.* 104-6. Pommeraye has a story, op. cit., p. 317, that the abbot of Saint-Ouen fell foul of the archbishop of Rouen over this sale, but no records now substantiate it.

² B.M. Stowe MS. 931, f. 10: she surrendered her life interest for 100 marks a year, July 1423. She had remarried after Doreward's death: *C.Cl.R. 1422–9*, p. 294.

³ Ibid., p. 300; *C.P.R. 1422–9*, pp. 472–4.

⁴ There formerly existed in the Cottonian collection 'copia alienationis factae per abbatissam monasterii S. Trinitatis de Cadamo in Normannia de terris suis in Angliae partibus cum chartis de avisamento justiciariorum de terris alienatis per eandem cum formulis aliarum chartarum de aliis alienationibus': T. Smith, *Catalogue of the Cottonian Library* (1696), sub Tiberius VII, f. 9. This alienation could have been such a sale: *C.P.R. 1413–16*, pp. 165, 257.

⁵ Seine-Maritime 7 H 57: it is followed by Richard II's grant of 21 April 1398, inspected and confirmed by Henry IV: 17 November 1400.

qui avoit le bailli de Wermingueust et auxi qui a eu tous ses biens et quils sont devenus'. By judicious inquiry from a man of Winchelsea, unnamed friends at Canterbury, and a gentleman in London, the agent was to discover 'sil est nulle maniere que on peut ravoir les terres que leglise a en Angleterre, soit par supplication devers le roy, ou par quelle autre maniere'. He was particularly to sound the English clergy about a proposal to appoint papal 'guardians' and whether 'ceux de par dela obeiroient point aux conservatoires que le pappe donrroit'. Finally the man was to ask the parson of Rye for 13 marks of silver, which he owed to the monastery every year: why this rent only was singled out is not explained.[1]

The foundation of the priory of Shene gave all the monks of Normandy a more tangible enemy and the Carthusians remained the object of Benedictine attack well into the century. Michael, abbot of Saint-Evroul, composed an ironical letter to Shene in October 1416, congratulating the monks on their foundation but asking them to consider carefully whether they would not pay, later, when they appeared before the eternal judge, for enjoying the rights of others. He reminded them of the maxim: 'nolite igitur in proximis committere quod in vobis non velletis admittere.' The papacy could not justify them, because it was effectively vacant; the king had no greater right to take away from the Normans than his predecessors had to give: how then could he defend his action? As to arguments drawn from the war, Michael dismisses them: 'nec quod nostrum est a nobis aufert, aut alteri tradit bellorum frequentia, quoniam a bellis excipimur, pacem poscimus pacem colimus odia dissidia bellorumque strages nescimus; sicut omni culpa belli caremus sic propter bella jure nostro privari non possumus.' Nor is distance an obstacle to the enjoyment of lands: 'nec obest terrarum distancia cum in longe distancioribus terris ex opibus regni possit susteneri religio.' The loss of his revenues caused the abbot to bewail the reduction of his community by half: 'xl

---

[1] Appendix VI: the reference to the pope is a little disconcerting: John XXIII had been deposed 29 May 1415; Gregory XII resigned 4 July 1415; only Benedict XIII, equally unacceptable in Normandy and England, was pope in 1416. Martin V was elected 11 November 1417.

Deo psallentes habebat, vix retinet xx religiosos'.[1] Not many stages of the Normans' campaign against Shene are known, but Michael's arguments were no doubt repeated wherever they presented their case. The abbot of Lire claimed in July 1417 that the monks of Ghent, Jumièges, Saint-Evroul, and others had already petitioned the assembled fathers of Constance, but nothing is known of its reception.[2]

The attitude of Martin V is also unknown, although he must have been the author of the bull authorizing the dissolution of the aliens which the abbot of Saint-Ouen asked Chichele to send him a copy of.[3] This bull may be the one formerly kept by the monks of Saint-Evroul in their English folder of documents.[4] Its contents have not been transmitted even in summary and it is possible that no bull frankly dissolving the priories was ever issued. Henry V would not have tolerated Martin's interference on the aliens' behalf and the most that Martin may have done was to order an inquiry to assess the value of the property as a prelude to the payment of some realistic compensation. John, bishop of Chichester, presided over an inquiry at Warminghurst into the value of Fécamp's property, apparently acting under instructions from Martin.[5] This John Kemp, bishop of Chichester, was chancellor of Normandy in 1421, before whom six monks were appointed to act at the inquiry: 'pro componendo de ecclesiis grangiis decimis terris et possessionibus que monasteria ecclesie atque conventus francie et normannie . . . pretendunt habere in regno anglie atque ipsos rationabiliter et debite recompensari.'[6]

There was a flurry of activity in 1421 due to the different attitude of Henry V to the monks after the treaty of Troyes.

---

[1] E. Martène, *Thesaurus Anecdotarum*, i. 1746–8: 27 October 1416 = *Annales Ordinis Cartusiensis*, ed. C. Le Couteulx, vii. 416–18: 'Epistola ad Shenenses scripta cum aliis documentis hoc negotium tangentibus a R. P. Hyppolito Gemeticensis Abbatiae procuratore congregationis S. Mauri olim perhumaniter nobis communicata sunt cujus epistolae apographum hic subjicimus.'

[2] Eure H 590, chapter 97, no. 103: 24 July 1417.   [3] See above, p. 129.

[4] Orne H 555, p. 2: 'Inventaire du chartrier de l'abbaye de Saint-Evroul' written in 1791. The bull of Martin V was kept with letters of the earls of Leicester and bishops of Lincoln, and therefore presumably concerned England.

[5] Seine-Maritime 7 H 57: the inquiry was to be made 5 July 1421.

[6] Seine-Maritime 7 H 57: 16 March 1421. The monks of Fécamp were also ill-used by the English in Normandy: P.R.O. 31/8/140 A, no. 235: 10 October 1421.

Henceforward he had French as well as English subjects, and even if he had no intention of restoring the priories to their former owners,[1] he might have planned some gesture, like compensation, to soothe the monks. The abbot of Caen reminded him of his glorious forebear, William the Conqueror, the abbey's founder, and asked for restoration of his lands, probably at this triumphant stage in the king's career: 'faire recevoir ung de vos dis religieux au gouvernement dudit manoir de Frantonne avecques ses dependances qui puisse jouir et vivre de lespirituel en la fourme que le dit Fratre Raoul faisoit; jusquesaceque au regard du temporel soit par vous ordonne et ce leur vieulles ottroier et ils priront dieu de mieux en mieux pour votre royal maieste et votre noble conseil'.[2] Whatever the king's reaction to such petitions may have been he ordered all holders of alien churches and property to produce evidence of their titles in October 1420[3] because final peace had been made with France and Edward III's order of 1369, taking the aliens' lands into custody, was therefore at last obsolete. Thus the king simply ignored the developments of the period since 1378, including the Statute of Leicester which had officially dissolved the alien priories, and reopened the whole question by reverting to the position of 1369.

There is no contemporary evidence of what the government tried to do in these months before Henry's sudden death, but later Henry VI's government summoned the abbot of Bourne to show by what right he continued to enjoy the manor of Wilsford, formerly part of Bec's endowment, after the treaty of Troyes, since he held it by a grant of June 1419 *durante guerra* and ought therefore to have surrendered it in peace-time under the terms of the statute of Leicester.[4] This curious incident shows only that a

---

[1] *Histoire de Jumièges*, ed. J. Loth, ii. 166: Henry V is said to have confirmed the abbey's privileges, and to have declared his formal intention not to restore their rights in England. For a similar pronouncement by Henry VI, see A. Du Moustier, *Neustria Pia*, p. 427.

[2] Calvados H 1884; Appendix VIII. For Frampton see above, pp. 122–3. After Bedford's death in 1435, the priory passed to St. Stephen's, Westminster, provided that the farm was still paid: *C.F.R. 1430–7*, p. 335; *C.P.R. 1436–41*, p. 125; *C.P.R. 1461–7*, p. 163.   [3] Rymer, x. 26; *C.Cl.R. 1419–22*, p. 129.

[4] P.R.O. E 135/22/90. The abbot produced letters of Henry IV confirming the grant of Richard II to Thomas Holland, earl of Kent, of property worth 20 marks

memory of Henry V's realization that peace changed the position of the aliens lingered on after his death. It must have been Henry V who insisted on it. Whether he himself intended it or not, his order that all holders of alien property should produce evidence of title encouraged the Norman monks to hope for complete recovery. In March 1421 the prior of Sainte-Barbe-en-Auge and his community agreed to delegate to certain Norman abbots the task of negotiating with the king for this purpose, and they sent a memoir to the abbots describing the priory's own dealings with Cheyne more than thirty years before, insisting that the community had been cheated.[1] Most of these abbots met a few weeks later[2] in Rouen, where they discussed what should be done, and finally decided to send two of their number to England to see Henry and his parliament. In order to cover their expenses urgent letters were sent out to all Norman houses inviting contributions as soon as possible, at all events within a fortnight. The letter[3] is important for showing that the abbots had originally come together at the king's request, and also that they believed the parliament, summoned to meet in May 1421, would make decisions favourable to them.

Henry V's early death put an end to the hopes that he seems to have inspired in his years of victory. In the short interval between the abbots' meeting and Henry's death no general change in the monks' fortunes had been effected.[4] The abbot of Saint-Evroul, at least, was a Norman un-satisfied: in 1426 he went to Rome and appealed to the cardinal bishop of Piacenza, Branda de Castiglione,[5] for

a year during the war, and which Kent had given to Bourne, on condition that the community paid Bec 5 marks a year pension. The abbot told the king in 1444 that he had had to make many laborious journeys to Normandy for the purpose of bargaining with the monks for a permanent surrender.

[1] Appendix VIIA: Calvados 2 D 170: 10 March 1420/1. Henry is described as Regent and Heir of the kingdom of France, so that it must be later than the treaty of Troyes.

[2] They probably met in April if they anticipated going to England for the parliament of 2 May. Henry V was in England from 3 February to 10 June 1421.

[3] Appendix VIIB: Orne H 898.   [4] For Fécamp see above, p. 132.

[5] After the treaty of Troyes he received the administration of the diocese of Lisieux and only surrendered it when his own nephew Zano became bishop in 1425. Zano was translated to Bayeux in 1432, and remained influential in English councils till Charles VII occupied Normandy. The death of the cardinal was reported to England by the chapter of Bayeux: Bayeux Chapter MS. 5, f. 17.

justice. The latter caused his junior colleague, the Carthusian
Nicholas de Albergatis, to examine the abbot's case, and,
surprisingly, the Cardinal Carthusian accepted it and wrote
urging his brethren at Shene to surrender their ill-gotten
gains: 'ut praefato Reverendo Patri Domino Abbati sine
contentione et lite dignaremini restituere bona sui monasterii quae non jure de facto videmini occupare licet regia
auctoritate et manu quasi militari dicta occupare defenda-
mini'.[1] Needless to say they ignored his letter. The matter
did not rest there, however, for Bekynton found it necessary
to brief the English representatives to the council of Basel
about what to say if the dissolution of the priories was discussed there. According to the apologia he outlined, the
aliens had failed to fulfil the conditions of their foundation
in war-time, Martin V had blessed the new monasteries (not
dissolved the old), and what is most interesting, if true, the
monks had themselves refused compensation when it was
offered by Henry V: 'Henricus quintus dictorum monasteriorum et ecclesiarum alienigenarum praelatis coram
praedictis judicibus ad hoc legitime citatis et vocatis recom-
pensam congruam juxta vim formam et effectum dictarum
literarum apostolicarum obtulit et fecit offerri'.[2] Although
this is not as surprising as it may appear at first sight, for
the monks constantly held out for restitution, not compensation, it would be unwise to take Bekynton's word as it stands.
At all events the monks of Ghent, the first to receive an
English endowment, were amongst the last to defend it.
Their intention to raise the matter at Basel was known at
Shene in 1433[3] and the council entrusted the case to Branda
de Castiglione, since promoted from St. Clement's to Portu-
ensis. A judgement in favour of Ghent was actually pro-
nounced by James Clant, canon of Saint-Severin, Cologne,
and approved by Eugenius IV, but it was reversed by
Nicholas V in 1451.[4] With this decision the church let the
matter rest. Survival had become a matter of individual
initiative, not collective action.

[1] Le Couteulx, *Annales*, vii. 559: 31 May 1427.
[2] T. Bekyngton, *Correspondence* (Memorials of the Reign of King Henry VI, ed.
G. Williams, London, 1872), ii, letter 274, heading 6, pp. 263–5.
[3] Bodleian MS. Rawlinson D 138, ff. 123^v–4.
[4] *C.Pap.L. 1447–55*, pp. 237–8.

What is surprising is the success with which some priors combated the forces of dissolution at least in their own lifetimes. The priory of Lancaster was destined for the nuns of Syon, but they had to wait for the death of the prior in 1428 and even then to buy out the claims put forward by the archdeacon of Richmond.[1] Six years later the government summoned the (dead) prior and Sir Richard Houghton, his co-farmer, to pay the arrears of the farm owing since 1413, and although the arrears were pardoned it is interesting that the government expected one or other of the farmers to be in occupation and made no reference to the legal position of the nuns.[2] In the same year the prior of Loders, John Bellamy, last heard of in 1403, was also sued, with William Wynard, for arrears of farm since 1413, so that the government thought that he too was still in possession of his priory.[3] At Stogursey, where the conventual life of the priory was stronger, the monks certainly took the custody, so that Eton College, to whom the property was given in 1440, contrary to the provision allowing for the survival of conventual houses, had to wait until 1465 before entering into possession.[4] Similarly at Modbury new priors were appointed by the abbot of Saint-Pierre-sur-Dives both in 1422[5] and in 1430,[6] when the abbot sent three monks to Henry VI to allow the king to choose a prior for the abbey's other priory at Tutbury, which had become denizen.[7] The last prior of Modbury was not very happy in his office. He was threatened by the monks of Cowick who desired to dispossess him and he had to appeal for protection to the archbishop of Canterbury and the pope;[8] a local gentleman, Sir Philip Courtenay, wrote to him in English abruptly remind-

[1] *Rot. Parlt.* v. 552; *Formulare Anglicanum*, nos. c, cclxx.
[2] P.R.O. E 135/22/3, no. 123/3.
[3] Ibid., no. 4. Cf. above, p. 123, no. 3.
[4] *Stogursey Charters*, nos. 82, 86–87, 88–89; P.R.O. E 106/12/41: one of these monks, Robert Vyse, is styled *monachus firmarius et occupator prioratus*: 1 November 1438. [5] Eton College, Modbury Charter no. 47: 11 March 1422.
[6] Ibid., nos. 52, 350; appointed under an agreement for alternate presentations by the abbot and the patron Hugh Champernown: ibid., no. 124: 11 February 1429.
[7] This and the appeal for the restoration of the Tutbury revenues to the abbot were not successful: ibid., nos. 48, 57. All three monks eventually settled at Modbury: ibid., nos. 130–1.
[8] Eton College, Modbury Charters, nos. 59–60: 28 February 1433.

ing him that it was his duty, not the vicar's, to say mass,[1] which for some reason he was afraid to do.[2] He was sure enough of his position in 1438, however, when Queen Joanna died, to petition in English for the restoration of all the priory's revenues in excess of the ancient apport of 40s., which is what the king was legally entitled to under Henry IV's last order, the priory being conventual. The prior resented paying £22 more than the apport to which the king had no legitimate right. John Fortescue had already received a grant of the farm for seven years after the queen's death, but in deference to the prior's wishes this grant was reduced by £10 immediately and by another mark at the end of seven years.[3] Although the prior was not allowed to send money to Normandy, he sent a *tabula* made of alabaster from Poole harbour after paying the tolls in 1442[4] and he also received monks from Normandy in 1456 and 1470;[5] during his period of office receipts and accounts were kept in order.[6] The priory did not become denizen like Tutbury, Blyth, or St. Neot's, but the prior had proved that he was *institutus et indictus* and not *dativus et removibilis*[7] and was therefore covered by the terms of the statute which protected such status. The prior was only thirty when appointed and lived on at least till 1479[8] and the priory survived with him.

The legality of the position of the prior of Modbury saved his priory as Stogursey had been saved from immediate dissolution and distribution between Carthusians and Brigittines, but both fell victim to Henry VI's foundation, Eton.[9]

[1] Ibid., no. 315. [2] Ibid., no. 316.

[3] Ibid., no. 137: the prior's petition: 1438; granted in part: ibid., no. 66: 17 July 1438. The prior said that the priory was still in the king's hand although the *abbey* was faithful and obedient. Henry VI was still king of France and in effective control of Normandy at this time. Fortescue received the reversion: ibid. no. 62: 12 February 1438. Apart from the case of Wootton Wawen, discussed below, p. 138, see also M. Chibnall, *The English Lands of the Abbey of Bec*, p. 131, for a petition of the abbot of Bec in 1436, and p. 134 for a remission of farm at Cowick.

[4] Eton College, Modbury Charter, no. 133: 14 February 1442.

[5] Ibid., no. 135 and no. 79: the monk John de Musmer was allowed by his abbot to remain five years at Modbury if he were law-abiding: 18 October 1470.

[6] Ibid., nos. 271–306: Receipts; nos. 307–9: Accounts. [7] Ibid., no. 66.

[8] Exeter Registers:Lacy, i, f. 59b; for the stabilizing effect of the long priorate of William of Saint-Vaast at St. Neot's see M. Chibnall, *The English Lands of the Abbey of Bec*, p. 126–7.

[9] Eton College, Modbury Charter no. 67: 20 March 1442. See M. Chibnall, op. cit., p. 133.

Why was this? Was it that by 1440 their position looked anomalous, that the king allowed nothing to stand in the way of his wish to raise a pious memorial, that the English position in France roused a new wave of hostility to the survivors of the aliens, or only that 'the covetousness of neighbouring English abbeys' converted the surviving conventual priories, not actually protected by letters of 'naturalization', to other religious purposes during the years of Henry's own government?[1] Pembroke about this time was annexed to St. Alban's[2] and Wootton Wawen was added to King's College, Cambridge, in 1448.[3] This priory had survived till that time on the same basis as Modbury. The prior, John Severayn, had been restored to the priory in 1400[4] and was still 'prior et rector ecclesie parochialis de Waweyne Wotton' in 1431. His imminent death caused a scramble for the appointment of a successor. The abbot of Castellion nominated a monk, John de Conches, as life prior in September 1436,[5] although he was not sent until the following March.[6] Meanwhile, Sir Roland Leynthal, who claimed to have enjoyed the custody of the priory for thirty-four years,[7] insisted that the next presentation belonged to him *per liberam donationem regiam* and persuaded the bishop of Worcester to accept his candidate, William Saunders, his own chaplain, as prior.[8] The king, a little late, nominated a monk of Westminster to the priory in July,[9] but by October had been won round by Leynthal and forbade the admission of anyone but Saunders.[10] The chaplain of

---

[1] Henry VI granted all the former alien properties to the archbishop of Canterbury and others in September 1440 and notified his intention to found Eton College at about the same time. Grants were also made to King's College, Cambridge: Rymer, x. 802–3. *C.P.R. 1435–41*, pp. 454, 471, 513, 557.   [2] Knowles and Hadcock, p. 73.

[3] *C.Cl.R. 1447–54*, p. 64; *C.P.R. 1446–52*, pp. 112, 174. Leynthal received £20 for what he had lost from the priory by the king's gift of it to King's College: *C.P.R. 1441–6*, p. 103. See below, n. 7.

[4] *C.P.R. 1399–1401*, p. 170: 7 October 1400.

[5] King's College, Cambridge, II. i. S 11.

[6] Ibid. II. ii. III. S 2a. Severayn resigned his office 21 June 1427: ibid. III. S 2c. This suggests he must have been reappointed till his death.

[7] He had in fact received it for the service of a rose: 20 April 1418: *C.P.R. 1416–22*, p. 331.

[8] King's College, II. 2. III. S 2b: Leynthal's letter is dated 9 March 1437.

[9] *C.P.R. 1436–41*, p. 62: the late prior was said to have died after Easter.

[10] King's College, III. S 2d.

Wootton then invoked the priory's patron, the earl of Stafford and Perche, to oust Leynthal. The last prior had no sooner died, he wrote, than Leynthal's son came and took 'la prieure et de tous les biens et dient qui ny ara plus nulz religieux fransois mez dient qui luy mettront prestres seculiers'.[1] The next year all the ancient Toesny and Stafford charters to the priory were inspected, presumably to confirm the Staffords' position,[2] and Castellion's candidate to the priory was finally inducted by royal letters patent in May 1438.[3] The Normans, through their old patrons, had triumphed over their lay custodian. Yet within ten years the priory was surrendered to King's College. These three examples seem to prove that during the 1440's new hostility engulfed priories which had weathered all previous storms. It is true that Eton did not enter into possession until later, but for the priories' future it was fatal that a religious institution stood waiting for the death of the actual priors. In this connexion, however, it is interesting to notice that the abbess of Syon was still not in possession of all Fécamp's property 1474–6, because Robert Modo, prior of St. John, had been made parson of Steyning and still lived to enjoy it sixty years after Fécamp's property had first been given to the nuns.[4]

The Norman cause was therefore not snuffed out completely in 1414. Monks continued to come to England and even to enjoy some official recognition.

The Carthusians of Mountgrace presented a petition to Humphrey, duke of Gloucester, while still Protector, against Canon John Burdett, who had been presented to Haugh priory by the canons of Cherbourg, in defiance of the Carthusians' rights.[5] There are references to the proctors of Lire and Newent in 1423.[6] The author of the history of

---

[1] Ibid., S 62. The earl, Humphrey de Stafford, was probably in Normandy and may have been pressed from Castellion to act on the monks' behalf.   [2] Ibid.

[3] *C.P.R. 1436–41*, p. 170; W. Dugdale, *Warwickshire*, ii. 816–17; Eure II F 148, ff. 32, 32ᵛ, 35.

[4] P.R.O. E 135/22/78. Elizabeth, abbess of Syon: she occurs after 1448 and probably lived into the sixteenth century. *M.A.* vi. (1820), 541. The date proposed was suggested by the keepers of the P.R.O.

[5] P.R.O. Ancient Petitions 295/14704: 1422-30. A John Burdett occurs 1423: *C.Cl.R. 1422–9*, p. 483; and in 1434: *C.P.R. 1429–36*, p. 347.

[6] *Hereford Registers: Spofford*, p. 14.

Jumièges believed a monk was admitted as prior of Hayling in 1462 and in 1470 and again in 1475. Although he claimed to have authority for this belief,[1] the fact that the documents concern Queen Margaret of Anjou, who had no influence at all in England 1462–70 or after 1471, makes his testimony almost worthless. Perhaps monks were appointed in Normandy but never accepted in England. The monks of Le Tréport rediscovered at this time a charter of the count of Eu, in which he proposed to establish monks in place of the canons of Hastings castle. On the strength of this charter, and this alone, the monks believed that they had the right to appoint the 'prior' of Hastings, although no precedent is known, probably because the count had never completed the necessary arrangements. The English property had become matter for legend to the Normans and they overlooked their sale of the English assets to Robertsbridge in 1290. The newly appointed prior was sent to England with a petition addressed to the queen, presumably Margaret of Anjou, asking for the restoration of the priory.[2] Even more extraordinary are letters issued by the abbot of Saint-Wandrille in August and September 1477 appointing James Pseaulme (or William Cortoirt) prior of Ecclesfield in succession to the last prior, Robert William, who had died. The terms of the appointment suggest nothing odd: 'mandantes preterea omnibus et singulis subditis nostris tam religiosis quam aliis tam in dicto prioratu quam alibi existentibus'.[3] Yet the priory is last heard of in 1385, when it was given to the Carthusians of Coventry and a prior Robert William occurs in 1356.[4] The documents do not belong to the previous century and Abbot John de Brametot who issued them was a man of long experience in the abbacy. It is true that the name of the prior is uncertain since James's

[1] *Histoire de Jumièges*, ed. J. Loth, ii. 215–16.

[2] The letters appointing the priors were printed by Laffleur de Kermaingant, *Cartulaire de l'abbaye de Saint Michel du Tréport*, nos. CCLXVIII, CCLXIX: 29 September 1470. The petition addressed 'A tres haulte et tres excellente princesse la royne dengleterre' is Seine-Maritime 18 H 2 = P.R.O. 31/8/140A, no. 291; for the others see ibid., nos. 359, 379.

[3] B.N. MS. Lat. 17133, nos. 33–34: 7 August, 21 September 1477. Abbot John de Brametot reigned 1447–83. See J. Eastwood, *History of Ecclesfield*, pp. 513–14, who quotes another document since disappeared, dated 1492.

[4] *C.F.R. 1347–56*, p. 152; *C.F.R. 1356–69*, pp. 2–3, 12; see above, p. 118, n. 1.

name is scratched through and substituted with William's, but even if this is a mere draft it is mysterious what circumstances lie behind its composition. In 1475 the monks of Valmont took the trouble to have a long record of all their English possessions, including the names of the books in the priory, inspected,[1] although it is impossible to guess the use of such a document except to keep alive the Normans' hope of ultimate recovery.

However ill founded, the expectations of the Norman monks were encouraged by the survival of some priors and priories into the late fifteenth century, by negotiations, like those between Henry VI and Grestain as late as 1449[2] for compensation, and by the political restlessness which threatened Henry VI's religious foundations and created rival claims to the former monastic lands.[3] The fate of the aliens was still, it seemed, in the balance.

The aliens' fate is more closely related to changing social conditions than has been stressed hitherto. Simplification of so few examples may lead to rash generalization, but it is roughly true that the aliens were exploited, but not appropriated, as long as the king was powerful; when the king was too weak to resist the pressure of the land-hungry, needy nobility, he was unable to prevent them dissolving the priories to their own, not to his, greater profit. In the long run, this property was recovered for religious or educational purposes by royal foundations of monasteries and colleges, but it was Lancastrian royal piety alone which salvaged something from the dissolution, and for generations the lay occupiers, Leynthal and his fellows, enjoyed the taste of monastic property. As Sir John Cornewaile told Fécamp: 'durant nos vies nous sumez surez assys'. Weak kings like Richard II as a minor, Henry IV in old age, Henry VI, as incompetent, could not resist the demand for expulsion of monks and quiet possession by secular farmers. Politically these same conditions produced the disorders of the fifteenth

---

[1] Seine-Maritime 19 H 2.

[2] Eton College x. 9, 10: 23 April 1449.

[3] e.g. C.P.R. 1413–16, pp. 151, 355, 395; C.P.R. 1416–22, p. 395; C.Ch.R. 1341–1417, pp. 469–70, 479–80. Monks Sherborne was granted to Queen's College, Oxford, but also, ineffectively, to Eton College: C.P.R. 1461–7, p. 116, and C.P.R. 1467–77, p. 394: 1473. See M. Chibnall, The English Lands of the Abbey of Bec, pp. 132–4.

century; ecclesiastically, it was the aliens, the weakest members of the church, who suffered. In the name of politics, because of their foreign allegiance, they were sacrificed and their religious privilege trampled upon for secular considerations. The authority of the king was invoked to override clerical privilege, but it was not the king but the aristocratic supporters of the Lancastrians who benefited immediately from the dissolution.

NOTES

A. A fourteenth-century copy of this letter survives in Rouen: 7 H 57 = P.R.O. 31/83/140 A, no. 504. 'Chers et bons amis nous vous avons escript plus' que vous vousissiez traictiez dacorder aveques nos de transport' un vostre manoir en Engleterre appele Bury en nostre main et de recevoir de nos la value du dit manoir en peccune noviee pour convertir en autres heritages et appliquier a vostre moust' si come vos verrez estre miex a faire pour le bien et utilite de votre dit moust' A fin que la chose soit plus au profit de vous et de votre dit moust' nos vous prions que vos envoies par devers nos en Engleterre un ou pluseurs certaines personnes par qui ou quieux la value du dit manoir aveques les apertenances soit seue et qui ait ou aient povair de traictier et dacorder oveques nos sur la matiere desus touchie et si vuillies metre conseil que un bon homme de votre college soit envoie pour gouverner vos heritages et autres choses en Engleterre car si come nous avons entendue per relacion des gens a qui nous avons bonne foi celuy que vous y avoiz envoie nest pas bien agreable au pais ne profitable a vostre dit moust' . . . Escript en Avignon, le quart jour de fevrier.' The earl went to Avignon on royal business 1343–4, 1348, 1350, and 1354. If the agent referred to was John Palmer (see above, p. 95) the letter was probably written 4 February 1344. Arundel had written previous letters to Fécamp and had talked to the almoner of the abbey probably at Avignon, the court of Clement VI, formerly abbot of Fécamp.

B. Grestain had to dispose of its English property in 1348 in order to raise the money for its loan to the patron, Jehan de Melun sire de Tancarville, captured at Crécy and in need of ransom money. Tancarville gives a gloomy picture of how useless these English possessions were to the monks, but it is unlikely that they would have disposed of them if they had not been forced to it or had not found Norman lands to buy in exchange, namely Tancarville's barony of Mezidon: 'c'est assavoir que pour chacune troys mille livres florin à l'escu prix pour seize solz huit deniers tournois ou autres monnoies à la vallue nous leur baillerons et deslivrerons perpétuellement cent livres tournoiz de annuel rente des fruictz yssues et revenues . . . jusques à la vallue et somme d'argent qu'il nous bailleront': 14 April 1347, C. Bréard, *L'abbaye de Notre-Dame de Grestain* (Rouen, 1904), pièce justificative no. XXVI, pp. 235–8. The lands in England were leased for a 'thousand years': ibid. no. XXVIII; *C.P.R. 1348–50*, p. 221; *C.Cl.R. 1354–60*, pp. 659–60; Dénifle, *Désolation des Églises*, ii. 75, n. 1; *C.Pap.L.* iii. 276, 338.

1046

Charter of Edward the Confessor granting the monks of Saint-Ouen, Rouen, part of the island of Mersea, Essex.

A. Original lost. B. Copy of the original made in the fifteenth century now in the Archives of the Seine-Maritime: 14 H 145, 34 cm. × 40 cm. C. A later version of the charter, with a different description of the land boundaries, formerly existed in the Colchester archives. D. Copy of the Colchester text made and printed by Philip Morant without witnesses' names in his *History of Essex*, i. 426, n. F.

In nomine summi tonantis dei scilicet omnipotentis qui cuncta ex nichilo formavit. quique protoplastum hominem Adam videlicet cuncivem esse celestis Jerusalem condidit. illumque serpentina seductione precipitatum immensa pietate atque predestinatione ad culmen angelice beatitudinis proprio cruore redemptum provexit.[1] Nunc ut omnibus necesse est christianis quamdiu hic in mortali vita persistunt[2] de perituris celestia de caducis eterna mercari. Ego rex Eaduuardus hoc fretus sum consilio. quia eadem veritas dicit. date et dabitur vobis.[3] et item scriptura intonat. Divicie viri redempcio anime eius.[4] Et Salomon Fili elemosina animam a morte liberat et non patitur ire in tenebris.[5] Quapropter istorum preceptorum necnon aliorum auxiliatus adminiculo Ego rex[6] Eaduuardus superius prenotatus Anglorum atque northunhymbrorum do regi omnium regum[7] domino sanctoque petro. necnon (almo antistiti Audoeno sibique)[8] servientibus qui proprius fiscus attenus meorum antecessorum fuit quandam partem insule quae vocatur mersege cum (omnibus terrisque sibi adjacentibus)[8] et cum pratis. silvisque piscaturiis sicuti integram hanc et possessivam[9] habui curriculo duorum dierum postquam dei gratia (ad apicem regiminis)[8] perveni. Si quis vero homo[10] hanc meam donationem infringere temptaverit sciat se coram christo et angelis eius[11] ac sanctis suprascriptis in tremendo examine redditurum et

---

[1] *pervexit* in D. [2] *persistant* in D. [3] Luke vi. 38.

[4] Proverbs xiii. 8: Redemptio animae viri divitiae suae.

[5] Tobias iv. 11: quoniam elemosyna ab omni peccato et a morte liberat et non patietur animam ire in tenebras. [6] Omitted in D.

[7] Miss F. Harmer tells me this phrase is unique in Anglo-Saxon documents.

[8] These words cannot be read in B without the help of an ultra-violet lamp, owing to a stain on the manuscript.

[9] *poscessinam* in D. [10] *hominum* in D. [11] Omitted in D.

funditus dampnaturum nisi hic prius[1] emendare satagerit[2]. þis is þ

Hee sunt

landgemere æt meresege þ is ærest on pantan streame oð hit cymð to

terre eorum date apud Mersege.   Ibi est rivus super   Pone   Streme   et extendit usque ad

ðam dican betwyx east meresege [and west meresege.]

quoddam fossatum vocatum Deramy's[3] Diche inter   Est-Mersey   et West-Mersey

ðonne of ðam dican into ðam fleote. ðonne of ðam fleote into ðære

et a   Deramy's-Diche usque ad Deramy's-Flete   et a Deramy's-Flete usque ad quandam

stræte   þ hit cymð to ðære petan.   þonne

Stratam vocatam Deramy's-Strete et ibi extendit se usque ad le Peete[4] vocat(um) Deramy's-Peete

on   fingringaho   æ[t] ðam stane fram ðam stane   to bricsfleotes

villa de Fyngeryngho   ad Deramy's-stone et a   Deramy's-stone   usque ad Brigflete

orde æft fram ðam stane to Winnanbricse[5] fram Winnanbricse   to

ex parte orientali et a Deramy's-stone   usque ad

peltandunes meowte

Weldene-Downes Meowte.

Acta est hec prefata donatio anno dominice incarnationis millesimo quadragesimo sexto ✠ Ego Eaduuardus rex Anglorum hanc donationem libere concedo et manu propria hoc signo confirmo.

✠ Ego Eadsigus Cantuariorum archiepiscopus cum signo sancte crucis roboravi.

✠ Ego Ælfricus[6] archiepiscopus cum virtute sancte crucis consignavi
✠ Ego Rotbertus[7] episcopus confirmavi
✠ Ego Stigandus[8] episcopus corroboravi
✠ Ego Ælfwinus[9] episcopus conclusi
✠ Ego Wulfsigus[10] episcopus confortavi
✠ Ego Hearmanus[11] episcopus confortavi
✠ Ego Wulnoð abbas[12]
✠ Ego Lyfnoð abbas[13]
✠ Ego Ælfwine abbas[14]
✠ Ego Godwine dux
✠ Ego Harolt dux

[1] *plene* in D.   [2] *sategerit* in D.
[3] See below, p. 149.
[4] See below, pp. 146–7.
[5] There are nine strokes visible before 'an' in the copy. 'Winnan' is conjectural.
[6] Archbishop of York.   [7] Bishop of London.
[8] Bishop of Elmham.   [9] Bishop of Winchester.
[10] Bishop of Lichfield.   [11] Bishop of Ramsbury.
[12] Abbot of Westminster.   [13] Unknown.
[14] Abbot of New Minster (?) Winchester.

✠ Ego Lyfrac dux
✠ Ego Sweyn dux
✠ Ego Siwerð dux
✠ Ego Birn dux
✠ Ego Befkytel minister
✠ Ego Utfer minister
✠ Ego Manni minister

Dorso: hec est copia carte S. Edwardi regis Anglorum que pertinet abbatique conventui monasterii SS. Petri et Pauli S. Audoeni Rothomag' Henricus Chichele archiepiscopus Cantuariensis habet originalem Et est registratus sive signatus in cartaria S. Audoeni Et est sine sigillo

NOTE ON THE *LAND-DESCRIPTION*

This text is difficult to understand without the help of three Anglo-Saxon wills[1] of the late tenth century and the information supplied by Domesday Book. Edward the Confessor grants part of Mersea island with lands adjacent to it with fields, woods, and fishing rights, as he held them at the time of his accession. This estate which had been intended for a monastery at Stoke, presumed to be across the Essex county border at Stoke-by-Nayland, probably comprised several pieces of property mentioned in these wills: the church of St. Peter and an estate at Mersea, Fingringhoe, with the six hides on which the minster stands, a woodland at Totham (in the hundred of Thurstable), and an estate at Peldon.

In 1086, as in 1066, the estate of Saint-Ouen in Essex was reckoned as 2,460 acres. The monks had held a house in Colchester for this manor, but it had been taken away by Waleran who subsequently gave it to the monks of Caen. Although the estate is called Mersea, Round believed that it included Fingringhoe for which there is no entry in Domesday.[2] Henry I granted the abbot of Saint-Ouen the manor of Fingringhoe 1108/1112,[3] but this need not be proof that Saint-Ouen had not held the land, or part of it, in 1086 or earlier. Peldon is surveyed as the property of William the Deacon:[4] there is nothing to connect it with Saint-Ouen. However, it is interesting to notice that a considerable proportion of its estimated 600 acres had been taken away by Hamo Dapifer before 1086: 200 acres of coastal marsh and 80 acres of arable land. In addition St. Ouen enjoyed rights outside the manor of Mersea

[1] D. Whitelock, *Anglo-Saxon Wills*, Cambridge, 1930: wills II, XIV, XV.
[2] *V.C.H. Essex*, i. 454, n. 4; D.B. f. 22, tenant XVII.
[3] Johnson and Cronne, no. 1010.
[4] D.B. f. 94b, tenant LXVI.

holding two-thirds of the soke rights in Winstree hundred.[1] These had been infringed by Ingelric before 1066, who had taken half a hide and 30 acres of two sokemen of the hundred and added them to the manor of Langenhoe.[2] The other sokemen had been taken by the king and added to his manor of Layer.[3] The two sokemen taken by Ingelric may be the men mentioned under Little Wigborough;[4] I wonder, however, whether they may not rather be sought in Langenhoe parish itself which at one time thrust a finger of land into west Fingringhoe and split the parish into three parts.[5]

There is no known grant to Saint-Ouen of these rights other than this charter of Edward, so the description may fairly be interpreted as granting them. Probably the boundary description, like others of its kind, was intended to guide a man walking round the boundaries. The description follows first the line of the shore of the river Blackwater to a ditch or dyke between East and West Mersea. There is no evidence that a ditch ever completely divided the island, although it is not impossible. In the earliest description of the bounds of East Mersea that I have seen (1606)[6] there is no mention of a ditch. From the shore the boundary proceeds 'partim borealiter et orientaliter partim usque ad terram vocatam Northams'. The present parish boundary in the north of the island follows a channel for a short distance and it is highly probable that this channel once cut much more deeply into the island and served as a sufficient guide to the partition of the island.

The ditch runs into a *fleot*. This word in Old English means 'a tidal channel or creek' and in this case doubtless refers to Pyefleet. The boundary then returns to the west along the shore and crosses to the mainland by the *stræt* or Strood—an old Roman causeway[7]—and thence to the *Pete*. Mr. Reaney takes this word to be the same as Middle English *pete*, a form which is found first in the Scottish Latin documents of the thirteenth century and gives our modern English *peat*.[8] The word is derived from the Latin. But as the word *pete* in the charter occurs so much earlier and in the south of England, this derivation is unlikely. Mr. Norman Blake of Liverpool University has alternatively suggested that the word might be related to the Dutch dialect word *piete* (a weak feminine or masculine noun) found in Flanders and Brabant, meaning 'a covered watercourse, small bridge'. The similarity

---

[1] These were extended by Stephen; v. Appendix 1B.

[2] D.B. f. 27b, *V.C.H.* i. 463a. [3] D.B. f. 4b.

[4] D.B. f. 55b; *V.C.H.* i. 501b.

[5] These divisions may be seen on the Ordnance Survey 2½-in. map of 1895. Civil parishes restored a more rational division after 1888.

[6] Essex County Record Office, Manorial Survey D/DR c, M6/1, 2.

[7] J. H. Round, 'The Roman Road from Colchester to Mersea', *Transactions of the Essex Archaeological Society*, xvi (1923), 273–6.

[8] P. Reaney, *Essex Place-names*, p. 322.

of the terrains in the Low Countries and Essex makes it probable that bridges of this type were necessary for crossing from field to field. Adopting Mr. Blake's suggestion I propose that the name Pete (O.E. weak fem. *Pēte*, dat. *Pētan*) comes from the existence of a bridge carrying the strood or causeway over a creek that formerly flowed beyond the strood. This creek with the strood can be seen clearly on maps of 1788 and 1804, and the bridge is still named Peat Tie bridge in the former;[1] a neighbouring field was known as 'Bridge field' in 1558.[2] This bridge gave its name to the manor of Peet, Peet Tie Hall, and Pete Tie Common.

It now becomes more difficult to interpret the description. The next phrase means 'then in Fingringhoe to that stone', so that this stone must have been somewhere in Fingringhoe and can have nothing to do with a stone called *Deramy's stone* which according to Mr. Laver was somewhere close to the ditch between East and West Mersea.[3] From the stone the boundary goes in two directions. First it goes to *Bricsfleotes ord*. This *fleot* or creek is probably to be sought in the channels between the rivers Colne and Blackwater. It cannot refer to the Colne which is a river, the Old English name for which is *stream*, and the name Colne itself is old even though early references to this particular river are not found. There appear to be two possibilities: the channel coming up to the Peet, which is improbable as that would mean doubling back on our tracks, or one or other of the creeks called Geedon creeks in the fourteenth century. That they have different names later is of no great significance as the creeks in this area appear to have changed their names often. The exact sense of *ord* is difficult to determine. In Old English the word means 'a point' and in place-names it usually refers to 'a spit of land, a headland or the point of a hill stretching out into a plain'. It is not elsewhere used of creeks in Old English. But from parallel usages in Dutch and Scandinavian Mr. Blake suggests that it means 'the head of a bay or creek, i.e. the highest point reached by the tide in the creek'. This would provide a very suitable boundary mark. No later form of *Bricsfleot* is known, and the meaning of the first element remains obscure. Possibly it is an error for O.E. *bricg/brycg* 'bridge' (cf. Morant *brigfleet*), but this is unlikely as *brycg* does not usually occur as the first element in place-names. Another possibility is that it comes from O.E. *birce* 'a birch'; but most probably the first element contains a personal name. Tentatively I would like to suggest that the boundary line was drawn between the stone in Fingringhoe and the head of one of the Geedon creeks. It is still not clear, however, what portion of land is delimited by this boundary, particularly when

[1] Essex County Record Office D/DH t, P26, D/DC 37.
[2] G. Benham, *Essex Review*, li (1942), 96–97.
[3] *Transactions of the Essex Archaeological Society*, xvi (1923), 314–15.

the description does not continue from *Bricsfleotes ord*, but returns to the stone and apparently sets out in another direction. The boundary now runs from the stone to *Winnanbricse* and thence to *Peltandunes meowte*. Morant's charter has *Weldene* for the latter, and the manuscript *p* could be either a *p* (as in *Pantan*) or an attempt to write the Old English *w*. But as *Peltandun* is a well-attested form in the Old English documents,[1] the charter must surely read *Peltandunes*. The word *meowte* is completely unknown in English. Assuming that it is a genuine form, Mr. Blake suggests that it contains the Indo-European element **meu* or **meu-d-*, meaning 'wet, damp' and that the word could mean 'marshes or low-lying meadows'. Domesday mentions that Peldon had valuable sea-marshes. There remains the problem of *Winnanbricse*, apparently situated somewhere west of the strood, and probably on the confines of Mersea and Peldon in the manor of Peet, which lay across these two parishes. The first element *Winnan* is an assumed form to fit in with the nine minims plus *an* which is found twice in the text. Other readings are possible, but as the personal name *Winna/Wynna* is found in place-names in the district, this reading was adopted. *Bricse* is possibly a scribal error for *bricge*, and in the first example of the word the reading of *s* is doubtful. It must be remembered that O.E. *brycg*, *bricg* can mean 'a causeway' as well as 'a bridge', both of which must have been common in this marshy terrain. The name has however disappeared without trace together with the conditions which made the feature a significant boundary point.

No mention has been made of Morant's Latin version of this description, recently republished with a commentary by Mr. Hart.[2] Morant claims that the document came from the Colchester archives. By this I understand him to conceal the fact that he was using here, as elsewhere, a transcript made by Thomas Jekyll. Jekyll copied many Essex documents and in his lifetime West Mersea was the property of Thomas d'Arcy created Viscount Colchester 1621. Colchester may well have inherited a copy of Edward's charter from the former owners of the manor. Jekyll certainly refers to him in those documents of his which survived his death,[3] though by his later title Earl Rivers (creation of 1626). If I am right, Jekyll's transcript must have been made in the early 1620's. There is no reason to suppose that the Colchester archives refer to the deeds of St. John Colchester, which was quite unconnected with the estate.

This seventeenth-century transcript is not an accurate translation of

---

1 P. Reaney, op. cit., p. 321.
2 C. Hart, *Early Charters of Essex: The Norman Period*, Leicester, 1957. Appendix A, III, pp. 23–25.
3 British Museum Harley MSS. 4723, 5190, 5195, 6677–8, 6684–5; Additional MSS. 19985–9.

the Old English text, where they overlap, and suggests that the translator either could not read Old English or did not understand it. The
first phrase gives 'These are their lands given at Mersea' instead of
'This is the land-boundary at Mersea'. The second translates *ærest*
'first' with *rivus* and the seventh renders *orde* with *ex parte orientali*.
These show that the translator understood the general sense of the
description, while suggesting that he did not understand the exact
meaning. Morant's version omits *Winnanbricse* altogether. It is in-
conceivable furthermore that a translator familiar with the terrain
could render *Peltandunes* as Weldene-Downes. *Meowte* baffled the
translator as it mystifies us.

Lastly there is the strange recurrence of *Deramy's* in the Latin
version. The form itself is not Latin and the genitive in *'s* cannot be
earlier than the sixteenth century. It is very unusual for *all* the features
of an estate to be called after the same man, for if all were Deramy's
the distinctiveness of the name would be lost and the element dropped.
It is moreover interesting that it is only the stone that is called Deramy's
stone without explanation. Elsewhere we find the forms, as it were
glosses: vocatum Deramy's Diche, vocatam Deramy's Flete, vocatam
Deramy's strete, vocat' Deramy's Peete. There was a stone in West
Mersea close to the ditch known locally as Deramy's stone, and the
name might have been popularly extended to the ditch and beyond. The
manorial documents of the fourteenth and sixteenth centuries preserve
no echo of the name, not even in field-names.

Attempts have been made to get over this difficulty by supposing
that Deramy refers to Deorman, an English personal name attested in
the late eleventh century. Even granted that the form Deramy is
derived from Deorman, which is improbable, there is still no direct
evidence that the Deorman of Domesday and elsewhere had anything
whatsoever to do with this manor.[1] Saint-Ouen held this manor
apparently unchallenged from 1046 to 1421 when it was sold to
Chichele.

Morant's text is highly unsatisfactory and I consider that its testimony when it conflicts with the Rouen transcript should be set aside.
For what it is worth my guess is that Jekyll himself attempted a translation of the Old English in the charter he found before him and which
he hardly understood. I cannot explain where the 'Deramy's' comes
from—but I am certain that Mr. Hart's explanation[2] is unsatisfactory.

---

[1] A Deorman held a house in Colchester, possibly the moneyer; D.B. f. 105.
Davis, no. 399, refers to a connexion between the manor of Deorman and Eudo
Dapifer.   [2] Op. cit., pp. 43–45.

1148–54

Charter of Theobald, archbishop of Canterbury, confirming to the monks of Saint-Ouen the hundred of Winstree, given them by King Stephen

A. Original lost. B. Copy of the original made in the fifteenth century now in the Archives of the Seine-Maritime: 14 H 145, 34 cm. × 40 cm.

Theobaldus dei gratia Cantuariensis Archiepiscopus Anglorum primas et apostolice sedis legatus universis sancte ecclesie fidelibus Salutem. Noverit universitas tam presencium quam futurorum quoniam deo et monasterio sancti Audoeni Rothomagi et eiusdem loci monachis firmam hundredi de Wenestre quod illustris anglorum rex Stephanus eis in perpetuam pro dei amore et salute anime sue contulit elemosinam juste et canonice possidendam in perpetuum concedimus ac confirmamus precipientes quatinus predicti fratres bene et honorifice et libere et in pace possideant et teneant sicut iam dictus rex eis dedit et carta sua confirmavit et sicut eiusdem carta testatur. Valete.

Originalis istius littere adhuc est in cartaria sancti audoeni.

Apports and farms paid by some priories and monasteries to the first three Edwards

Monastery or priory	'De redditu transmarinis'		Rates of farm		'Ancient farms temp. Edw. III'
	1294-5[1]	1295-6[2]	1295[3]	1324[4]	14th c.[5]
Aumâle, Birstall	£50	£50	£170	£170	£266-13-4
Aunay	£20	£20	£41-6-8	£46	£46
Beaulieu, Patricksbourne	..	..	£9	£10	£10
Bec, Cowick	£12	£12	£26-13-4	£40	£40
Goldcliff	£1	£1	£100	£66-13-4	£20
Ogbourne	£213-6-8	£213-6-8	..	£520	..
St. Neot's	£1-10	£1-10	£150	£160	£170
Bernay, Creeting and Everdon	..	..	£15	£16	£18
Eye	..	..	..	£160	£140
Blanchelande, Cammeringham	£3	£3	£30	£33-6-8	£33-6-8
Boscherville, Avebury	..	..	£20	£24	..
Edith Weston	..	£6-13-4	£30	£30	..
Caen, Frampton	£16-13-4	£33-6-8	£75	£90	£90
Panfield and Well Hall	£22-13-4	£22-13-4	..	£75	£60
Cérisy, Monks' Sherborne	..	..	..	£20	£60
Cherbourg, Haugh	£10	£10	£70	£73-6-8	£73-6-8
Cormeilles, Newent	£40	£40	£120	£130	£130
Evreux, St. Taurin, Astley	£13-6-8	£13-6-8	£24	£16-13-4	..
Fécamp, Coggs	..	..	..	£10	£10
Warminghurst	£266-13-4	£266-13-4	£300	£333-6-8 [6]	
Grestain, Wilmington	..	£100	£165-10-10	£170	£170
Jumièges, Hayling	£10	£26-13-4	..	£120	£120
Lire, Carisbrooke	..	..	£40	£80	£113-6-8
Wareham	£40	£40	£45-10	..	..
Liver's Ocle	£66-13-4	..	..	£120	£120
Longueville, Newington	£53-6-8	£93-6-8	£90	£95	£105
Lonlay, Folkestone	£4	£6	£26-16-8	£30	£30
Stogursey	13-4	13-4	£28	£30	£30
Mont Saint-Michel, Otterton	£73-6-8	£73-6-8	£81-13-4	£100	£110
St. Michael's Mount	..	..	..	£13-6-8	£13-6-8
Montebourg, Appuldurcombe	£10-16-8	£9-6-8[7]	£41-9-8	£50	£66-13-4
Loders	£13-6-8	£26-13-4	£65-6-8	£70	£80
Mortain	£26-13-4	£7-6-8	£30	£30	..
Pont Audemer	£20	£20	..	£20	£21-6-8
Préaux, Tofts	£26-13-4	£26-13-4	£100	..	£110
Sainte-Barbe-en-Auge	£26-13-4	£26-13-4	£72	£80	£80
Sainte-Cathérine, Rouen, Blyth	£2	£2	£80?	£13-6-8	£13-6-8
Harmondsworth	£26-13-4	£26-13-4	£75	£80	£80

[1] P.R.O. E 106/3/10. [2] Ibid. 3/19, m. 1 [3] Ibid., mm. 5–11.
[4] Ibid. E 106/5/2, m. 4. [5] Ibid. E 106/7.
[6] During the abbatial vacancy 25 March–29 April 1336 the bailiff farmed the lands at £400 p.a.:
C.P.R. 1334–8, pp. 233, 258. [7] The priory also offered three 'pisas' of cheese worth 30s.

Monastery or priory	'De redditu transmarinis'		Rates of farm		'Ancient farms'
	1294–5	1295–6	1295	1324	14th c.
Saint-Evroul, Noion	£13–6–8	£26–13–4	£53–6–8	£55	£50
Ware	£166–13–4	£166–13–4	£220	£230	£245
Saint-Ouen, Rouen,					
Mersea	£30	£30	£50	£50	£55
Saint-Pierre-sur-Dives,					
Modbury	£2–10	£2–10	£10	£10–13–4	£10–13–4
Tutbury	..	..	£60	..	£66–13–4
Wolston	£26–13–4	£26–13–4	£36	£30	..
Saint-Sever, Haugham	£1–13–4	£3–6–8	..	£26–13–4	£46
Saint-Sauveur-le-					
Vicomte, Ellingham	..	..	..	£2–13–4	£4
Saint-Victor-en-Caux	£10–13–4	£10–13–4	£42	£45	..
Saint-Wandrille,					
Upavon	£10	..	£30	..	..
Ecclesfield	£13–6–8	..	£80	£13–6–8	£13–6–8
Savigny	£13–6–8	£13–6–8	£106	£100	£100
Saint-Martin, Séez,					
Arundel	£27–1–11¾	..	..	£35	..
Atherington	£66–13–4	£66–13–4	£80–10	£66–13–4	..
Lancaster	£10	£20	£90	£66–13–4	£66–13–4
Pembroke	..	..	..	£80	£20–6–8

APPENDIX III

1378–99

(*a*) Names of Norman monks who obtained permission to leave England in February 1378, excluding those who subsequently remained

These names have been taken from P.R.O. Treaty Roll 76 no. 61 mm. 11–1 and arranged under names of parent monasteries in alphabetical order.

Aumâle		Brother Martin de Rouen, monk
Aunay		John Frankes, monk
Bec	Cowick	Thomas de Turgevill, monk
		John de Petra Fida, monk
		Nicholas de Besovill, monk
		Peter de Bernay, monk
		Peter Mountbourk, clerk
	Goldcliff	Peter de Becco, monk
		Thomas de Bronia, monk
		John de Vesenell, monk
		Ralph de Vilers, monk
		John de Malnyk, monk
	St. Neot's	Peter de Becco, monk
		Peter de Bernay, monk
		Robert de Turgevill, monk
	Stoke by Clare	Richard Roon, monk
		Richard Vesenill, monk
		Roger de Panylly, monk
		Reginald de Week, monk
		Reginald de Tartre, monk
		Robert de Week, monk
		William Buchell, monk
Bernay	Eye	John Foukes, monk

		William Leskyret (Leskelene), monk
		Geoffrey Raynere (Reveer), monk
		Richard Treusell (Trousett), monk
Blanchelande	Cammeringham	John Newewe, confrater prioris
Boscherville		Stephen Fosse, monk
		John Sauntell, monk
		William Busey, valet
		Thomas Diant, valet
Caen, Saint-Etienne		John Letur, monk
Castellion (or Conques?)		Nicholas de Cheyne, proctor
		Peter de Courville, monk
		William Gibelot
Cérisy		Giles Ingeram, monk[1]
		Thomas le Priost
		James de Mount
		John de Gran
Cormeilles		Nicholas de Rate, monk
		John Pasdinile
Fécamp		Stephen, monk
Lire	Lyresocle	John Roverel, socius prioris
Lonlay		William Coderell, monk
		Gervase Denys, monk
		John Angelard
Sainte-Barbe-en-Auge		Henry Levee, canon
		Nicholas Monus, valet
Sainte-Catherine, Rouen	Blyth	William Hornet, monk
		John de Campis, monk
		Matthew Pouble, monk
		Peter de Merketis, monk
		Geoffrey Penewell, monk
		John Russel, valet
		Martin Daungeyn, valet
Saint-Ouen, Rouen		Stephen Fouk[1]
Saint-Pierre-sur-Dives		Gervase Gaudon, monk[2]
Saint-Wandrille		Lawrence Mathete, monk

[1] These monks may be the persons, with similar names, who remained: see Appendix III B.

[2] This monk was allowed one horse, 20s., and 40s. for expenses, when he went oversea: P.R.O. T.R. 76, no. 61, m. 7.

		William Blaunk
		John Bourdet
		Richard de Riparis, alienigena
Saint-Martin, Séez	Lancaster	Thomas Akayre, monk
		Oliver Miche, monk
		William Blesteboys, monk
		Michael Micert, monk
	Arundel[1]	
	Pembroke	Gervase Lubrayk, monk
		John Chivaler, monk
		William de Glene, monk

The following are names of monks from other French monasteries:

Saint-Vincent du Mans,	Abergavenny	Gilbert de St. Vincent, monk
		John Chevel, monk
		William Beaufitz, monk
		John Keyn, monk
Saint-Florent-lès-Saumur	Monmouth	John Caron, monk
		William de Portu, monk
		John Skarcy, monk
		John Aout, monk
	Sele	Nicholas Comyn, prior
		Robert Fouke, monk
Marmoutier	Holy Trinity, York	Thomas de Greges, monk
		John de Castello, monk
Cluny	Wenlock	John Chaii, monk
		John Wally, monk
Cîteaux		Roger de villa de richeto
Tywardreath priory		John Powelast
		John Mirebeau
		Thomas Coupe

The following names occur in groups, but their priory or monastery is not stated:

Richard le Chevalier, monk
Philip le Roverier, clericus eius

---

[1] The abbot of Séez claimed that eighteen of his monks had been expelled in 1378; some of these must have been from Arundel: *C. Pap. L.* iv. 239–40.

Brother Radulf de Saint-Medard, monk
John Launds, monk
Radulf Motet, monk
John de Maryns
Peter Coneys

Brother Dionysius Pate, monk
William Cowete, monk
Martin Phelip, monk
William Petite, monk

Brother William Vaundon, monk
William Dagenet, monk
John Pessevill, monk
Thomas Faure, monk
Nicholas Chivaler, monk
Peter Bavet, monk

Stephen de Lyre
John Petit

Brother Gerald de Bonoanus, monk
Raymundus Martin, monk
William Petit, monk
Peter de Tillio, monk
Peter Symond, monk
Robert Letoure, monk
Radulf Bellenger, clericus
John Burdeville, monk
William Danyel, canon of Saint-Mary, Welliportus, Brittany
William de Montibus
Peter Roket

(*b*) Names of religious who obtained permission to remain in England after 1378, or who are known to have been there 1378–99

Almenesches	Katherine de l'Isle, prioress of Lyminster[1]
Aumâle	*Thomas de Séez, prior of Birstall[2]
	*John de Harmesthorpe[2]

* P.R.O. T.R. 76, no. 61, mm. 11–1.
[1] *C.F.R. 1377–83*, pp. 168, 170; ibid. *1383–91*, p. 4.
[2] *C.P.R. 1381–5*, p. 606.

Aunay	*Henry Fulconis, proctor[1]
Bec	*John de Saint George, monk of St. Neot's
	*William Appeville, monk of St. Neot's
	*John Saint Martyn, monk of St. Neot's
	*John Cleevebeek, monk of Goldcliff
	*John de Aquila, monk of Stoke by Clare
	William de Saint Vedast[2]
	*John Seint Clut, monk of Ogbourne
Bernay	*Nicholas de Avems, monk of Eye
	*Robert Aunfray, monk of Eye
	*James Caney, monk of Eye
	*Roger Fevere, monk of Eye
Blanchelande	Peter Richere, prior of Cammeringham[3]
Caen, Saint-Etienne	A monk had permission to visit his abbey in 1382[4]
Castellion	*John Mawebrede, prior of Wootton Wawen
Cérisy	Ingeram de Buysson, prior of Monks Sherborne[5]
Cherbourg	*John Smyth, prior of Haugh
	Richard Beaugrant, prior of Haugh[6]
	*Giles, socius et canonicus ipsius prioris
Cormeilles	*John Fabri, prior of Newent[7]
	William Auger, prior of Chepstow[8]
Evreux, Saint-Taurin	Richard de la Fountaigne, monk of Llangenith[9]
	Richard de Hampton, prior of Astley[10]
Fécamp	Hugh Veretot, bailiff of Warminghurst[11]
Grestain	*Thomas Auncell, prior of Wilmington[12]

---

* P.R.O. T.R. 76, no. 61, mm. 11–1.

[1] *C.F.R. 1377–83*, p. 247.

[2] He was prior of St. Neot's; M. Chibnall, *The English Lands of Bec*, p. 126.

[3] *C.F.R. 1383–91*, p. 209.   [4] P.R.O. T.R. 76, no. 66, m. 4.

[5] *C.F.R. 1377–83*, p. 345.

[6] *C.F.R. 1391–9*, pp. 109, 235.

[7] *C.F.R. 1377–83*, p. 160.

[8] *C.F.R. 1383–91*, pp. 164–5, 286; ibid. *1391–9*, pp. 70, 261–2; *C.P.R. 1396–9*, p. 469.

[9] *C.F.R. 1377–83*, pp. 129, 248.

[10] *C.F.R. 1377–83*, p. 212; *C.P.R. 1381–5*, p. 461.

[11] *C.F.R. 1383–91*, p. 57.

[12] *C.F.R. 1383–91*, p. 230.

Jumièges	John Bucket, prior of Hayling[1]
Lessay	Priors of Boxgrove[2]
Lire	Ralph Maylock, proctor[3]
	Thomas de Vallosoul, prior of Carisbrooke[4]
	Stephen de Barra, prior of Wareham[5]
	Michael Anfrey, prior of Hinckley[6]
Longueville	*John Boyt, monk of Newington
	*John Fabri, commonachus of Newington
Lonlay	Nicholas Barbarote, prior of Folkestone[7]
	Richard Amys, prior of Stogursey[8]
Montebourg	Peter de Mouster, prior of Appuldurcombe[9]
	Monks at Loders?[10]
Mont Saint-Michel	Simon Garyn, prior of Otterton[11]
	Thomas Payn, prior of Otterton[11]
	Richard Harepath,[12] prior of St. Michael's Mount
	Richard Auncell,[13] prior of St. Michael's Mount
Pont-Audemer	*Richard Ruceole, proctor[14]
Préaux	*Clement Hulyn, prior of Tofts[15]
Sainte-Barbe-en-Auge	*Robert de Rotes, prior of Beckford
	*John Muget, capellanus
	*Stephen de Scaus
Sainte-Catherine-du-Mont	*Nicholas Nichole, monk of Blyth
	*Nicholas Anglici, prior of Blyth[16]

* P.R.O. T.R. 76, no. 61, mm. 11–1.

[1] *C.F.R. 1377–83*, pp. 16, 161, 284, 295; ibid. *1391–9*, pp. 111–12.

[2] See above, p. 46.

[3] *C.F.R. 1377–83*, pp. 68, 274; ibid. *1383–91*, pp. 304, 356; ibid. *1391–9*, pp. 186–7, 218.

[4] *C.F.R. 1377–83*, p. 89; May 1378.

[5] *C.F.R. 1377–83*, p. 17; he was prior again in 1403: *C.F.R. 1399–1405*, p. 193; there are no farmers mentioned for the intervening period.

[6] *C.F.R. 1377–83*, p. 17; ibid. *1383–91*, p. 304; ibid. *1391–9*, p. 204.

[7] *C.F.R. 1377–83*, p. 17; ibid. *1383–91*, pp. 148, 212: he was a leper.

[8] *C.F.R. 1377–83*, p. 194; ibid. *1383–91*, p. 331; *Stogursey Charter*, no. 223: he had a life title.

[9] *C.F.R. 1377–83*, p. 75.

[10] No farmers are known for this priory, so that monks may have been there.

[11] *C.F.R. 1383–91*, p. 177; *C.P.R. 1396–9*, p. 148.

[12] *C.F.R. 1383–91*, p. 13.

[13] *C.F.R. 1383–91*, pp. 127, 213.   [14] Ibid., p. 176.

[15] Ibid., pp. 225, 263.   [16] *C.F.R. 1383–91*, p. 126.

Robert de Beauchamp,[1] prior of Harmondsworth

*John d'Anseuyll,[1] socius prioris

Saint-Evroul   *William Heberd, prior of Ware[2]

*Ralph Auzeree, prior of Noion[3]

Nicholas Champyny, prior of Noion[4]

Saint-Ouen   *Stephen, prior of Mersea

Saint-Pierre-sur-Dives *Charles de Bruera,[5] monk

*Bernard Gaudouen,[5] monk

*John Fouke, monk

John, prior of Tutbury[6]

*John Chatel, prior of Wolston[7]

Saint-Victor-en-Caux   *Nicholas de Balomer, prior of Clatford[8]

*Nicholas Lassimer, prior of Clatford[8]

Savigny   *Michael Roger, prior of Long Bennington[9]

Saint-Martin, Séez   *Richard le Verrier, prior of Wenghall[10]

John de Rugecok, prior of Pembroke[11]

*William Umfrey, monk of Pembroke

John Innocent, prior of Lancaster[12]

Richard Surone, proctor[13]

Giles Louvel, proctor[14]

Prior of Atherington[15]

Valmont   Richard Tudenham, monk[16]

The following aliens also received permission to remain in England
after February 1378:

John Codmore, subprior of Monks Kirby[17]

* P.R.O. T.R. 76, no. 61, mm11. –1.
[1] See above, p. 117.
[2] C.F.R. show no farmers.
[3] C.F.R. 1377–83, p. 242; ibid. 1383–91, p. 181.
[4] C.F.R. 1391–9, p. 240.
[5] These two monks had permission to stay on 1 February and to leave on
15 February 1378. Did they leave or stay? P.R.O. T.R. 76, no. 61.
[6] C.F.R. 1377–83, p. 82.
[7] C.F.R. 1377–83, pp. 79–80; ibid. 1383–91, p. 183.
[8] These two are probably the same person as Nicholas Loloyer: C.F.R. 1377–83,
p. 71.   [9] C.F.R. 1377–83, p. 256.
[10] C.F.R. 1377–83, p. 71; ibid. 1383–91, pp. 38–39.
[11] C.F.R. 1377–83, pp. 155–6.
[12] C.F.R. 1377–83, p. 17, p. 253; ibid. 1391–9, p. 187: he died in 1396.
[13] C.F.R. 1369–77, p. 64; ibid. 1383–91, p. 331.
[14] C.F.R. 1391–9, p. 187.
[15] P.R.O. E 106/11/2: 16 November 1378.
[16] C.P.R. 1377–81, p. 305; C.F.R. 1377–83, p. 161.
[17] P.R.O. T.R. 76, no. 61, mm. 6–7.

*Peter, almoner of Monks Kirby
*James, cellarer of Monks Kirby
*Michael, sacristan of Monks Kirby
*Michael de Malley, monk of Holy Trinity, York
*Michael Marquis, monk of Holy Trinity, York
*John Bochelere, valet
*John Choseato, valet
*John Renard, monk of Tywardreath
*Otto de Floriaco, monk of Wenlock
*John Drieu, prior of Tickford
*Peter de Castronovo, custos of Scarborough church, proctor of
    Cîteaux
*Colin de Jaherenta, prior of Ravendale
*Nicholas Johann, prior of Ravendale
*Simon, prior of Minting
*Robert, socius of Minting
*Nicholas Gynard, monk of Lenton
*John Gosselyn, monk of Lenton
*Michael de Plecio, monk
*Laurence Taillon, monk
*Nicholas de Plecio, monk

* P.R.O. T.R. 76, no. 61, mm. 6–7.

Conditions of leases drawn up by monks for would-be farmers

(*a*) *Saint-Wandrille's conditions for the farming of Ecclesfield priory by Sir John Luvetot*[1]

A. Original draft: B.M. Add. MS. 27581, no. 4.

Comme messire Jehan de Louvetot chevalier engloiz ait en volonte de prendre et gard(er) a la vie de lui et de N( ) son filz la prieurie de Ecclefeld appartenant aus religieux abbe et couvent de S. Wandrille oveques toutes les revenuez et appurtenancez dicelle. Et se soit ycelui chevalier pour ce entremiz davoir fait parler aus dis (religieux) pour avoir par escript et savoir sur leur planiere volente.

Les quelx religieux pour ce assemblez en leur capitre par la manere acoustumee tous ensemble dun commun conscentementz et meisme volente sont touz prestz de faire parfaire et acomplir le dit bail au dit chevalier par mand' et condicion que suiz. Et pour ce aient baillie ceste cedule par manere de memoire et advis.

Premierement lez diz religieux vouldroient que la dicte prieurie qui de present est empeesch' par le (roi?) dangleterre leur fust mise en delivre par le pourchas dicelui chevalier affin que yceulx religieux y peussent p(rendre?) paisiblement apres le decez diceulx chevalier et de son filz, le quel sera nomme en dit bail par son propre nom. Et que yceulx religieux aient de ce lettre de delivrance.

Item ilz vouldroient avoir un des religieux de leur eglise de Saint Wandrille par dela en la dicte prieurie pour servir dieu estre demontrez et avoir son vivre vestir chaucer aus propres cous et despens diceulx chevalier et de son filz. Et le quel religieux ilz pourroient envoier a seurte par dela et ycelui mander oster mettre commettre et envoier un autre concessorz et quant il leur plairoit le temps du dit bail durantz.

Item les diz religieux vouldroient que la dicte prieurie et les appurtenances fussent tenuez gouverneez maintenuez le temps durant, et rendues aus diz religieux apres le trespassement et decez diceulx chevalier et de son filz en bon estat et suffisant.

---

[1] This John Luvetot was probably the one born 1361/2: J. Hunter, *Hallamshire*, pp. 428. The priory passed to the Carthusians in 1385.

Et pour ycelui bail entremez par la manere et condicion dessus devisee a la vie diceulx chevalier et de son filz qui est une tres grant chose les diz religieux vouldroient bien avoir. Et leur semble que ycelle prieurie ovecques lez appartenances ou il a plusieurs belles et grandes revenues peut bien valoire de quatre a chinc mille francs.

Item ils vouldroient que la dicte somme dargent leur fust paie avant les mains apportee et rendue a seurte en royaume de France en la ville de Paris ou aillieurs ovecques toutes les lettres et delivrances qui a cause de ce seront faictes passez et acordez.

Dorso (almost illegible):

	Recepte	
	£ s.	d.
	93 10	
	11 10	3
voiages	7 17	9½

(b) Saint-Evroul's conditions for Mr. Carnallay's lease of the English lands

A. Original lost.   B. Copy of about 1400 in B.N. MS. Lat. 11056, f. 196–196ᵛ.

Memoire du fait dengleterre.

Premierement monss' de Carnallay prendra tout ceu que nous avons en engleterre, tant du chief comme des membres: cest assavoir, de Noion et de Neuf-marchie, iuscques au terme de etc. par la somme de etc. a paier avant la main pour tout le temps q'il tendra, par telle condition que se devers le temps dessus dit par pais entre les roys, ou autrement, les choses dengleterre estoient generalement rendues aux religieux de par dela, il seroit tenu avoir paier pour chacun an iuscques a la fin de son terme atant comme le roy y prent par chacun an.

Item il sera tenu paier L mars monnoie de France par chacun an au[x] religieux qui de Noion y seront ordenes pour lour vivre.

Item il maintendra touz les maisons et autres ediffices a nous appurtenans en bon estat et les levra en aussi bon estat comme il les prendra.

Item il soustendra touz proces et empetrement a ses despens et mettra affin a eux.

Item il rendra a ses perils et a ses despens en la ville de Caen toutes les summes dargent q'il sera tenu paier le terme durant.

Item toutz fois q'il lui ou ses heirs en aiant cause deffandront des choses dessus dicts ou daucuns dicelles nous pourions repondre de leur autorite sans ordre de ( ) ces possession de noz choses et demander restitution de ceu q'ilz nairont dument acompli.

Item il sobligera a toutz les choses dessus dicts et a rendre paisible possession de noz choses ainssi tenues en estat et hors de pestilent comme dit est en la fin du terme sans aucun preiudice de nous et nos predecesseurs.

Item il procurera a ses despens touts les choses dessus dictes estre confirmes par le roy dangleterre, affin doster et de toute doubte de possessions autrement.

Item pour faire les despens a ceulx qui yront par dela pour pour-chacier tout les choses dessus dictes il prestra ij^c mars devant toute ( ) ainsi que se le contrault se parfait, ils lui feront deffoncer sur la somme ou se non, on lui donera povair de ley r( ) sur noz biens dengleterre.

[v°]

Et touz les choses dessus dicts et toutes autres qui seront ainse a notre proffit et seurte et a lonneur et prouffit dudit chevalier selon la coustume du pais, et tout en la meilleur maniere q'il se pourra faire, il sobligera pour lui et ses hoirs et les fera confirmes de roy dengleterre.

APPENDIX V

2 JUNE 1409

Letter of Sir John Cornewaile to the abbot of Fécamp

A. Original in the Archives of the Seine-Maritime 7 H 57; 29 cm. x 28 cm.; autograph on paper; fragment of red seal. B. Transcript made by Déville, P.R.O. 31/8/140 A, no. 484.

Honorez sires labbe et covent de Fiscamp / ieo vous salue tressovent et de tout mon coer / Et voillez savoir que Cassyn et un vostre esquier / en sa compaignie memparlerent si ieo voloie treter avec vous pour certeins terres tenements et possessions queux appartenent a vostre abbeye en Engleterre qeux nostre seignour le roi par auctorite de parlement et par assent des seignours et de son conseill / par sez lettres patentz ad done et graunte a moi et a ma dame — ma compaigne et a mon fitz durant noz vies / qeux estoient en sez mains a cause de la guerre. Et ore est ensi que ore tarde vostre moigne Hugh Veretot est mort lendemayn de seint George et est ensi que iay tout la charge dez ditz terres et tenementz sanz que y nest nully depar vous / Et ore devant ienvoiay a vous par Cassyn esquyer davoir trete avec vous depar moi dez ditz terres et tenementz pour c ans ou cxx ans / vous donant une certeine somme de monoie come nous pourions acorder et ieo nay hieu null respons de cella / Et ore ieo vous certefie que ieo fuy depar de cea la meer a Lile en Flaundres pour certeins armes faire devant le duc de Burgoigne Sur quoi ienvoie devers vous mon tres cher et bon ame Geffray Furneis portour de cestes pour mesme la cause de savoir vostre volunte si vous voillez treter de dite matiere avec moi ou non. Et si vous voillez treter avec moi / envoiez un vostre procurour aiant vostre plein poer' avec le portour de cestes a Lile en Flaundres / ou ie demeure iuscques al xvᵒ iour de ceste mois de juyn / Et en cas que nous pourons acorder vous serrez bien graciousement paiez / mez me coviendra davoir licence du roi. depuis que nous averons trete avant que ieo puisse faire fyn de nostre covenant / qar sanz licence ne pourra ie rien faire / mez ie ne me doute poynt de cella / si non que me costerra graunde somme devers le roi et son counceill. Et si vous ne voillez treter avec moi / mandez a moi ieo vous empri' par le portour de cestes en tout haste / Et voillez penser et regarder par entre vous labbe et le covent quelz graundz profitz ent sont venus a votre meson de xxx ou xl ans. en cea et regardez par entre vous si vous vaut meulz davoir une somme dor pour certaines ans ou le lesser en le manere come il est maintenant / qar durant noz vies nous sumez surez assys / Et voillez doner foi et credence al porter de cestes de ce qil vous dirra par bouche / Priant a la benoite Trinite que vous ait en sa garde / Escript a lile en Flaunders le seconde iour de juyn.

(*Written in same hand*) Jehan Cornewail chevalier

Memoir of instructions for an agent of Fécamp visiting England

A. Original, Archives Départementales de la Seine-Maritime 7 H 57; paper; 29 cm. × 40·5 cm.

Memoire a Craquet qui ira a Saint Thomas en Angleterre.
Premiere(ment)

De soy' enquerir a un homme de Wincheneel nomme Jehan More qui parla a Sandrum quant il fu en Angleterre, qui cest qui a les lettres touchans leglise de Fescamp. lesquelles je disois quil savoit bien qui les avoit. Et de faire tout que on les ait.

Item de savoir qui a eu les lettres tiltres et autres choses qui avoit le bailli de Wermingheust et auxi qui a eu tous ses biens et quils sont devenus.

Item de savoir se on pourroit parler aux hoirs de celluy qui estoit senescal de la m[anoir] durant le temp que le bailli y' fu, lequel je croy quil avoit nom Jehan equin' Start.

Item de savoir a Saint Thomas de Cantobie se ceulx de par dela obeiroient point aux conservatoires que le pappe donrroit.

Item de savoir quelx prelatz seroient bons pour estre juges de la dicte conservatoire et de les apport' par estr'.

Item de savoir se on y dimoyeroit aucun pour savoir comme le spiritualite sy gouverne, sil y seroit receu et pour donner con que de faire clers etc.

Item de savoir a Saint Thomas sil y a nul que se voulsist chargier destre procureur en la court de conservatoires.

Item de savoir se len voit temps et lieu, sil est nulle maniere que on peut ravoir les terres que leglise a en Angleterre, soit par supplication devers le roy, ou par quelle autre maniere.

Item denvoier le cousin damp' Thomas [　]anglors jusques a Londres et quil senquiere quelz gentz ce sont que Jehan Dart et Jehan de Straole[1] que se dient de Coulogne sur le Rin, et ou ils demeurent

¹ These two men were merchants of Cologne. The van Stralen family occurs often in the Hansa records during the fifteenth century. The abbot of Fécamp was accused by merchants of Cologne of detaining these two men, when an appeal was presented by the men of Cologne to the Emperor Sigismund on their behalf, late June 1416. This memoir was therefore probably written about this time, when the abbot was trying to find out more about the merchants. The appeal to

a la ( ) combien il a quelz y demeurent et sil est vray quilz se meslent de merchandise de peleter et quelz gens se sont, silz sont point maries, et de quel estat ilz sont.

Item quil senquiere de messire Rogier Seglen chevalier, quel homme cest et quil avoit vaillant et de quel pais il est, com[ ] quil se dit dalemaigne.

Item de savoir de un nome Georget, qui se dit varlet dudit chevalier, quel homme cest et ou il demeure(t) a present.

Item de demander au cure de la Rye xiii marcs dargent, quil doit a leglise de Fescamp chacun an.

the emperor does not make it clear how they fell into the abbot's hands. The relevant portion is as follows: 'Uren coenynckligen gnaten begeren wir vlelich zo wissen, daz unser burger zwene, as mit names Johan Dasse ind Johannes van Stralen, vurtzijden, uff deme mer gefangen worden sint van otzlingen reuoveren ind sint die selve zwene unse burgere also vortan zo gefencknis bracht ind komen in hant eyns abtz in Franckrijch mit namen genant der abt van Vekamp; van wilchen abte unse burgere doch gheyne wijs leidlich noch qwijt werden en kunnen ind werdent uns weder Got, ere, reicht ind alle bescheit vurunthalden, ind en hilft uns nyet, so wat wir darumb geschreven, gesant oder gedadingt haven, ind willen umber sagen, daz sij den Engilschen zogehoerich soelen syn. Ind want, gnedichster alreliefster herre, die selven unse burgere oevel ind unschuldentlich zo dem gevencknis koment synt, Johan Dasse, unse ingesessen burger ind Johannes van Stralen unse geboeren burger sint ind uns zo verantwerden steent, ind wir ind unse stat ouch mit dem vurseid ind abte van Vekamp noch den synen in den getzijden, do unse burgere vurschreven gevangen wurden, ind ouch noch hude zo dage van geynrekunne viantschaf en wissen, gaentz oder usstaentz zo haven, ind dar emboyven so blivent unse burgere doch allis gefangen zo yren groissen unschuldentlichen schaden ind unwillen . . . .' *Hansisches Urkundenbuch* (ed. K. Kunze, Leipzig, 1905), vi. 1415–33, no., 82, pp. 36–37: Verzeichnete Mitthl. a.d. Stadtarchiv von Köln 7, 87.

(a) The prior of Sainte-Barbe-en-Auge entrusts to certain Norman abbots the negotiations for the recovery of his English property from Henry V

A. Original in the Archives Départementales du Calvados: 2 D 170; 29·5 cm. × 16 cm.; fragments of two seals.

Universis presentes litteras inspecturis Jacobus permissione divina humilis prior monasterii Sancte Barbare o.s.a. lex. dioc. totusque eiusdem loci conventus salutem in domino sempiternam. Noveritis quod nos, utilitatem dicti monasterii nostri pensantes unanimi concurrentes assensu in capitulo nostro ad sonum campane, ut moris est, solemniter congregati, melioribus modo forma et viis quibus potuimus et possumus, reverendos in christo patres dominos Estoldum Fiscampnensem, Nicholaum de Gemeticis, Guillelmum S. Wandregisilli, Michaelem S. Ebrulphi, Symonem de Lira, Guillelmum S. Trinitatis in monte Rothomagi, Guillelmum de Conchis, Johannem S. Georgii de Boquervilla, abbates Jacobum de Longgvilla, et Guillelmum S. Laudi Rothomagi[1] priores, fecimus constituimus nominavimus et ordinavimus ac tenore presentium facimus constituimus nominamus et ordinamus procuratores et commissarios nostros et dicti monasterii nostri, sub tali condicione, quod id quod per maiorem et saniorem partem eorum in hiis que sequuntur actum fuerit valeat, viz. ad faciendum constituendum nominandum eligendum et deputandum nuncios et procuratores tales quales sicut prefatis dominis abbatibus commissariis seu maiori et saniori parte eorundem placuerit, pro comparendo nominibus nostris ac dicti nostri monasterii coram serenissimo et illustrissimo principe ac domino Domino Henrico dei gratia rege Angliae, herede et regente regni Franciae ac domino Hybernie, eiusque parlamento aut consilio ac etiam coram quibuscunque principibus dominis temporalibus aut spiritualibus et coram omnibus aliis et singulis personis aut iudicibus ecclesiasticis et secularibus, quacunque auctoritate dignitate seu potestate fungentibus et quocunque nomine censeantur; dantes et concedentes nominibus nostris et dicti monasterii nostri dictis procuratoribus et nuntiis per prefatos patres reverendos nominandis pro ut supra et deputandis plenam et liberam potestatem ac mandatum speciale comparendi nomine nostro et pro nobis et dicto monasterio nostro coram prefatis serenissimo principe et aliis superius dictis, recuperationemque deliberationem et restitutionem

[1] I have not discovered that the canons of Saint-Lô, Rouen, had English possessions.

fructuum reddituum maneriorum beneficiorum prioratuum nostrorum iurumque et pertinentium eorundem existentium in regno Anglie aut sub dominio eiusdem serenissimi principis nobis ratione prefati nostri monasterii et ex fundatione seu dotatione ipsius spectantium et pertinentium, prosequendi petendi humiliter, et requirendi et obtinendi quascunque litteras circa has necessarias petendi impetrandi et obtinendi; nosque et dictum monasterium nostrum in veram et realem dictorum fructuum reddituum maneriorum beneficiorum prioratuum predictorum ac iurum et pertinentium eiusdem possessionem ponendi restituendi, si opus fuerit, manutenendi et defendendi; et insuper dicta loca beneficia prioratus et alia nobis pro ut, ut supra, pertinentia tam in spiritualibus quam in temporalibus reformandi et in eisdem officiarios et ministros ponendi et instituendi usque ad beneplacitum nostrum; et generaliter omnia et singula circa deliberationem restitutionem et recuperationem predictorum necessariorum facienda que nos faceremus et facere possemus si presentes et personaliter interessemus; proviso tamen quod dicti nuntii seu procuratores nominandi nullam commutationem conventionem vendicionem seu contractum possint facere de dictis redditibus beneficiis prioratibus et aliis pro ut supra nobis pertinentibus; concedendo etiam dictis reverendis patribus facultatem taxandi salaria et expensas dictorum nuntiorum et procuratorum et nos in quantum nos et dictum monasterium nostrum tangere poterit, summas pecunie quales sibi rationabiliter visum fuerit expedite pro solutione dictarum expensarum et salariorum imponendi; promittentes bona fide et sub obligatione omni et singulorum bonorum mobilium et immobilium nostrorum et dicti monasterii nostri presentium et futurorum. Nos gratum ratum firmum habere et perpetuo habiturum totum et quicquid per dictos reverendos patres aut maiorem et saniorem partem eorundem ac per nuntios et procuratores per eos nominandos actum dictum factum procuratum et ordinatum fuerit in premissis seu gestum. In quorum omnium et singulorum premissorum testimonium et fidem sigilla nostra quibus in talibus utimur presentibus litteris duximus apponenda. Datum et actum in dicto capitulo nostro hora capituli die decima mensis martii anno domini millesimo quadringentesimo vicesimo.

(*b*) Circular letter sent by the monasteries' representatives sitting in Rouen (?) describing their proposals for approaching Henry V about the recovery of their English lands

A. An original from the Archives Départementales de l'Orne, which may have been the draft composed at the meeting. It has two large holes in it.

Reverende in christo pater ac domine precarissime cordiali recommendacione premissa. Sciatis precepto regis omnes prelatos et alios in hac regia civitate[1] convenisse qua propter opportunitate captata, nos omnes abbates et priores monasteriorum ducatus Normannie et domini dicti nostri regis plures in unum congregati super facto recuperationis et restitutionis prioratuum beneficiorum maneriorum reddituum ac iurum nobis singulis ac monasteriis nostris pertinentium et existentium in dominio dicti nostri regis in suo regno Anglie et alibi ultra mare, concordes fuimus regis presentiam adire restitutionem et recuperationem iurum nostrorum p(redictorum) hinc postulare et prosequi. Quod nequivimus propediente dicti nostri regis ad angliam repentino redditu, recessum matura deliberatione prehabita considerantes et in nobis revolventes tam strenue et ardue ([2]) advicem de quo coram districtissimo iudice reddituri sumus rationem et ad quod obligamur (re-?)presso proprio iuramento et de vestro consensu et auditorio ad huius sancti negotii et cause necessarie prosecutionem providimus et elegimus mittere ad dominum nostrum regem et suum consilium etiam in suo parlamento in Anglia nuncios solempnes reverendos in christo patres dominos Michaelem[3] abbatem S. Ebrulphi o.s.b. et Guillelmum[3] abbatem monasterii Mortuimaris ordinis Cisterciensis sacre theologie professorem, patres utique probos maturos prudentes et in agendi expertos unacunque uno iuris peritos quatinus maturitate sufficientia et honestate nunciorum pensatis tam ([4]) rei negotium et in nobis per necessarium melius et facilius suum sortiatur effectum ad cuius negotii prosecutionem vestram ex parte ac etiam omnium nostrorum requiritur procuratorum seu commissionum cuius copiam unacunque presentibus vobis transmittimus. Et quia tam arduum negotium per tam maturos patres sine magnis expensis inchoari ad effectum deduci non potest, decens et necessarium omnes quos tangit manus porrigere adiutrices, hinc est reverende pater quod consideratis ex(pensis) necessariis dictorum nuntiorum ac omnium nostrorum facultatibus pensatis, videtur nobis omnibus quod ([4]) facto vestro et monasterio vestro habetis effectualiter persolvere et in auro, quam ([4]) per latorem presentium, de quo considimus unacunque procuratorio predicto ([4]) nobis secure si pl(acetis) certum nuntium et citiusque poteritis, ut tam sanctum et utile negotium dei auxilio suum ([4]) effectum ad dei laudem fundatorum nostrorum intentionum ac nostrarum conscienciarum ([4]) et de oneratione. Verum reverende pater, per quendam religiosum de abbatie de Lire, qui nunc app(aret) in hac civitate veraciter fuimus informati quod edicto regis enotatum est parlamentum regni Anglie in iocundo adventu domini nostri regis et

---

[1] Probably Rouen. [2] This word cannot be read.
[3] These names have been inserted later, by the same hand.
[4] There are two great holes in the middle of the text, which make the words difficult, or impossible, to read at this point.

proclamatum publice quod omnes habentes et detinentes (bona) omnium ecclesiarum et monasteriorum existentium extra regnum apportent et differant litteras evidentiarum suarum, et sperat dictus religiosus quod in hoc parlamento aliquid concludetur in facto redditum nostrorum. Per vos hortamur in visceribus domini nostri Jhesu Christi, et recuperationem reddituum vestrorum et ne in tantum ac perutile negotium differatur quatinus velitis accelerare et mittere totam summe predicte vestre tangent' unacunque dicto procuratorio et ad tardius infra quindenam.

Vestri abbates: Fiscamp' S. Audoen' de Gemiticis, S. Wandregisili, S. Ebrulphi, de Lira, de Bello Becco, de Conches, de Longavilla.

APPENDIX VIII

1420–1 (?)

Petition of the monks of Caen to the king of England

A. Original ? in the Archives of Calvados, H 1884; 37 cm. × 21 cm. B. Transcript by Léchaudé: P.R.O. 31/8/140 B I, pp. 197–9, no. 27.

Au roy notre souverain Seigneur.

Supplient tres humblement vos humbles religieux et orateurs labbe et couvent de saint estienne de caen fondes par prince de glorieuse recordation Guillaume jadis roi dangleterre et duc de normendie, comme le dit glorieux leur eust donne en leur fondacion pluseurs manoirs et grans revenues en engleterre, et par especial le manoir de Frantonne avecques ses despendences, a estre gouvernes par deux des religieux de votre dit moustier qui communiement avoient le spirituel pour eulx vivre par de la et doivent envoier a votre dit moustier la revenue du temporel avecques autres emolumens pour la substantacion diceulx. Et par especial la despouille des religieux qui la estoient quant ils alloient de vie a trespassement qui de droit appartient a votre abbe dudit lieu de caen comme droit et raison est partout en cas semblable. Et pour ce que frere Raoul des nues qui des longtemps a este gardien du dit lieu de Frantonne est alle de vie a trespassement puis nagueres comme len dit, Que de votre benigne grace et autorite royal ladicte noble fondacion faite par vos nobles predecesseurs qui de toute leur volente ont icelle tousiours augmentee, comme il apparut par le dit glorieux prince votre noble predecesseur qui si grandement la fonda tant en edifices grandes et notables que chascun sait, et que cest de present a la recommandacion et honneur de votre glorieux lignie et demonstraunce du droit que vous avez en votre duchie de normendie, et mesmement leur donna pour monstrer la singuliere volente quil avoit a votre dit moustier alors de son trespassement sa precieuse couronne, dont il estoit couronne es haultes festes, son ceptre avecques sa verge dor, son precieux galice, ses oriettes dautel plas candelabres et ses precieux ornemens royaux, dont vos religieux furent longement pocesseurs, jusques a ce que son filz guillaume, dit le roux, les retray devers lui, dont ils neurent aucune recompensacion[1] excepte la confirmation des manoirs dessus dis et du manoir de briditonn, qui pour ce leur fut donne par henry premier filz dudit glorieux fondeur

---

[1] On the contrary, Rufus gave them the manor of Creech in Somerset: Davis, no. 397.

considerant que lesdit joyaulx valloient mieux que tout ce quilz avoient
en engleterre.[1] Et encore de ce que le dit glorieux fondeur fist mettre
votre dit moustier en la sauve garde de leglise de Rome avecques toute
leur fondation et apres le fist faire semblablement Henry le segond en
fulminant grants paines de droit contre ceulx qui icelle diminuroient
et apetisseroient. Il vous plaist a fin que le divin service chacun jour
est dit et celebre en votre dit moustier pour vos nobles predecesseurs
et vous a faire recevoir ung de vos dis religieux au gouvernement dudit
manoir de Frantonne avecques ses despendences qui puisse jouir et
vivre de le spirituel en la fourme que le dit fraire Raoul faisoit; jusques
a ce que au regard du temporel soit par vous ordonne et ce leur vieulles
ottroier et ilz priront dieu de mieux en mieux pour votre royal maieste
et votre noble conseil.

[1] Johnson, no. 601.

BIBLIOGRAPHY

PRIMARY SOURCES

Abbreviatio Rotulorum Originalium in Curia Scaccarii, ed. H. Playford, 2 vols., London, 1805, 1810.

L. D'ACHÉRY, *Acta Sanctorum Ordinis Sancti Benedicti*, ed. J. Mabillon, Paris, 1668–1701.

Ancient Deeds, Catalogue, 6 vols., London, 1890–1915.

Annales Monastici, i, ed. H. R. Luard, R.S., London, 1864.

Annales Paulini, Chronicles of Edward I and Edward II, ed. W. Stubbs, London, 1882.

ARNULPH OF LISIEUX, *Letters*, ed. F. Barlow, Camden Society, 3rd Series, lxi, London, 1939.

ASSER, *Life of Alfred*, ed. W. H. Stevenson, Oxford, 1904.

A. BALLARD, *British Borough Charters 1042–1216*, Cambridge, 1913.

—— 'The Early Municipal Charters of the Sussex Boroughs', *S.A.C.* lv (1912), 35–40.

BATH AND WELLS, *Bishops' Registers: Giffard*, ed. T. S. Holmes, Somerset Record Society xiii, 1899.

—— —— *Drokensford*, ed. Hobhouse, Somerset Record Society i, 1887.

BAYEUX, *Antiquus Cartularius Ecclesiae Baiocensis, Liber Niger*, ed. V. Bourrienne, S.H.N. 2 vols., Rouen, 1902–3.

BEC, *Select Documents of the English Lands of the Abbey of Bec*, ed. M. Chibnall, Camden Society, 3rd Series, lxxiii, London, 1951.

T. BEKYNTON, *Correspondence*, ed. G. Williams, R.S., London, 1872.

M. M. BIGELOW, *Placita Anglo-Normannica*, Boston (Mass.), 1879.

W. DE GRAY BIRCH, *Cartularium Saxonicum*, London, 1885–93.

Book of Fees (Testa de Neville), 3 vols., London, 1921–31.

M. BOUQUET, *Rerum Gallicarum et Francicarum Scriptores*, Paris, 1783–1904.

BOXGROVE, *Cartulary of Boxgrove Priory*, ed. L. Fleming, Sussex Record Society, vol. lix (1960).

Bruton Priory, Cartulary, ed. H. C. Maxwell-Lyte, Somerset Record Society viii, 1894.

J. BURTON, *Monasticon Eboracense*, York, 1758.

Calvados, Inventaire-Sommaire des Archives Départementales antérieures à 1790, Série H, vol. i, ed. A. Bénet, Caen, 1905.

Cartae Antiquae, Royal and Private Charters prior to 1200, ed. J. H. Round, P.R.S. vol. x, London, 1888.

Cartae Antiquae Rolls 1–10, ed. L. Landon, P.R.S., N.S., xvii, London, 1939.

J. J. CHAMPOLLION-FIGEAC, *Lettres de Rois, Reines et autres personnages des cours de France et d'Angleterre*, 2 vols., Collection des Documents Inédits sur l'histoire de France, Paris, 1839–47.

Chancery Warrants, Calendar of, i, 1244–1326, London, 1927.

CHARTER ROLLS: *Rotuli Cartarum 1199–1226*, ed. T. D. Hardy, Record Commission, London, 1837.

CHARTER ROLLS: *Calendar 1226–* , London, 1903–27.

P. A. Chéruel (ed.), *Normanniae Nova Chronica*, M.S.A.N. xviii, Caen, 1850.
Chichester, *Cartulary of the High Church of Chichester*, ed. W. A. Peckham, Sussex Record Society xlvi (1946).
—— *Bishop's Registers: Rede*, ed. C. Deedes, Sussex Record Society viii and ix (1908, 1910).
Close Rolls: *Rotuli Litterarum Clausarum*, Record Commission, London, 1833–44.
—— *1227–72*, London, 1902-48.
—— *Calendar 1272–*. London, 1892.
G. E. Cokayne, *The Complete Peerage*, new edition by V. Gibbs, H. A. Doubleday, Lord Howard de Walden, and G. White, London, 1910– .
Colchester, *Cartularium Monasterii Sancti Johannis Baptistae de Colcestria*, ed. S. A. Moore, Roxburghe Club, 2 vols., London, 1897.
Bartholomew Cotton, *Historia Anglicana*, ed. H. R. Luard, R.S., London, 1859.
Coutumiers de Normandie, ed. E. J. Tardif, 2 vols. in 3, S.H.N., Rouen, 1881–1903.
Curia Regis Rolls: *Rotuli Curiae Regis*, ed. Sir Francis Palgrave, 2 vols., Record Commission, London, 1835.
—— *Calendar, Richard I–* , London, 1923– .
—— *A Roll of Richard I*, ed. F. W. Maitland, P.R.S. xiv, London, 1891.
Daniel, Walter, *Vita Ailredi*, ed. F. M. Powicke, Edinburgh, 1950.
H. W. C. Davis, *Regesta Regum Anglo-Normannorum 1066–1100*, Oxford, 1913.
L. V. Delisle, *Rouleaux des morts*, S.H.F., Paris, 1866.
—— *Cartulaire normand de Philippe Auguste, Louis VIII, St. Louis, et Philippe le Hardi*, M.S.A.N., Caen, 1852.
—— 'Lettre de l'Abbé Haimon', *B.E.C.* xxi (1860), 113–39.
L. V. Delisle and E. Berger, *Recueil des actes d'Henri II roi d'Angleterre et duc de Normandie*, Acad. des Inscriptions, 3 vols., Paris, 1909–27.
G. Demay, *Inventaire des Sceaux de la Normandie*, Paris, 1881.
H. Denifle, *La Désolation des églises monastères et hôpitaux en France pendant la Guerre de Cent Ans*, Paris, 1897–9.
E. Déville, 'Notices sur quelques manuscrits normands conservés à la bibliothèque de Ste. Geneviève: analyse d'un ancien cartulaire de l'abbaye de St. Etienne de Caen', *Revue Catholique de Normandie*, xiv, xv (1903–5).
Domesday Book, Liber Censualis, 4 vols., Record Commission, London, 1783–1816.
D. C. Douglas, *The Domesday Monachorum of Christ Church Canterbury*, London, 1944.
A. Du Chesne, *Historiae Normannorum Scriptores Antiqui*, Paris, 1619.
Dudo de St. Quentin, *De moribus et actis primorum Normanniae Ducum*, ed. J. Lair, Caen, 1865.
W. Dugdale, *Monasticon Anglicanum*, 3 vols., 1655–73.
—— ibid., ed. J. Caley, H. Ellis, B. Bandinell, 6 vols. in 8, London, 1846.
A. du Moustier, *Neustria Pia*, Rouen, 1663.
Eadmer, *Vita Anselmi*, ed. M. Rule, R.S., London, 1884.
Edward I and Edward II, Chronicles of, ed. W. Stubbs, i, R.S., London, 1882.

Eure, Inventaire-Sommaire des Archives Départementales antérieures à 1790, *Série G*, ed. G. Bourbon, Evreux, 1886; *Série H*, ed. G. Bourbon, Évreux, 1893.

Exeter, Bishops' Registers, ed. F. C. Hingeston-Randolph, 10 vols., London, 1889–1915.

Eynsham Abbey Cartulary, ed. H. E. Salter, O.H.S., 2 volumes, Oxford, 1907–8.

W. FARRER, *Lancashire Pipe Roll and Early Lancashire Charters*, Liverpool, 1902.

W. FARRER and C. T. CLAY, *Early Yorkshire Charters*, 10 vols., Wakefield, 1914–55.

FÉCAMP, 'Epistolae Fiscannenses', ed. J. Laporte, *Revue Mabillon*, xi (1953), 5–31.

—— 'De miraculis quae in ecclesia Fiscannensi contigerunt', ed. A. Långfors, *Annales Academiae Scientiarum Fennicae*, Series B, xxv (1), Helsinki, 1950.

Feudal Aids 1284–1431, London, 1899–1921.

FINE ROLLS: *Rotuli de Oblatis et Finibus . . . tempore regis Johannis*, ed. T. D. Hardy, Record Commission, London, 1835.

—— *Fines sive Pedes Finium 1195–1214*, ed. J. Hunt, Record Commission, London, 1835, 1844.

—— *Feet of Fines*, P.R.S., xxiv, 1900.

—— *Calendar, 1272–* , London, 1911– .

FLORENCE OF WORCESTER, *Chronicon ex Chronicis*, ed. B. Thorpe, 2 vols., London, 1848–9.

Gallia Christiana in Provincia Ecclesiastica distributa, xi, Rothomagensis, Paris, 1894.

GIRALDUS CAMBRENSIS, *Speculum Ecclesie*, ed. J. S. Brewer, R.S., London, 1873.

R. GLABER, *Vita S. Guillelmi Abbatis Dinonensis*, P.L. cxlii. 698–720.

R. GROSSETESTE, *Letters*, illustrative of the social conditions of his time, ed. H. R. Luard, R.S., London, 1861.

Hansisches Urkundenbuch, vi, ed. K. Kunze, Leipzig, 1905.

F. E. HARMER (ed.), *Anglo-Saxon Writs*, Manchester, 1952.

C. H. HASKINS, 'A Charter of Canute for Fécamp', *E.H.R.* xxxiii (1918), 342–4.

—— *Norman Institutions*, Harvard Historical Studies xxiv, Cambridge (Mass.), 1918.

HEREFORD, *Charters and Records of the Cathedral 840–1412*, ed. W. W. Capes, Hereford, 1908.

—— *Bishops' Registers, 1275–1448*, ed. R. G. Griffiths, W. W. Capes, J. H. Parry, 6 vols., Cantilupe Society, Hereford, 1906–16.

Herefordshire Domesday, ed. V. H. Galbraith and J. Tait, P.R.S., n.s. xxv, London, 1947–8.

Historical Manuscripts Commission, Reports.

W. HOLTZMANN, *Papsturkunden in England*: 1. Band, *Bibliotheken und Archive in London*, Abhandlungen der Gesellschaft der Wissenschaften zu Göttingen, Philologisch-historische Klasse, Neue Folge, Band xxv, Berlin,

1930; 2. Band, *Die Kirchlichen Archive und Bibliotheken*, ibid. Dritte Folge, Band xv, Berlin, 1936; 3. Band, *Oxford, Cambridge, Kleinere Bibliotheken und Archive und Nachträge aus London*, ibid. Dritte Folge, Band xxxiii, Göttingen, 1952.

HUNDRED ROLLS: *Rotuli Hundredorum*, ed. W. Illingworth and J. Caley, Record Commission, London, 1812–18.

INQUISITIONS, *Calendar of Inquisitions post mortem*, Henry III–Edward III, London, 1904–52.

—— *Calendar of Miscellaneous Inquisitions*, Henry III–Edward III, London, 1916–37.

C. JOHNSON and H. A. CRONNE, *Regesta Regum Anglo-Normannorum 1100–35*, Oxford, 1956.

JUMIÈGES, *Chartes l'abbaye de Jumièges, 825–1204*, ed. J. Vernier, 2 vols., S.H.N., Rouen, 1916.

—— *L'abbaye royale de St. Pierre de Jumièges*, ed. J. Loth, S.H.N., Rouen, 1882–3.

WILLIAM OF JUMIÈGES, *Historiae Normannorum*, ed. J. Marx, S.H.N., Rouen, 1914.

J. KEMBLE, *Codex Diplomaticus Aevi Saxonici*, 6 vols., London, 1839–48.

P. LABBE, *Novae Bibliothecae manuscriptorum librorum* tomi duo, Paris, 1657.

P. LABBE and G. GOSSART, *Sacrosancta Concilia*, 15 vols., Paris, 1671–72.

—— —— ibid. ed. G. D. Mansi, Venice, 1759–98.

Lancaster Priory: Materials for the History of the Church of Lancaster, ed. W. O. Roper, Chetham Society xxvi, xxxi, 1892, 1894.

A. L. LÉCHAUDÉ D'ANISY, *Catalogue des Archives du Calvados*, 2 vols., M.S.A.N., Rouen, 1834.

C. LE COUTEULX, *Annales Ordinis Cartusiensis*, vii, Montreuil-sur-Mer, 1890.

LINCOLN, *Bishops' Registers: Hugh de Welles*, i–ii ed. W. P. W. Phillimore, iii ed. F. N. Davis, L.R.S. iii, vi, ix, Lincoln, 1912–14.

—— —— *Grosseteste*, ed. F. N. Davis, L.R.S. xi, Lincoln, 1914.

—— —— *Gravesend*, ed. F. N. Davis, L.R.S. xx, Lincoln, 1925.

—— —— *Sutton*, ed. R. M. T. Hill, L.R.S. xxxix, xliii, lxviii, Lincoln, 1948, 1950, 1954.

LODERS PRIORY: *Cartulaire de Loders*, ed. L. Guilloreau, Évreux, 1908.

LONDON, *Early Charters of the Cathedral Church of St. Paul*, ed. M. Gibbs, Camden Society, 3rd Series, lviii, London, 1939.

A. LONGNON, *Pouillés de la province de Rouen*, Paris, 1903.

LONGUEVILLE: *Chartes du Prieuré de Longueville*, ed. P. Le Cacheux, S.H.N., Rouen, 1934.

HERBERT DE LOSINGA, *Epistolae*, ed. R. Anstruther, London, 1846.

F. LOT, *Études critiques sur l'abbaye de St. Wandrille*, Bibliothèque de l'école des hautes études, histoire et philologie, fasc. 204, Paris, 1913.

J. MABILLON, *Annales Ordinis Sancti Benedicti Occidentalium Monachorum Patriarchae*, Paris, 1703–9.

—— *Vetera Analecta*, ed. L. F. J. de la Barre, Paris, 1723.

T. MADOX, *Formulare Anglicanum*, London, 1702.

WILLIAM OF MALMESBURY, *De Gestis Regum*, ed. W. Stubbs, 2 vols., R.S., London, 1887–9.
—— *De Gestis Pontificum Anglorum*, ed. N.E.S.A. Hamilton, R.S., London, 1870.

Manche, Inventaire-Sommaire des Archives Départementales antérieures à 1790, *Série G*, Répertoire Numérique, ed. P. Le Cacheux, Saint-Lô, 1913; *Série H*, i-ii, Saint-Lô, no date; iii, ed. F. Dolbet, Saint-Lô, 1912; iv, part 1, ed. P. Le Cacheux, Saint-Lô, 1914; iv, part 2, ed. MM. Le Cacheux, Thomas, Lacroix, Legoy, Saint-Lô, 1942.

P. MARCHEGAY, 'Chartes françaises en Angleterre', *B.E.C.* xvi (1855), 127–35.
—— 'Les prieurés anglais de St. Florent près Saumur', *B.E.C.* xl (1879), 154–94.
—— *Chartes anciennes du prieuré de Monmouth*, Les Roches Baritaud, 1879.
—— 'Chartes normandes de l'abbaye de St. Florent près Saumur', *M.S.A.N.* (1889), 663–711.

E. MARTÈNE, *Thesaurus Novus Anecdotarum*, 5 vols., Paris, 1717.

E. MARTÈNE and V. DURAND, *Veterum Scriptorum et Monumentorum amplissima collectio*, 9 vols., Paris, 1724–33.

L. A. MIDGLEY, *Ministers' Accounts of the earldom of Cornwall*, Camden Society, 3rd series, lxvi, lxviii, 1942, 1945.

B. DE MONTFAUCON, *Bibliotheca Bibliothecarum Manuscriptorum Nova*, Paris, 1739.

Newington Longueville Charters, ed. H. E. Salter, Oxfordshire Record Society, iii, 1921.

J. NICHOLS, *A Collection of all the Wills . . . of the Kings and Queens of England*, 1780.

NORMAN ROLLS: *Rotuli Normanniae*, ed. T. D. Hardy, London, 1835.
—— *Magni Rotuli Scaccarii Normanniae sub regibus Angliae*, ed. T. Stapleton, 2 vols., London, 1840–4.

NORMANDY, ARCHIVES: Les Archives de Normandie et de la Seine-Inférieure: *Recueil des facsimilés d'écritures du xie au xviiie siècle*, ed. P. Le Cacheux and J. Vernier, Rouen, 1911.

G. OLIVER, *Monasticon Diocesis Exoniensis*, Exeter, 1846–54.

H. OMONT, *Catalogue Général des Manuscrits des Bibliothèques de France*, Départements I-II, Paris, 1888.

ORDERICUS VITALIS, *Historia Ecclesiastica*, ed. A. Le Prévost, S.H.F., 5 vols., Paris, 1838–55.

Orne, Inventaire-Sommaire des Archives Départementales antérieures à 1790, *Série H*, ed. L. Duval, 4 vols., and an index, Alençon, 1891–1910.

Osney Abbey Cartulary, ed. H. E. Salter, O.H.S. 6 vols., Oxford, 1929–36.

OTTERTON, 'Chartes d'Otterton', ed. L. Guilloreau, *Revue Mabillon*, v (1909), 167–206.

OXFORD, *Facsimiles and Early Charters in Oxford Muniment Rooms*, ed. H. E. Salter, Oxford, 1929.

PAPAL LETTERS, *Calendar, 1198–   *, ed. W. H. Bliss and J. A. Twemlow, London, 1894–   .

PAPAL PETITIONS, *Calendar of Petitions to the Pope 1342–1419*, ed. W. H. Bliss, London, 1897.

PAPAL REGISTERS, 1227– , published by the Bibliothèque des écoles françaises d'Athènes et de Rome, Deuxième série, Paris, 1884– .

MATTHEW PARIS, *Chronica Majora*, ed. H. R. Luard, 7 vols., R.S., London, 1872–83.

PARLIAMENT ROLLS: *Rotuli Parlamentorum*, vols. i-v, London, 1783.

—— *Memoranda de Parliamento* (1305), ed. F. W. Maitland, R.S., London, 1893.

PATENT ROLLS: *Rotuli Litterarum Patentium 1201–16*, ed. T. D. Hardy, Record Commission, London, 1835.

—— *Calendar 1216– ,* London, 1893–

J. PECKHAM, *Epistolae*, ed. C. T. Martin, R.S., 3 vols., London, 1882–6.

Pipe Rolls, 31 Henry I and 5 Henry II– , P.R.S., London, 1884– .

WILLIAM OF POITIERS, *Gesta Guillelmi Ducis Normannorum et Regis Anglorum*, ed. R. Foreville, Paris, 1952.

PRIVY COUNCIL, *Proceedings and Ordinances*, i, 1386–1410, ed. Sir N. H. Nicholas, Record Commission, London, 1834.

W. PRYNNE, *History of King John, Henry III and Edward I*, vol. iii, London, 1670.

Quo Warranto, Placita de, ed. W. Illingworth, Record Commission, London, 1818.

J. RAMACKERS, *Papsturkunden in Frankreich*, 2. Band: *Normandie*, Abhandlungen der Gesellschaft der Wissenschaften zu Göttingen, Philologisch-Historische Klasse, Dritte Folge, Band xxi, Göttingen, 1937.

O. RIGAUD, *Journal des Visites*, ed. T. Bonnin, Rouen, 1852.

J. H. ROUND, *Calendar of Documents preserved in France, 918–1206*, London, 1899.

T. RYMER, *Foedera, Conventiones, Litterae*, i-xi, London, 1704–10.

—— ibid., ed. A. Clarke, J. Caley, J. Bayley, F. Holbrooke, J. W. Clarke, Record Commission, London, 1816–69.

SAINTE-BARBE-EN-AUGE, *Chronique*, ed. R. N. Sauvage, Mémoires de l'Académie de Caen, Caen, 1906.

SAINTE-TRINITÉ DU MONT, Rouen, *Cartulaire*, ed. J. A. Déville, as Appendix to *Cartulaire de St. Bertin*, Collection des Documents Inédits de l'histoire de France, 1835, 1841.

SAINT-VALÉRY, *Chartes des Abbés*, ed. C. Brunel and H. E. Salter, Abbeville, 1910.

SALISBURY, *Register of St. Osmund*, ed. W. H. Rich-Jones and W. D. Macray, R.S., London, 1883–4.

—— *Sarum Charters and Documents*, ed. W. H. Rich-Jones and W. D. Macray, R.S., London, 1891.

R. N. SAUVAGE, *Les Fonds de l'abbaye de St. Etienne de Caen*, Caen, 1911.

Seine-Maritime, Inventaire, *Série G*, ed. C. de Robillard de Beaurepaire, 7 vols. and index, Rouen, 1868–1900.

—— Inventaire-Sommaire des Archives Départementales antérieures à 1790, *Série H* i, ed. J. Vernier, Rouen, 1921; ii-iv, ed. P. Le Cacheux, Rouen, 1927–38.

SELBORNE PRIORY: *Calendar of Charters and Documents*, ii, ed. W. Dunn Macray, Hampshire Record Society, 1894.

Sele Priory Cartulary, ed. L. F. Salzmann, Cambridge, 1930.

T. SMITH, *Catalogue of the Cottonian Library*, 1696.

Statutes of the Realm, ed. A. Luders, Sir T. E. Tomlins, J. F. France, W. E. Taunton, J. Raithby, J. Caley, W. Elliott, 11 vols., Record Commission, London, 1810–28.

J. STEVENS, *History of Ancient Abbeys additional to Dugdale's Monasticon*, 2 vols., London, 1722–3.

Stogursey Priory Charters, ed. T. D. Tremlett and N. Blakiston, Somerset Record Society lxi, 1949.

Taxatio Ecclesiastica Angliae et Walliae auctoritate papae Nicholai, circa 1291, ed. S. Ayscough and J. Caley, Record Commission, London, 1802.

J. B. A. T. TEULET, *Layettes du Trésor des Chartes*, Paris, 1863.

Thame Abbey Cartulary, ed. H. E. Salter, 2 vols., Oxfordshire Record Society, 1947–8.

Theobald Archbishop of Canterbury (Acta), ed. A. Saltman, London, 1956.

ROBERT OF TORIGNY, *Chronicle*, ed. R. Howlett, R.S., London, 1890.

—— ibid., ed. L. V. Delisle, S.H.N., 2 vols., Caen, 1872–3.

LE TRÉPORT, *Cartulaire de l'Abbaye de St. Michel du Tréport*, ed. P. P.Laffleur de Kermingant, Paris, 1880.

Valuation of Norwich, ed. W. E. Lunt, Oxford, 1926.

Vita Sancti Vitalis, ed. E. P. Sauvage, *Analecta Bollandiana*, i (1882), 355–90.

T. WALSINGHAM, *Gesta Abbatum Monasterii Sancti Albani*, ed. H. T. Riley, London, 1867.

H. WHARTON, *Anglia Sacra*, 2 vols., London, 1691.

D. WHITELOCK, *Anglo-Saxon Wills*, Cambridge, 1930.

Winchester, Bishop's *Register: Wykeham*, ed. T. F. Kirby, 2 vols., Hampshire Record Society, London, 1896, 1899.

—— Cathedral, *Compotus Rolls of the Obedientiaries of St. Swithun's priory*, ed. G. W. Kitchin, Hampshire Record Society, 1892.

Worcester, Bishop's *Registers: Giffard*, ed. J. W. Willis-Bund, Worcester Historical Society, Oxford, 1902.

—— —— *Sede Vacante 1301–1435*, ed. J. W. Willis-Bund, Worcester Historical Society, Oxford, 1894–7.

WILLIAM OF WORCESTER, *Itinerarium sive Liber Rerum Memorabilium*, ed. J. Nasmith, Cambridge, 1778.

J. WYCLIF, *De ecclesia*, ed. J. Loserth, Wycliffe Society, 1886.

—— *De eucharistia*, ed. J. Loserth, Wycliffe Society, 1885.

—— *De blasphemia*, ed. M. Dziewicki, Wycliffe Society, 1893.

Year Books: Edward III, Years 11–12, ed. A. J. Horwood, R.S., London, 1883.

—— —— *12–13*, ed. L. O. Pike, R.S., London, 1885.

—— —— *14–15* and *15*, ed. L. O. Pike, R.S., London, 1889, 1891.

York, Bishop's *Register: Gray*, ed. J. Raine, Surtees Society lvi, London, 1872.

SECONDARY AUTHORITIES

J. ADIGARD DES GAUTRIES, *Les noms de personnes scandinaves dans les noms de lieux normands de 911 à 1066*, Nomina Germanica, Uppsala, 1955.

P. N. BACKMUND, *Monasticon Praemonstratense*, ii, Staubing, 1952.

A. BEARDWOOD, *Alien Merchants in England 1350–77*, Cambridge (Mass.), 1931.

BEAUNIER, *Recueil historique chronologique et topographique des archevêchez evêchez abbayes et prieurés de France*, ed. J. M. Besse, Archives de la France Monastique, vii, *Province de Rouen*, Paris, 1908.

C. DE BEAUREPAIRE, '*Pouillés de la Province de Rouen*, par A. Longnon', *B.E.C.* lxiv (1903), 596–617.

V. BERTIÈRE, 'L'exercice du ministère paroissial par les moines', *Revue Bénédictine*, xxxix (1927), 227–50, 340–64.

A. BESNARD, *Monographie de l'église et de l'abbaye de St. Georges de Boscherville*, Paris, 1899.

M. M. BIGELOW, *History of Procedure in England 1066–1204*, London, 1880.

J. BIRDSALL, 'The English Manors of La Trinité at Caen', *Anniversary Essays in Medieval History presented to C. H. Haskins*, Boston, 1929, pp. 25–44.

F. BLOMEFIELD, *Topographical History of Norfolk*, continued by C. Parkin, 11 vols., London, 1805–10.

H. BÖHMER, *Kirche und Staat in England und in der Normandie*, Leipzig, 1899.

C. BRÉARD, *L'Abbaye de Notre-Dame de Grestain*, Rouen, 1904.

Z. N. BROOKE, *The English Church and the Papacy*, Cambridge, 1931.

M. BURROWS, *Cinque Ports*, London, 1888.

C. U. J. CHEVALIER, *Répertoire des sources historiques du moyen âge*, *Topo-bibliographie*, Montbéliard, 1894.

M. CHIBNALL (*née* Morgan), 'Inventories of Three Small Alien Priories', *J. Br. Arch. Assn.*, 3rd Series, iv (1940), 141–9.

—— 'The Abbey of Bec-Hellouin and its English Priories', *J. Br. Arch. Assn.*, 3rd Series, v (1940), 33–62.

—— 'The Suppression of the Alien Priories', Historical Revision xcix, *History*, xxvi (1942), 204–12.

—— *The English Lands of the Abbey of Bec*, Oxford, 1946.

C. T. CLAY, 'The Early Treasurers of York', *J. Yorkshire Archaeological Society*, xxxv (1940), 7–34.

G. M. COOPER, 'Illustrations of Wilmington Priory and Church', *S.A.C.* iv (1851), 37–66.

F. B. COQUELIN, *Histoire de l'abbaye de St. Michel du Tréport*, ed C. Lormier, S.H.N., Rouen, 1879.

J. N. DALTON, *The Collegiate Church of St. Mary Ottery*, Cambridge, 1917.

L. V. DELISLE, *Études sur la condition de la classe agricole et l'état de l'agriculture en Normandie au moyen âge*, Évreux, 1851.

—— *Le Cabinet des Manuscrits de la Bibliothèque Impériale*, 3 vols., Paris, 1866.

—— *Histoire du château et des sires de Saint Sauveur le Vicomte*, Valognes, 1867.

—— 'Livres d'images destinées à l'instruction religieuse et aux exercices de piété des laïques', *Histoire littéraire de France*, xxxi, Paris, 1893, pp. 213–85.

L. V. DELISLE, 'Philippe Auguste et Raoul d'Argences, abbé de Fécamp', *B.E.C.* lxv (1904), 390–7.

J. DEPOIN, 'Les premiers anneaux de la maison de Bellême,' *Bull. hist. et phil. du comité des travaux hist. et scient.* (1909), 147–67.

J. C. DICKINSON, *The Origins of the Austin Canons and their Introduction into England*, London, 1950.

D. C. DOUGLAS, 'The Norman Episcopate before the Norman Conquest', *Cambridge Historical Journal*, xiii (1957), 100–15.

A. C. DUCAREL, *Anglo-Norman Antiquities*, London, 1767.

W. DUGDALE, *The Antiquities of Warwickshire*, London, 1656.

—— *The Baronage of England*, 2 vols., London, 1675–6.

E. DUMONT and MARTIN, *Histoire de Montivilliers*, Fécamp, 1886.

J. DUNCUMB, *Collections towards the History and Antiquities of the county of Hereford*, vol. ii, Hereford, 1812.

J. EASTWOOD, *History of the Parish of Ecclesfield*, London, 1862.

H. ELLIS, *General Introduction to Domesday*, Record Commission, London, 1833.

ENGLISH PLACE-NAME SOCIETY, Publications, Cambridge, 1933– .

R. W. EYTON, *Antiquities of Shropshire*, 12 vols., London, 1854–60.

W. FARRER, *Honors and Knights' Fees*, 3 vols., Manchester, 1923–5.

H. P. R. FINBERG, *Tavistock Abbey*, Cambridge, 1951.

H. DE FORMEVILLE, *Histoire de l'ancien evêché-comté de Lisieux*, Lisieux, 1873.

E. A. FREEMAN, *History of the Norman Conquest*, Oxford, 1867–79.

—— *The Reign of William Rufus*, Oxford, 1882.

W. H. FRERE, 'The Early History of Canons regular as illustrated by the Foundation of Barnwell Priory', *Fasciculus J. W. Clark*, Cambridge, 1909.

V. H. GALBRAITH, 'Monastic Foundation Charters', *Cambridge Historical Journal*, v (1934), 205–22, 296–8.

—— *Studies in the Public Records*, London, 1948.

R. GÉNÉSTAL, *Du rôle des monastères comme établissements de crédit*, Paris, 1901.

—— 'Les vicomtes normands', *Nouvelle revue d'histoire du droit français et étranger* (1904), 766–75.

S. E. GLEASON, *An Ecclesiastical Barony of the Middle Ages: the Bishopric of Bayeux 1066–1204*, Cambridge (Mass.), 1936.

R. GRAHAM, *English Ecclesiastical Studies*, London, 1929.

—— 'Four Alien Priories of Monmouthshire', *J. Br. Arch. Assn.* 2nd ser. xxxv (1929), 102–21.

C. GUÉRY, *Histoire de l'abbaye de Lyre*, Évreux, 1917.

—— 'L'abbaye de Lyre: quelques additions au chapitre de ses possessions anglaises', *Revue Catholique de Normandie* (1921), 261–7.

L. GUILLOREAU, 'Les fondations anglaises de l'abbaye de Savigny', *Revue Mabillon*, v (1909–10), 290–335.

—— 'Les possessions des abbayes mancelles et angevines en Angleterre d'après le Domesday Book,' *Revue Historique et Archéologique du Maine*, lx (1906), 5–23.

D. Gurney, *The Records of the House of Gournay*, London, 1848–58.

L. W. Vernon Harcourt, *His Grace the Steward and Trial of Peers*, London, 1907.

R. A. R. Hartridge, *History of Vicarages*, Cambridge, 1930.

C. H. Haskins, *Norman Institutions*, Harvard Historical Studies xxiv, Cambridge (Mass.), 1918.

C. Hippeau, *L'abbaye de St. Etienne de Caen 1066–1790*, Caen, 1855.

G. A. Holmes, *The Estates of the Higher Nobility in fourteenth-century England*, Cambridge, 1957.

G. Hubert, 'Les prieurés anglais de l'abbaye de Lonlay', *Bull. de la Soc. de l'histoire de l'Orne*, xli (1922), 190–207.

J. Hunter, *Hallamshire, the History and Topography of the parish of Sheffield*, ed. A. Gatty, London, 1869.

J. Hutchins, *History and Antiquities of the county of Dorset*, 4 vols., 3rd ed. London, 1861–70.

E. F. Jacob, 'English University Clerks in the Later Middle Ages: the Problem of Maintenance', *Bull. John Rylands Library*, xxix (1946), 304–25.

Jumièges, *Congrès de Jumièges 1954*, 2 vols., Rouen, 1955.

N. Ker, *Medieval Libraries of Great Britain: a list of surviving books*, Royal Historical Society, London, 1941.

T. F. Kirby, *Annals of Winchester College*, 1892.

—— 'Charters of Harmondsworth, Isleworth, Heston, Twickenham and Hampton on Thames', *Archaeologia*, lviii (1903), 341–58.

M. D. Knowles, *The Monastic Order in England*, Cambridge, 1949.

—— *The Religious Orders in England*, Cambridge, 1948, 1955.

—— 'Essays in Monastic History: vi, Parish Organisation', *Downside Review* li (1933), 501–22.

M. D. Knowles and R. N. Hancock, *Medieval Religious Houses in England and Wales*, London, 1953; 'Additions and Corrections' to this in *E.H.R.* lxxii (1957), 60–87.

J. Laporte, 'Les origines du monachisme dans la province de Rouen', *Revue Mabillon*, xxxi (1941), 1–13, 25–41, 49–68.

G. A. de la Roque, *Histoire généalogique de la maison d'Harcourt*, Paris, 1662.

P. E. Lebeurier, *Notice sur l'abbaye de la Croix Saint Leufroy*, Evreux, 1866.

M. J. Le Cacheux, *Histoire de l'abbaye de St. Amand de Rouen*, B.S.A.N. (1937), 1–289, Caen.

P. Le Cacheux, 'La date de la fondation de l'abbaye Blanche de Mortain', *Revue Catholique de Normandie*, x (1900–1), 309–23.

J. Leclerq, *Jean abbé de Fécamp*, Paris, 1946.

J. F. Lemarignier, *Études sur les privilèges d'exemption et de juridiction ecclésiastique des abbayes normandes depuis les origines jusqu'en 1140*, Archives de la France monastique xliv, Paris, 1937.

—— *L'Hommage en marche et les frontières féodales*, Lille, 19–45.

R. G. Lennard, 'Peasant Tithe Collectors in Norman England', *E.H.R.* lxix (1954), 580–96.

M. Le Pesant, 'Notice d'un manuscrit trouvé dans les archives de l'Eure', *Annales de Normandie*, iii, 1ᵉ livraison, 87–90.

—— 'Les manuscrits de Dom Lenoir sur l'histoire de Normandie', *B.S.A.N.* l (1946–50).

A. Le Prévost, *Mémoires et notes pour servir à l'histoire du département de l'Eure*, 3 vols., ed. L. V. Delisle and L. Parry, Évreux, 1862–9.

E. Levien, 'Wareham and its religious houses', *Journal of British Archaeological Association* xxviii (1882), 154–70, 244–58.

W. Levison, *England and the Continent in the Eighth Century*, Oxford, 1946.

L. C. Loyd, *The Origins of Some Anglo-Norman Families*, Harleian Society, ciii, ed. C. T. Clay and D. C. Douglas, Leeds, 1951.

H. C. Maxwell Lyte, *History of Eton College*, London, 1889.

P. Morant, *The History and Antiquities of Essex*, 2 vols., London, 1768.

A. Morey, *Bartholomew of Exeter*, Cambridge, 1937.

G. A. Moriarty, 'The Barony of Coggs', *Reports of the Oxfordshire Archaeological Society*, no. 75 (1930), 309–20.

W. A. Morris and J. R. Strayer, *The English Government at work: II. Fiscal Administration*, Medieval Academy of America xlviii, Cambridge (Mass.), 1947.

H. Navel, 'L'enquête de 1133 sur les fiefs de l'évêché de Bayeux', *B.S.A.N.* xlii (1934), 5–80.

—— 'Les vavassories du Mont St. Michel à Bretteville sur Odon et Verson', *B.S.A.N.* xlv (1937), 137–65.

C. W. New, *History of the Alien Priories in England to the confiscation of Henry V*, Wisconsin, 1916.

R. Newcourt, *Repertorium ecclesiasticum parochiale Londinense*, 2 vols., London, 1708–10.

J. Nichols, *History and Antiquities of the County of Leicester*, 4 vols. in 8, London, 1795–1815.

T. Oleson, *The Witenagemot in the Reign of Edward the Confessor*, London, 1955.

H. Omont, 'Les prieurés anglais de l'abbaye de Bec', *B.S.A.N.* xxvii (1909), 242–57.

W. Page, 'Some Remarks on the Churches of the Domesday Survey', *Archaeologia* lxvi (1915), 61–102.

E. Perroy, *L'Angleterre et le Grand Schisme d'Occident*, Paris, 1933.

F. Pommeraye, *Histoire de l'abbaye de St. Ouen*, Rouen, 1662.

A. L. Poole, *The Obligations of Society in the Twelfth and Thirteenth Centuries*, Oxford, 1946.

R. L. Poole, *The Exchequer in the Twelfth Century*, Oxford, 1912.

A. A. Porée, *Histoire de l'abbaye de Bec*, 2 vols., Evreux, 1901.

E. Power, *The Wool Trade in English Medieval History*, Oxford, 1941.

F. M. Powicke, *The Loss of Normandy*, Manchester, 1913.

—— *The Thirteenth Century*, Oxford, 1953.

H. Prentout, *Essai sur les origines et la fondation du duché de Normandie*, Mémoires de l'Académie de Caen, Caen, 1911.

—— 'Dudon de St. Quentin', *B.S.A.N.* xxxiii (1918), 193–225.

—— *Études sur quelques points d'histoire de Normandie*, Mémoires de l'académie de Caen, n.s. iii, v–vi, 1929–31.

J. RAINE,*The History and Antiquities of the Parish of Blyth*, Westminster, 1860.
R. L. G. RITCHIE, *The Normans in England before Edward the Confessor*, Exeter, 1948.
ROMBAULT, 'St. Evroul aux xie et xiie siècles', *Bull. de la Soc. d'hist. et d'archéologie de l'Orne*, xv (1896), 448–61.
J. H. ROUND, *Geoffrey de Mandeville*, London, 1892.
—— *Feudal England*, London, 1895.
—— *The Commune of London*, Westminster, 1899.
—— *Studies in Peerage and Family History*, 2 vols., London, 1901.
—— *The King's Serjeants and Officers of State*, London, 1911.
—— *Family Origins and other studies*, ed. W. Page, London, 1930.
—— 'Some Early Sussex Charters', *S.A.C.* xlii (1899), 75–86.
—— 'The Family of St. John and of Port', *Genealogist*, N.S. xvi (1899), 1–13, ibid. xvii (1900), 137–9.
—— 'Some Notes on Anglo-Norman chronology', *Genealogist*, N.S. xvii (1900), 1–4.
—— 'The Castles of the Conquest', *Archaeologia*, lviii (1902), 313–40.
R. N. SAUVAGE, *L'abbaye de St. Martin de Troarn*, M.S.A.N., Caen, 1911.
W. G. SEARLE, *Onomasticon Anglo-Saxonicum*, Cambridge, 1897.
J. SELDEN, *The History of Tythes*, London, 1618.
Q. SENIGAGLIA, 'Le compagnie bancarie Senesi nei secoli xiii e xiv', *Studi Senesi*, xxiv (1906), 149–217; ibid. xxv (1908), 3–66.
W. A. SHAW, *The History of Currency, 1252–1894*, London [1895].
W. SOMNER, *The Antiquities of Canterbury*, ed. Butler, London, 1763.
F. M. STENTON, *The First Century of English Feudalism 1066–1166*, Oxford, 1932.
—— *Anglo-Saxon England*, 2nd ed., Oxford, 1947.
T. TANNER, *Notitia Monastica*, London, 1744.
T. TAYLOR, *Saint Michael's Mount*, Cambridge, 1932.
—— 'Saint Michael's Mount and the Domesday Survey', *Journal of Royal Institution of Cornwall*, xvii (1907–9), 230–5.
E. M. THOMPSON, *The Carthusian Order in England*, London, 1930.
R. THOROTON, *History of Nottinghamshire*, 3 vols., London, 1797.
S. L. THRUPP, 'Survey of the Alien Population of England in 1440', *Speculum*, xxxii (1957), 262–73.
M. A. TIERNEY, *History and Antiquities of the Castle and Town of Arundel*, 2 vols., London, 1834.
E. TURNER, 'The Priory of Boxgrove', *S.A.C.* xv (1863), 83–122.
L. VALIN, *Le Duc de Normandie et sa Cour*, Paris, 1909–10.
P.-E.VIARD, *Histoire de la dîme ecclésiastique jusqu'au décret de Gratien*, Dijon, 1909.
—— *Histoire de la dîme ecclésiastique en France 1150–1313*, Paris, 1912.
Victoria History of the Counties of England, London, 1901– .
P. VINOGRADOFF, *English Society in the Eleventh Century*, Oxford, 1908.
L. VOSS, *Heinrich von Blois*, Historische Studien, Berlin, 1932.
J. WARBURTON and A. C. DUCAREL, *Some Account of the Alien Priories and of such lands as they are known to have had in England and Wales, collected from their manuscripts and printed by J. Nichols*, London, 1786.

G. H. WHITE, 'The First House of Bellême', *T.R.H.S.*, 4th series, xxii (1940).

W. WILLIAMS, 'William of Dijon', *Downside Review*, lii (1934), 520–45.

S. WOOD, *English Monasteries and their Patrons*, Oxford, 1955.

R. WORSLEY, *The History of the Isle of Wight*, London, 1781.

J. H. WYLIE, *The History of England under Henry IV*, 4 vols., London, 1884–98.

—— *The Reign of Henry V*, 3 vols., London, 1914–29.

J. P. YEATMAN, *Feudal History of the County of Derby*, 2 vols., London, 1886.

J. YVER, 'Henri Prentout: 1867–1933, Notice Biobibliographique', *Mémoires de l'Académie de Caen*, N.S. vii, Caen, 1934.

INDEX

Numbers in italics refer to footnote references.

SELECTIVE SERVICE SYSTEM

GRADUATE OR PROFESSIONAL COLLEGE STUDENT CERTIFICATE

(Complete Appropriate Item or Items)

Form Approved
Budget Bureau No. 33-R-0202

Date _____ Sept. 19, 1972

Selective Service No.

11	10	49	64

1. Name and Current Mailing Address of Student

Dean Kukuck
614½ College Ave.
Lincoln, IL 62656

PART I - GRADUATE STUDENTS

2(a). The student identified above has been accepted for admission to graduate school for a full-time course of instruction leading to the degree of _____, in _____, in the class commencing _____ and being the first class commencing after he completed the requirements for admission.

2(b). The student identified above has entered upon a full-time course of instruction as a candidate for a graduate degree, which commenced on __9.4.72__, and currently is meeting degree requirements, and is expected to attain the degree of __Master of Divinity__, in __Theology__, on or about __6.1.76__.

PART II - PROFESSIONAL STUDENTS

3(a). The student identified above has been accepted for admission to _____ school in the first year class commencing _____ and being the first class commencing after he completed requirements for admission.

3(b). The student identified above has entered upon, the _____ year of his professional studies, and is satisfactorily pursuing a full-time course of study leading to graduation with the degree of _____ on or about _____.

PART III - GENERAL

4. The student identified above is (check one) ☐ Not eligible to continue   ☐ No longer enrolled full time
☐ Graduated _____
(Date)

5. Remarks

INSTRUCTIONS

Selective Service Regulations define a student's academic year as the twelve month period following the beginning of his course of study.

This form should be submitted when an individual has been accepted for admission as a graduate or a professional student to a college, university, or similar institution of learning (Item 2(a) or 3(a), and will be submitted promptly (1) at the beginning of a student's academic year (Item 2(b) or 3(b), or (2) when a student is no longer enrolled, not eligible to continue, or graduated (Item 4). When graduation occurs Item 4 should be completed, entering the date of graduation after that caption.

The original may be forwarded to the State Director of the State in which the institution is located, for distribution to local boards within the State, or to other State Directors of Selective Service, or direct to local boards. When the latter plan is followed the address of the registrant's local board should be in his possession on a Registration Certificate (SSS Form 2 or 2-A) or a Notice of Classification (SSS Form 110). A copy may be furnished to the registrant and a copy returned.

Submission of this form does not constitute a request for deferment.

Authentication of information on this form may be by any means evidencing that a responsible official of the institution has verified its preparation.

6. ADDRESS OF LOCAL BOARD

Local SS Board #10
605 S. Nell
Champaign, IL 61820

7. AUTHENTICATION

Registrar's Office
Lincoln Christian College
Box 178
Lincoln, IL 62656

Name and address of Institution

S S S Form 103 (Revised 10-11-67) (Previous printings are obsolete)